Maigret, Simenon and France

Maigret, Simenon and France

Social Dimensions of the Novels and Stories

BILL ALDER

Foreword by Stephen Knight

McFarland & Company, Inc., Publishers
Jefferson, North Carolina, and London

LIBRARY OF CONGRESS CATALOGUING-IN-PUBLICATION DATA

Alder, Bill, 1958–
    Maigret, Simenon and France : social dimensions of the novels and stories / Bill Alder ; foreword by Stephen Knight.
       p.   cm.
    Includes bibliographical references and index.

    ISBN 978-0-7864-7054-9
    softcover : acid free paper ∞

    1. Simenon, Georges, 1903–1989—Criticism and interpretation.
    2. Simenon, Georges, 1903–1989—Characters—Jules Maigret.
    3. Literature and society—France—History—20th century.
    4. Social change in literature. I. Title.
    PQ2637.I53Z56 2013
    843'.912—dc23   2012044027

BRITISH LIBRARY CATALOGUING DATA ARE AVAILABLE

© 2013 Bill Alder. All rights reserved

No part of this book may be reproduced or transmitted in any form or by any means, electronic or mechanical, including photocopying or recording, or by any information storage and retrieval system, without permission in writing from the publisher.

Front cover images © 2012 Shutterstock

Manufactured in the United States of America

McFarland & Company, Inc., Publishers
  Box 611, Jefferson, North Carolina 28640
    www.mcfarlandpub.com

To the memory of my father,
BERT ALDER

Acknowledgments

I would like to thank Professor Stephen Knight of the University of Melbourne and Doctor Heather Worthington of Cardiff University for their support and enthusiasm for this project. I have learned a great deal from them both. I have also benefited greatly from the comments of Doctor Maurizio Ascari of Bologna University and Professor Claire Gorrara of Cardiff University. I would like to thank Doctor Laurent Demoulin, curator of the Fonds Simenon at the University of Liège, for his hospitality and help during my visits. Tony and Sybil Clegg showed great kindness and generosity in their donation of their collection of Maigret texts.

Table of Contents

Acknowledgments vi
Foreword by Stephen Knight 1
Preface 5
Introduction 9

CHAPTER 1
The Fayard Maigret Novels: Narratives, Contexts, Settings and Themes, 1931   21

CHAPTER 2
The Fayard Maigret Novels: Narratives, Contexts, Settings and Themes, 1932   53

CHAPTER 3
The Fayard Maigret Novels: Simenon's Perspective   91

CHAPTER 4
Short Stories and Journalism: Maigret, Simenon and the Crises of the 1930s   114

CHAPTER 5
What Maigret Did Next   145

CHAPTER 6
Conclusions   173

Bibliography 197
Index 205

Foreword by Stephen Knight

Georges Simenon is one of the great forces of the crime fiction world. Not only did he create for Maigret 75 novels and 28 short stories, he produced well over a hundred other crime stories, notably the psychothrillers the French call *romans durs*, "hard novels." He was enormously successful in translation as well: only Edgar Wallace and Agatha Christie have matched his world dominion.

Like theirs, his style seems simple, his stories unelaborated. If this suggests that triumph in crime fiction depends on naivety, one contradiction is the ability of critics to see much in Simenon's fiction, and another, wholly Gallic, one is the range of French star filmmakers who have found inspiration in his work—Renoir, Clouzot, Carné, Autant-Lara, Melville, Tavernier, Chabrol, and Delannoy (starring Jean Gabin, no less).

More depth lies in the life of Simenon. Born half Belgian-French, half Flemish (one of the more difficult citizenships of Europe), he was at school with World War I brutally close. He grew up through the financially dramatic 1920s and, especially in France, the politically melodramatic 1930s; he then lived in rural France through World War II. We do not know what Simenon thought when the local Nazis, perhaps not the best informed, felt Simenon was the same as the Jewish surname Simon. What we do know is that none of these drastic contexts make any overt mark on Simenon's work. Bill Alder has written the first study to look closely at Simenon's France as well as his fiction. He focuses on the intimately local currents of history and society, the fears, arrogances, deceptions and ultimately the crimes that people feel they are backed into by a changing, frightening, local world.

Simenon started very young as a news reporter, and always had the power to write quickly: he could finish a book in a week. As he moved towards Maigret he published the hundred and fifty pulp novels in the period 1924–

1929: the first 19 Maigrets themselves came in just over three years from February 1931. There is also the local reporter style of writing about what is here and now, never drawing the long bow of history—yet he rendered human detail so well, it is in fact verifiable against history, as this study shows very clearly.

By tracing in detail the social roles and concerns of the characters, Alder is able to show how Simenon in the 1930s was charting both a set of real human anxieties and also the actual processes by which France was, for many people regrettably, changing its structures of work, of consumption, and sociopolitical attitudes. To bring this off critically, Alder is the first to use on Simenon a British cultural studies approach. Starting in the 1970s, this maintained the earlier tradition of reading the texts very closely for their thematic patterns, adding the full force of sociopolitical understanding. In the manner of Raymond Williams and Terry Eagleton, the text and the context were read as fully interlinked, and so fully revealing each other.

Through tracing the responses of people in the texts and studying with some detail the socioeconomic patterns of the time, Alder shows how Simenon's essential position is that of the much-harassed *petite bourgeoisie*, and how the "certain idea of France" that Simenon offers focuses on the distress of this subclass (to which he originally belonged), and shows how its enemies, both the rich and the poor and above all the irresistible agents of modernity, can be held at bay only with difficulty and sometimes with crimes.

Alder's study focuses first on the 1930s, when Maigret was created and came to dominate: the stories were successful from the start, and soon translated into English. True to his profession, his calling and his code of humane interaction, Maigret is one of the very few mythic figures of crime fiction, up there with Holmes, Poirot and Marlowe. With very careful analysis of the subtly moving novels that made Maigret famous, Alder is able to show him as a sort of pope for the *petite bourgeoisie*—yet also as the first serious police detective. We are so used to Maigret that his early uniqueness is forgotten. In one challenging argument, Alder links the character with Dashiell Hammett's detached yet deeply moral detectives.

Both Simenon and Maigret survived the war, but not without some embarrassment. Some thought Simenon was a collaborator, and he spent a number of years in the United States as an indirect result. Reflection suggests that a man of such strong feelings about human justice is very unlikely to have been a collaborator. It is much more likely that, as Maigret does in the novels, Simenon kept his head down, did the right thing at close quarters, and, like many French, waited for the storm to pass—and so could be picked on afterwards by enemies.

To a substantial extent Maigret and Simenon did not change much: as

Alder shows, the material in the many postwar novels (forty-eight Maigrets among them, usually with "Maigret" in the title, no doubt for well-earned commercial reasons) often looks back to the earlier world; threats that were seen as developing in the 1930s novels are now more fully formed, especially the move from the land into industry, the growth of the state and of service work in France.

The Maigret of the later novels is still the fully realized strong *doyen* expressing powerfully what Alder calls "social conservatism and humanism" together. That in itself has been enough to make him a fascinating figure—yet only because he appears in elegantly spare prose in stories that move with simple elegance to validate those core Maigret values: the fluent focused movement of the fiction is retained to the very end.

And this, as Alder makes clear, is the achievement. Simenon's personal conservatism does not mean he does not explore and expose France as it is. Alder brings in what Lukás said about Scott and Balzac: their personal politics did not stop them charting with searching accuracy the state of the world in which their characters—and their readers—lived and suffered.

So Simenon, as Alder describes him, and as he is represented in the French-language criticism that Alder has also assembled here, is not just a major producer of crime fiction (and, let us not forget, an inspirer of fine French films). He is also a major author in the full sense, and Bill Alder's very detailed, closely referential, always lucid account of his life and work tells us how he is great, thus explaining why so many have for so long wanted to read him.

This is a book Simenon has deserved—but Agatha Christie and Edgar Wallace also deserve the *Alder*native approach. While we cannot expect Bill Alder to produce seventy-five books of criticism, his approach is so illuminating and revealing we can only, as another great and serious populist put it, ask for more.

Stephen Knight is a research professor at the University of Melbourne, Australia, having retired from Cardiff University, Wales. He is the author of essays and books on crime fiction and other topics. His most recent study is The Mysteries of the Cities: Urban Crime Fiction in the Nineteenth Century *(McFarland, 2012).*

Preface

Georges Simenon (1903–1989) was one of the most successful twentieth-century authors of crime fiction, whose series of Maigret novels and short stories, published between 1931 and 1972, found international commercial and critical acclaim. In addition to being translated in print into over fifty languages, there have been more than a dozen films based on Commissaire Maigret's inquiries and a number of highly popular television series based on the character in France, Great Britain, Germany, Italy and Holland. A number of elements set Simenon and Maigret apart from their predecessors in the crime fiction canon: in particular, the author's deep interest in the social and psychological causes of crime, and his character's method of solving cases by immersing himself in a given social milieu, rather than by engaging in exercises of deductive reasoning to discover "Who-dunnit?" or tracking down criminals by feats of heroic individual action.

This book examines the importance of social class and social change in Georges Simenon's Maigret stories in order to draw out their meanings in terms of the social context in, by and for which they were produced. As such, it will particularly serve the needs of students in French language/French studies who are studying the Maigret narratives as part of twentieth century fiction modules or students in literature courses with a crime fiction component. It will also be of interest to readers of the Maigret series outside formal courses of study and lovers of crime fiction in general.

The book focuses in detail on the texts of the Maigret narratives, with a particular emphasis on the early and formative novels. The texts are studied in the context of developments in contemporary French society from a broadly Marxist methodological perspective. The book considers the role of social class and social change in the development of plot, characterization and the settings of the stories and seeks to establish the extent to which the depiction of French society is historically accurate, and explores the influence of the author's own class position and ideology on his fiction.

The road to this book has been a long one. Like many growing up in Britain in the 1960s, my parents were keen viewers of the BBC *Maigret* television series starring Rupert Davies. Indeed, the character's influence was so strong that whenever I asked my parents a difficult question, as young children invariably do, they would answer, "Who do you think I am? Maigret?" Nevertheless, I forgot all about the commissaire until I was learning French at school as a teenager. At the age of 17 or 18 I read a couple of Maigret stories, recommended by my teacher for the relative simplicity of the French, but quickly decided that this was mundane stuff and that the likes of Jean-Paul Sartre and Albert Camus, with their consciously "difficult" philosophical concerns, were far more exotic and interesting.

I crossed paths again with Maigret in the mid–1980s under unusual circumstances. At the time I was working the night shift in a steel foundry and my co-workers filled all possible nonworking time by playing cards. As a very bad card player, I had little interest, so I looked for something "simple" to read during meal and drinks breaks. The Maigret stories seemed a good choice—short and apparently not too demanding. Over a period of months I began to realize that there was something in Maigret's sympathy for the "little people," *les petites gens*, which I liked, although I was curious about what appeared to be a contradiction: Maigret seemed to have more in common with the artisans, shopkeepers, and even prostitutes he encountered than with the *juge d'instruction*, *procureurs*, politicians and members of the bourgeoisie he met; but how could a high-ranking police officer, an agent of the repressive apparatus of the capitalist state, be simultaneously a sympathizer of those with apparently the smallest stake in the society which the police defended?

Fast forward ten years. I was working as a teacher of French for 16 to 19 year olds and adults. Part of the syllabus allowed the teacher free choice of one or two French novels as a subject for students' coursework, the only restriction being that the novel(s) must deal in some depth with a particular French region. I chose Maigret and Paris. Over the years I became fascinated by the author's portrayal of the society in which the stories unfolded. On the one hand, Maigret, and by implication his creator, seemed very aware that the social environment in which he operated was that of a class society; on the other hand, both character and author appeared to favor a view of life based on the idea that beneath the surface, class distinctions were unimportant and that what really counted was the essential *humanity* of each individual, that there was an *homme nu*, somehow existing separately from his concrete social existence. I was also intrigued by Simenon's descriptions of French society, which seemed to confirm my own received ideas of what France was like at some indeterminate moment in the past. Yet I was simultaneously aware that Maigret's Paris and France bore little resemblance to the France I had known from the late 1970s onwards and that, moreover, the Maigret narratives spanned a forty-year period in which considerable change had occurred. Was the France of the novels a realistic representation of an historical epoch or had Simenon's literary vision somehow entered into the social imagination in place of a more accurate historical portrayal?

These questions remained in my mind for several years, but it was not until I received the opportunity to devote sufficient time and energy to sustained research of the subject that I was able to begin to try to answer them. This book is the result of research conducted in university libraries and other establishments, such as the Bibliothèque des Littératures Policières (BILIPO) and the Fonds Simenon, in France, Belgium and the United Kingdom. Much of its content is based on a Ph.D. thesis for the University of Cardiff examined in August 2009.

There is already a considerable amount of literature relating to Simenon in general and the Maigret saga in particular. Three major biographies were published in the 1980s and 1990s, and the critical evaluation of the author's writing began with Thomas Narcejac's *Le Cas Simenon* in 1950. It has continued through to the present day, although much more material exists in French than in English. The Maigret stories have been analyzed on several occasions in full-length books in French although there are no equivalent studies in English. Nevertheless, little has been written about the Maigret texts viewed in the context of contemporary social class relations and social change. In French, Jean Fabre and Jacques Dubois provide analyses of the Maigret narratives using an approach based on sociological criteria. However, interesting as these studies are, they are limited in the amount of attention they devote to close textual analysis of the narratives. Although the centenary of Simenon's birth in 2003 saw the reissue of a number of novels, both Maigret and non–Maigret, virtually nothing has been published in English on Simenon and/or Maigret in recent years. Publications on Simenon in French in the past decade have tended to be on aspects of his work other than the Maigret series, for example his travels or his photography.

This book concentrates on a clearly defined area of the Maigret saga, that is to say social class, social change and the representation of social reality in a series of crime fiction narratives. Readers wishing to explore in depth other themes pertinent to the series, such as the relation between the Maigret narratives and the non–Maigret *romans durs*, the commissaire's career in cinema and television or the author's literary techniques, will find a plethora of resources at their disposal. The websites of Stephen Trussel, in English (http://www.trussel.com/f_maig.htm) and the Centre d'Etudes Georges Simenon, in French (http://www.libnet.ulg.ac.be/simenon.htm) are the essential starting points.

Citations in this book from Simenon's fictional, journalistic and autobiographical writings are from published English-language editions. Where possible I have followed British and American spelling conventions according to the country of publication. Where no English-language edition exists, I have provided my own translations. The frequent use of ellipsis is Simenon's and not my work or that of other translators. Where French-language secondary sources are cited, these are generally my translations, excepting Pierre Assouline's biography of Simenon, where citations are from the published English-language edition.

Introduction

Why Should We Study the Maigret Stories?

As well as his 75 novels and 28 short stories featuring Maigret, Simenon also wrote more than 100 non–Maigret novels, another 200-plus novels and novellas under various pseudonyms and numerous volumes of autobiography and journalism. Simenon is the only non-anglophone crime fiction author who has found international renown with readers and critics alike. In addition to their extraordinary commercial achievements, the Maigret stories have been credited with establishing a new direction in crime fiction, emphasizing social and psychological portraiture rather than focusing on a "puzzle" to be solved or on "action" (Dulout, 1997, 32). Other critics see the Maigret investigations as a first step towards the police procedural novel of the post–1945 period (Mandel, 1984, 53). André Vanoncini goes so far as to propose that "few detectives have become mythical figures. The entire membership of this highly exclusive club consists of Sherlock Holmes, Hercule Poirot, Philip Marlowe and Jules Maigret" (2002, 56).

If we agree with the pre–Socratic Greek philosopher Parmenides that "nothing comes from nothing," then the following two questions present themselves: What were the circumstances that led to Simenon's creation of Commissaire Jules Maigret? What needs did these stories meet in order to make them so remarkably successful? This book will attempt to answer these questions.

"To understand literature, then, means understanding the total social process of which it is part," says Terry Eagleton (1976, 5–6). At the same time, an understanding of any given society inevitably involves an understanding of the literary forms it produces. Indeed, according to Engels, "One can learn more about the development of French society [in the early nineteenth century] from Balzac, despite his royalism, than from all the professional historians, economists and statisticians of the period put together" (1888, in Solmon, ed., 1973, 68). In this book I will examine how social class and social change, two key features of capitalist society and, indeed, all hitherto existing class-structured societies, manifest themselves in the literary forms of the Maigret novels and short stories composed by Georges Simenon, particularly those written in the 1930s. I will argue that a full understanding of the significance of these texts is made possible only by placing them in "the total social process of which [they are] part" (Eagleton, 1976, 6). First, however, I will briefly comment on the position of crime fiction in bourgeois society, the importance of the period between the 1914–1918 and 1939–1945 world wars and the centrality of Georges Simenon's Maigret texts in the history of the genre.

In the words of Ernest Mandel, "The history of the crime story is a social history, for it appears intertwined with the history of bourgeois society itself" (1984, 135). If the capitalist economic system is characterized by generalized commodity production (Mandel, 1973, 10–11), then crime fiction is a commodity par excellence. Mandel's argument finds support from numerous francophone crime fiction critics and practitioners. Jean-Jacques Tourteau argues that crime fiction is a commodity insofar as it is an object produced for its exchange value, rather than as an expression of the beliefs or feelings of its creator:

> The producers (publishers and authors) ... produce what sells rather than trying to sell what happens to be produced.... The publishers of crime novels look therefore for what will sell; then they produce it. Once the content has been decided, the product must be marketed: appearance, price, distribution, all require their full attention [Tourteau, 1970, 28–29].

It follows for Marc Lits that: "The crime novel ... has always had a direct relationship with its potential public, seeking to achieve the widest possible readership and the largest possible print runs, not denying its status as a 'commodity'" (Lits, 1999, 114).

Jean-Patrick Manchette, himself a successful crime fiction author, sees in the commodity status of the genre something which distinguishes it from forms of literary production characteristic of earlier modes of production:

> The crime novel is defined by the fact that it is produced directly for the market. Therefore it stands outside the traditional distinction between "highbrow" and "popular" artistic creation.... The crime novel is, and has been since its emergence as a distinct genre, an object of consumption [Manchette, 1983, 102].

For Franck Evrard, crime fiction shares many characteristic features with other forms of popular literature conceived and produced for mass consumption:

In its manner of production and consumption the crime novel embodies the characteristics of mass produced literature as described by P. Bourdieu. Amongst other things, these include the dominance of financial criteria; methods of promotion, advertising and marketing; the target readership (non-intellectual elements within the ruling class and other social layers); the hope for immediate short-term success; the orientation to existing tastes which requires an adaptation to dominant norms (themes, stereotypes, writing styles); the subordination of the author to the owners of the means of production and distribution and to the expectations of public opinion [Evrard, 1996, 26–27].

A commodity is a product created to be sold on the market, as opposed to one which has been made for direct consumption. Every commodity must have a use value or nobody would buy it, since the purchaser is concerned with the commodity's ultimate consumption and with satisfying some need. The commodity represented by crime fiction clearly satisfies a major social need, if sales figures are used as a measure. According to a UNESCO study, more than a billion copies of Agatha Christie's novels have been sold worldwide, Frédéric Dard has sold more than 100 million novels under the pseudonym of "San Antonio," and Georges Simenon's crime fiction sells more than one million copies per year (Dulout, 1997, 42). It follows that for a literary form to achieve this degree of popularity it must have a profound resonance with its readership and, if literary production and consumption are understood as being the expression of social relations and practices within class society, then a study of crime fiction constitutes an invaluable tool for understanding the ideology and social imagination of any given moment within the development of capitalist society. The importance of this perspective for the study of literature was recognized as early as 1970 by Jacques Dubois, who would become a prominent commentator on crime fiction in general and Georges Simenon in particular:

> One of the tasks of sociological criticism, which recognizes that classical literature is in fact the literature of a particular class, is therefore to break down certain barriers and to widen the field of literary study. So it takes an interest in texts that were formerly considered "popular" ... in order to show that between these writings and the traditional objects of literary criticism the differences are often only of degree and custom [1970, cited in Lits, 1999, 114].

The interwar period marks a significant moment in the history of capitalism. At an international level, the capitalist system underwent a roller-coaster ride of boom and bust, accompanied by immense political upheavals. The revolutionary upsurge during the period 1917–1921 saw the successful defense of the Russian Revolution and the removal of the czarist empire from the capitalist sphere, while also witnessing the defeats of the German and Hungarian revolutions. From 1921 to 1924 capitalism stabilized itself with parliamentary regimes holding firm in all countries except Italy, where Mussolini's Fascist movement seized power in October 1922. The years from 1924 to 1929 saw a continued expansion of capitalism in the United States, Britain and France but a developing economic and political crisis in Germany. The Wall Street crash of 1929 ushered in an international recession leading to the accession to power of the National Socialists in Germany in 1933 and the rise of the French Popular Front from 1935 to 1936. In 1936 civil war erupted in Spain between the parliamentary Republican administration and the forces of reaction headed by General Franco, and by 1939 Europe was at war again as the contending imperialisms of Germany on the one side and Britain and France on the other fought for access to and control of the markets of Central and Eastern Europe.

Simultaneously with these momentous political and social developments, capitalism was itself undergoing a major transformation. In 1917 Lenin and Bukharin published major texts noting the transition of capitalism from its "classical" nineteenth-century forms to the new stage of imperialism. According to Lenin:

> The old capitalism, the capitalism of free competition ... is passing away. A new capitalism has come to take its place, bearing obvious features of something transient, a mixture of free competition and monopoly.... Thus the twentieth century marks the turning point from the old capitalism to the new, from the domination of capital in general to the domination of finance capital.... Capitalism's transition to the stage of monopoly capitalism, to finance capital, is connected with the intensification of the struggle for the partitioning of the world [1978, 38, 39, 45, 74].

Lenin further predicted that while smaller-scale capitalist enterprises might be able to survive, and even prosper, in periods of expansion of the economy as a whole, such businesses would be disproportionately hit in times of recession. The petite bourgeoisie would be increasingly marginalized by the predominance of monopoly and finance capital and the increasing socialization of production. Although they might rail against "modern" capitalism, their protests would be ineffective, flying in the face of the actual material development of the mode of production: "Reactionary, petit bourgeois critics of capitalist imperialism dream of going *back* to 'free,' 'peaceful' and 'honest' competition," according to Lenin (27).

At the same time as the development of capitalism in the advanced economies of the United States, Britain and France was bearing out Lenin's analysis, crime fiction, an example in popular culture of the general economic trend, was undergoing a period of major expansion in quantitative terms. Magazines publishing crime stories, such as *Black Mask* in the United States, had massive circulations; the British middle-class reading public responded enthusiastically to authors such as Agatha Christie, Dorothy Sayers, Margery Allingham and J.D. Carr; in France, collections such as *Le Masque* and *L'Empreinte* introduced readers to the stories of anglophone authors such as Christie, Ellery Queen and Carr, as well as publishing domestically produced crime fiction. The emergence of the cinema as a new form of popular entertainment included at the center of its programming crime-based stories, such as *Underworld* (1927), released in France as *Les Nuits de Chicago*, *Scarface* (1931) and *Little Caesar* (1931).

Following the publication in Liège of journalistic articles, short stories and a novella, written while he was still a teenager, Georges Simenon made his literary debut in early 1920s France, producing the kind of "pulp" literature that met the needs of a capitalist publishing industry attracted by an expanding market of readers based on the immense progress in universal literacy in France that resulted from the introduction of free and compulsory education under the Third Republic. The comparative prosperity of the postwar period contributed, providing greater disposable income for leisure activities. Simenon's decision, in 1929, to write crime fiction novels and short stories and his creation of the character of Commissaire Jules Maigret was to have enormous consequences for both himself and the development of the genre.

The public response to Maigret was immediate and dramatic: from an income of 103,380 francs in 1930, Simenon's revenue tripled to 310,561 francs in 1931, the year of publication of the first Maigret novels (Assouline, 1997, 111), with receipts from Fayard, the publisher of his Maigret stories, as his biggest source of income. Three films based on the novels followed in 1932 and 1933, and Simenon's 1932 earnings increased to 372,921 francs, the vast majority of which came from Fayard's royalties and from film rights to Maigret novels (113). Simenon's popularity was not confined to France; by 1939 he was the most widely translated contemporary French-language writer in the world, with 18 translations (the great majority of which were Maigret stories), second only to Alexandre Dumas *père*, who with 22 held the record for non-contemporary French authors (153).

Simenon had been praised by authors as diverse as Céline, Colette, Cocteau and Mauriac, while the future Nobel laureate André Gide described him as "the greatest of all, the most genuine novelist we have had in literature" (Marnham, 1992, 2). By the time his last novel, *Maigret et monsieur Charles*, was published in 1972, Simenon had written 75 Maigret novels and 28 Maigret short stories. In 1982 his world sales (Maigret texts and other novels included) were said to be over 700 million copies in 55 languages, making him the most widely read living author in the world at that time (Perisset, 1986, 217).

If Antonio Gramsci is right that "the success of a work of commercial literature indicates ... the 'philosophy of the age,' that is, the mass of feelings and conceptions of the world predominant among the 'silent majority'" (1985, 348), then there could be no better starting point to examine social class and social change in crime fiction in a francophone context than the 1930s Maigret writings.

The Aims of This Book

There is no shortage of literature relating to Simenon in general and the Maigret saga in particular. Three major biographies have been published (Assouline, 1997, Eskin, 1987, and Marnham, 1992) by French, American and British authors respectively; the critical evaluation of the author's writing, as opposed to his life, began in earnest with Thomas Narcejac's *Le Cas Simenon* in 1950 and has continued through to the present day, although much more material is available in French than in English. The Maigret stories have been analyzed in full-length books by writers such as André Vanoncini (1990), Alain Bertrand (1994) and Bernard Alavoine (1999) and ephemeral studies on particular aspects of the Maigret corpus extend as far as *Madame Maigret's Recipes* (Courtine, 1975).

Nevertheless, little has been written about the Maigret texts viewed in the context of issues of contemporary social class relations and social change. Jean Fabre (1981), for the corpus as a whole, and Jacques Dubois (1980 and 1992), for the 1931–1934 Fayard series, provide sustained analyses of the Maigret narratives using an approach based on sociological criteria, and Thierry Gouttefangeas (1991) offers a historian's perspective on the early novels: the present study owes a great debt to all three. However, it could be argued that these scholars, immensely valuable as their studies are, are limited in the amount of attention they devote to close textual analysis of the stories themselves. Fabre (1981) proposes that "we must look in two directions: outside the text ... in the 'historical' relationship between the author and his/her output; then, and more implicitly, in the specific working out of each text" (21). Nevertheless, taken as a whole, Fabre's study places more emphasis on the former "direction" than the latter: he succeeds in establishing the petit bourgeois nature of Simenon's ideology in relation to his literary practice in the series, but there is much less on how the issues of social class and social change drive forward the narratives. Dubois (1980 and 1992) succeeds in establishing the importance of a sociological approach to the study of the early Maigret novels but, like Fabre, his focus is primarily on Simenon's class position at a global level, and his study of how the social relations of the interwar period structure the development of plot and character remains tantalisingly underdeveloped. Gouttefangeas (1991) presents an important overview of the extent to which the portrayal of inter-war French society in the Fayard novels corresponds to actual sociological data on the period, but social class and social change are considered more at a static, comparative level than in terms of their dynamic, determining role within the texts.

The present study attempts to focus on the texts themselves to draw out their meanings in terms of the social context in, by and for which they were produced. My approach is influenced in this by Stephen Knight's argument that:

> There are several reasons for taking some central examples ... and giving them a detailed ... treatment. A close analysis is necessary to establish just what is the implicit meaning of a story. [It is necessary to] concentrate on the nature and function of the texts themselves. This method helps to make criticism consider a work in terms of its social relations rather than only in terms of its relations with other works.... The content of the text, its omissions and selections, is important. Plot itself is a way of ordering events; its outcome distributes triumph and defeat, praise and blame to the characters in a way that accords with the audience's belief in dominant cultural values—which themselves interlock with the social structure [1980, 2, 3, 4].

A second major focus of the present work is to consider the 1930s Maigret texts in relation to their contemporary reality. Many critics, paradoxically including many of those who recognize the important role of social class in the Maigret stories, insist on the absence of history from the narratives. Fabre and Vanoncini both remark on the absence of explicit references to contemporary events in the Maigret series:

> Moreover the absence of historical references is evident in the [Maigret] series. The action unfolds against an almost blank historical backdrop.... Events in the real world are unclear or vague [Fabre, 1981, 30].

> Simenon systematically eliminates chronological historical and ideological references from his texts to such a degree that there is little point in attempting to read them from a "realist" perspective [Vanoncini, 1990, 62].

For Richard Vinen, *Le Chien jaune* is an exception to the norm of the Maigret narratives in its historical realism:

> If *The Yellow Dog* does not entirely belong to Simenon's usual world, it is rooted, more precisely than most Simenon novels, in historical reality. Generally, Simenon ignored history—a Martian who based his knowledge of France on the Maigret stories would never hear of Charles de Gaulle and would learn almost nothing about France's experiences of the Second World War [Vinen, 2003a, 2–3].

Christopher Shorley makes a similar point:

Further, Simenon is generally seen in the Maigret texts as downplaying the importance of history and politics in interwar France. It would certainly be difficult to deduce from them the current key events or controversies, let alone to identify Simenon's own sympathies. At the same time, he offers an acute awareness of individuals and their social backgrounds [Shorley, in Gorrara ed., 2009, 44].

There is a difficulty here. Fabre alleges "an almost blank historical backdrop," yet insists elsewhere (1981, 200ff) that Simenon is "a petit bourgeois intellectual in history." Does the "absence of historical references" contradict this latter assertion? Does the lack of *explicit* "chronological historical and ideological references" necessarily render a text less realistic? Does an author's stated disregard of history inevitably mean the latter is absent from his writing? If Simenon is acutely aware of the social backgrounds of individuals, these cannot be in some abstract sense: must they not exist within a definite, historically determined class society? The present work, in its approach to social class and social change in the Maigret stories, particularly those of the 1930s, will address all of these questions.

The Methodology of This Book

The approach and concepts used here are Marxist; that is to say, they are based on a methodological approach and a view of society developed by Karl Marx and subsequent thinkers influenced by him, principally Marx's co-thinker, Friedrich Engels; V.I. Lenin; Antonio Gramsci; and Nicos Poulantzas. Central to the methodological approach is the understanding that:

> In the social production of their life, men enter into definite relations that are indispensable and independent of their will, relations of production which correspond to a definite stage of development of their material productive forces. The sum total of these relations of production constitutes the economic structure of society, the real foundation, on which rises a legal and political superstructure and to which correspond definite forms of social consciousness. The mode of production of material life conditions the social, political and intellectual life process in general. It is not the consciousness of men that determines their being, but, on the contrary, their social being that determines their consciousness [Marx, 1859, in McLellan (ed.), 1980, 389].

From this it follows for Marx that:

> The ideas of the ruling class are in every epoch the ruling ideas, i.e. the class which is the ruling material force of society, is at the same time its ruling intellectual force. The class which has the means of material production at its disposal has control at the same time over the means of mental production.... The ruling ideas are nothing more than the ideal expression of the dominant

material relationships, the dominant material relationships grasped as ideas [Marx, 1845, in McLellan (ed.), 1980, 176].

This does not, however, mean that Marxism is a crude economic determinism in which all elements of social life, including literary production, can be simply reduced to the mode of production and the stage of development of the economy at a given conjuncture. Engels was at pains to point this out:

> According to the materialist conception of history, the *ultimately* determining element in history is the production and reproduction of real life. Other than this neither Marx nor I have ever asserted. Hence if somebody twists this into saying that the economic element is the *only* determining one, he transforms that proposition into a meaningless, abstract, senseless phrase. The economic situation is the basis, but the various elements of the superstructure ... also exercise their influence upon the course of the historical struggles and in many cases preponderate in determining their *form* [1890, in Marx, Engels, Lenin, 1972, 294].

In short, the Marxist view of the world is an integrated one rather than a series of structural "strata." A mode of production does not exist in the abstract in Platonic ideal forms of feudalism, capitalism, and so on. Rather, economic production is a concrete activity, carried out by real people: it takes place as part of a given society, not separately from, and still less prior to, the social formation within which it exists. Each society has developed its own specific historical path in which social and political forms have a degree of relative autonomy and in which existing social practices and ideologies influence the practical forms taken at each new stage of development. In terms of literature, this may include the influence of preceding literary traditions and writers, or the specific background, beliefs and personal agenda of an individual author.

However, just as literature cannot be understood as a simple "reflection" of society, neither is it inspired by a mysterious artistic muse or explicable purely in terms of the author's personal life experience and psychology. Literary production constitutes an individual's way of interpreting the world, but that vision of the world is experienced in relation to the dominant ideology of the age, the way in which the material class relations of everyday life are embodied conceptually in the social imagination. In short, ideology is a definite, historically relative structure of perception which underpins the position of a particular social class. People are not free to choose their ideology, any more than they are free to choose their social class position; they are constrained by the nature and stage of development of the mode of production and their position within class society.

> An ideology is never a simple reflection of a ruling class's ideas; on the contrary, it is always a complex phenomenon, which may incorporate conflicting,

even contradictory views of the world. To understand an ideology, we must analyze the precise relations between different classes in a society; and to do that means grasping where those classes stand in relation to the mode of production [Eagleton, 1976, 6–7].

Although all societies are based on a dominant mode of production, they may contain in their concrete forms elements of several economic systems. Thus, for example, European capitalist societies in the period leading up to the Great War contained remnants of the feudal mode of production and simple commodity production, that is, the form of transition from feudalism to capitalism. However, their dominant mode of production was capitalism, which existed in both its "classical" competitive form and the emerging monopoly-imperialist form identified by Lenin. Following the war, monopoly capitalism consolidated its dominance within the capitalist mode of production as a whole, while feudal production largely disappeared and simple commodity production entered into a phase of dissolution. These developments had a profound effect on social class structure and class relations. While each historical mode of production is fundamentally based on the opposition of two classes (e.g., lords and serfs under feudalism, capitalists and proletarians under capitalism), because all existing societies are composed of various forms of production, they necessarily involve several complexes of social classes.

So, alongside the principal classes of capitalists and proletarians, early twentieth-century Western European societies also included the remnants of the feudal aristocracy, the peasantry and a declining urban petite bourgeoisie engaged in simple commodity production. In addition, the transition from "classical" to monopoly capitalism involved the expansion of a social layer which, while it was not petit bourgeois in the classical sense of being made up of small property owners and commodity producers, held a position within society which was premised on its role in assuring the reproduction of the existing social division of labor. Poulantzas (1974) characterizes this group as the nouvelle petite bourgeoisie, suggesting that it includes managerial, professional and technical elements within both the private and public sectors.

One criterion for judging the success of realist fiction is the extent to which it succeeds in portraying the society it describes in its full social richness. To succeed fully in these terms, literature should not only present the principal social classes in their relation to the society as a whole and to each other but should also indicate the tendencies of development within the society—its presentation of reality will be dynamic rather than static. It is my contention that Simenon's work in the Fayard novels represents its society in its rich complexity; but that the author's failure to grasp the inherent directions of change in twentieth century capitalism reduces his capacity to sustain the correspondence between his narratives and a changing social reality in the post–1945 period.

In this introduction I have established the key points underpinning the chapters that follow. I argue that an understanding of literature requires an understanding of the society in and by which it is produced and that by seeking to understand literature we can better understand that society. I propose that social class and social change are fundamental features of all societies and that an important criterion for judging the success of fiction is the extent to which it is able to explore how these categories manifest themselves through plot, characterization, settings and themes, and that a successful realist narrative should realize a broadly accurate portrait of contemporary society. I contend that the huge popularity and social weight of crime fiction in the twentieth century renders it eminently suitable for this kind of study and that the importance of the inter-war years in the transformation of capitalism makes it a particularly significant period in the development of the genre.

My study focuses on the 1930s Maigret writings of Georges Simenon which, in their commercial success and critical acclaim, stand out as being seminal to the history of French-language crime fiction. In Chapters 1 and 2 I consider in depth seven of the 19 Maigret novels published between 1931 and 1934 and analyze their relation to the development of French society. In Chapter 3 I draw out Simenon's perspective as articulated through the narratives in terms of his own class position and ideology. Chapter 4 looks at the Maigret short stories of the period 1936–1938 and Simenon's contemporary journalism. Chapter 5 compares the 1930s Maigret narratives with Simenon's continuation of the saga from the end of the Second World War to 1972. Finally, Chapter 6 synthesizes the arguments in the form of a general conclusion.

CHAPTER 1

The Fayard Maigret Novels: Narratives, Contexts, Settings and Themes, 1931

Introduction

Between 1924 and 1929 Simenon produced about 150 pulp fiction novels, mostly tales of love or adventure, and a few crime stories with an "action" slant, under seventeen pseudonyms (Baronian et al., 2004–2007, "Le Roman de Georges Simenon," 19, 27). He described these as *littérature alimentaire*, which he defined as:

> a work which does not correspond to the author's personality, to his need for artistic expression, but to commercial demand. The "roman populaire" is merchandise ... corresponding fairly closely to the range of goods found in a department store. Thus the popular novelist is an industrialist or an artisan [Cited in Eskin, 1987, 63].

By late 1929 Simenon felt that he was ready to move on in his literary career: "What should I write next? For some time I had the feeling that my apprenticeship was drawing to a close. I was still hesitant to launch into a more difficult, if not more serious vein" (cited in Eskin, 74). Caught between pulps and his feeling of insecurity about writing "real" literature, he developed a theory of the *roman semi-littéraire*, a midway step (Assouline, 1997, 90–91). After some experimentation with what Eskin (1987, 75) calls "pre-" or "proto–Maigrets," in which Commissaire Maigret features briefly (Brulls, 1930 and 1932; Sim, 1932), which were all written before the Maigret series, although some were published after a delay of several years, Simenon approached one of his main publishers, Arthème Fayard, in the spring of

1930 with the manuscript for *Pietr-le-Letton*. Simenon later claimed to have written this novel in September 1929, although Claude Menguy and Pierre Deligny (1989) argue convincingly that it was composed in early 1930, and he proposed a major "launch" to the publisher. Fayard's response, according to Simenon's account, was "We're going to lose a lot of money, but I'll try it anyway" (cited in Eskin, 79), and a contract was duly signed on May 26.

Fayard published 19 Maigret novels between February 1931 and April 1934 and, contrary to his fears, they were a huge commercial success. Fayard's archives were later lost in a fire, so no exact sales figures exist. However, using criteria such as contemporary press reviews, the rapid adaptation to the cinema of a number of the texts and the number of translations into other languages, it is reasonable to say that the nineteen novels were immensely profitable. This can be seen in the dramatic increase in Simenon's income from 103,385 francs in 1931 to 717,216 francs in 1934 (Assouline, 1991, 111, 193).

Although the character of Maigret necessarily undergoes some development throughout the series, the short period of composition imposes a degree of coherence and consistency on the texts and their contexts. Thus Dubois (1992, 173) proposes: "As, moreover, the different stories mesh together as a result of recurring features, we are led to treat the nineteen novels as a single large text." From this body of work I will concentrate my analysis on seven books: *Monsieur Gallet décédé*, *Le Chien jaune*, *La Tête d'un homme*, *L'Ombre chinoise*, *L'Affaire Saint-Fiacre*, *Chez les Flamands* and *Le Port des brumes*, all published in 1931 or 1932. These texts have been chosen for two reasons: first, they cover a wide variety of geographical settings (Paris and the provinces, large and small towns, urban and rural locations); secondly, they show the detective operating in a broad range of social milieus, from the aristocracy to the popular classes, passing through various strata of the bourgeoisie. They therefore show us both a "horizontal" and a "vertical" cross-section of French society in the inter-war period.

Monsieur Gallet décédé: *Petit-Bourgeois Mediocrity and Ambition in a Changing Society*

Monsieur Gallet décédé and *Le Pendu de Saint-Pholien* were the first Maigret novels to be published, simultaneously in February 1931. Although *Monsieur Gallet décédé* was not any less well received at the time than its companions, modern critiques of it have been somewhat disparaging (Eskin, 1987, 87; Dubois, 1992, 176). Unlike several of the other Fayard Maigret novels, *Monsieur Gallet décédé* has not been produced as a film and is rarely discussed in Simenon criticism. Nevertheless, a close reading reveals a deep consideration by Simenon of social relations between and within classes and a working out through the story of how these relations affect the behavior of individual characters.

In *Monsieur Gallet décédé* Emile Gallet, apparently a salesman, is found dead in a hotel room in Sancerre. For 18 years, unknown to his wife, he had been dishonestly obtaining money from Royalists under the name M. Clément, using the subscription lists from his father-in-law's Royalist newspaper, *Le Soleil*, to find his sources. Maigret discovers that Gallet had been to see the owner of the neighboring estate, Tiburce de Saint-Hilaire, attempting to raise the 20,000 francs he needed to pay off a blackmailer, whose identity he did not know, who was threatening to reveal his dual existence. When Maigret locates the "blackmailer," Monsieur Jacob, he is revealed to be a newspaper seller who merely received the packages of money on behalf of Gallet's son's fiancée, Eléonore Boursang, who with Henry Gallet, the son, was the agent of the blackmail. A visit to a tax inspector who had known Gallet in Indo-China leads Maigret to the discovery that Gallet and Saint-Hilaire had switched identities many years earlier, when Gallet had discovered that Saint-Hilaire was to be the beneficiary of a large inheritance. At the time Saint-Hilaire was impoverished, and so had agreed for a financial consideration. Since then, after discovering the truth, he had visited Gallet (now "Saint-Hilaire") from time to time to ask for money. This time, unable to pay his debts, Saint-Hilaire (now "Gallet") had worked out an elaborate suicide to look like murder, so that his wife could receive the 300,000 francs life insurance policy he had been paying for the past five years.

The dating of the story in *Monsieur Gallet décédé* is extremely precise ("le 27 juin 1930," *Monsieur Gallet décédé*, 7), unlike most of the other Fayard Maigret stories, which are "contemporary" without being specifically dated. The locations are real places (Saint-Fargeau and Sancerre) and Simenon draws on his own recent travels aboard the *Ostrogoth*, as well as his earlier employment as personal secretary to the marquis de Tracy, to make the description of the settings convincing. The economic and social conjuncture in France in June 1930 was one in which the middle classes lived in an atmosphere of complacency. Although the depression of the 1930s had been heralded by the Wall Street crash of 1929, and although the economic situation in Britain was following closely behind, the French economy remained apparently untouched. At worst, the situation appeared to be one of stagnation after a period of sustained growth from 1920 to 1929 (Braudel and Labrousse, 1979–1980, 22). As late as December 1930, Tardieu, the head of the administration, was describing the financial situation as "altogether satisfying" (Dard, 1999, 13).

Nevertheless, although the middle classes as a whole had prospered throughout the 1920s, certain sectors had done better than others. Montero (2001, 62) explains that:

> In the interwar years, the middle classes were the mainstay of the republican administrations. But this position came at a high price. Even if they did not lead to a loss of social status, devaluation and inflation affected living standards and levels of consumption and unsettled returns on savings. Social mobility was high as a result of the enrichment of some and the impoverishment of others. The problem was particularly serious for retirees and small investors and savers, whose situation was in contrast to the spectacular success of those who profited from inflation: industrialists, bankers, businessmen and large-scale farmers.

Madame Gallet perhaps expresses the disillusionment of certain layers of the middle classes when she explains: "We live a rather lonely life, like all who have known better days do in this post-war period with its brutality and vulgarity" [*Monsieur Gallet décédé/Maigret Stonewalled*, 12].

Berstein and Becker (1990, 339) describe the economy as "dualistic," with certain sectors in industry, commerce and agriculture operating in a thoroughly "modern" fashion, while others still lived "to the rhythms of the nineteenth century on their farmsteads and in their shops and small workshops." This division was also evident within the aristocracy. Whilst many had managed to integrate fully into the economic life of the more advanced sectors of capitalism, others, particularly those who depended on income from unproductive tenant farmers or sharecroppers (*métayers*), often in the less fertile center or fringe areas of the country, faced an uncertain future (Zeldin, 2003, 283–284). Although their economic difficulties were relative, they faced a future in which the aristocratic prefix "de," while it may still have commanded a certain deference in some quarters, was no longer an absolute guarantee of wealth, position or power.

The principal locations in *Monsieur Gallet décédé* are a housing development at Saint-Fargeau, 35 kilometers south of Paris, where the Gallet villa is situated, and Sancerre, a small town about 160 kilometers south of Paris, known for its wine production and scenic position on the Loire, where Gallet's body had been found at the Hôtel de la Loire and where the chateau of Saint-Hilaire is located. Although the main development of Paris in the interwar period was in the working class inner-suburbs, such as Ivry, Aubervilliers, Saint-Denis, Boulogne-Billancourt and Bobigny, where the population increased by 35 percent between 1921 and 1931 (Montero, 57), the greater Paris region as a whole also saw an expansion, with the development of *lotissements*, where land could be bought for construction purposes. This was partly due to the efficiency of the French railroad services (witness Mai-

A small workshop in 1925. The economy was "dualistic," with certain sectors in industry, commerce and agriculture operating in a thoroughly "modern" fashion, while others still lived "to the rhythms of the nineteenth century on their farmsteads and in their shops and small workshops." (Courtesy Bibliothèque nationale de France.)

gret's rapid movements between the different locations) and, significantly, although most of the houses are unfinished, the railroad station in Saint-Fargeau has been completed.

On Maigret's arrival in Saint-Fargeau he encounters symbols of a society in change:

> The development area was nothing more than a huge wood, which at one time must have been part of a country estate. All that had happened so far was that a geometrical pattern of paths had been cut ... and the electric cables which would one day supply light to the houses had been laid.
> Opposite the station, however, there was a square already laid out with fountains and pools in mosaic. A wooden notice board read ESTATE SALES OFFICE. Alongside was a plan showing that these uninhabited clearings had already been named after generals and politicians [*Monsieur Gallet décédé/ Maigret Stonewalled*, 6].

It is symbolic indeed that on the one hand the old aristocratic order is being replaced by capitalist property development, yet, on the other hand, as with France's dual economy, the development remains only partly completed. The electricity cables are also an important symbol: by 1932, 82 percent of communes had household electricity against a figure of 17 percent in 1919 (Abbad, 1993, 20).

The Gallets have a servant. According to Berstein and Becker (1990, 370) this would place them in the *moyenne bourgeoisie* (a petit bourgeois family might have a daily cleaner, the wealthier bourgeois and aristocrats would have several servants). Nevertheless, the villa is described as "ordinary" (*Monsieur Gallet décédé/Maigret Stonewalled*, 24) and, although the decor is "ordinary but of good quality" (37), what strikes Maigret is that everything is an imitation of the style of the grande bourgeoisie—"imitation Persian rug" (37), "an enormous vase of fake Sèvres" (39). This aspirational imitation of the lifestyle of the rich was, according to Montero (2001, 61–62), one of the defining features of middle-class consumption habits in the 1920s and indicative of a certain type of snobbery.

This snobbery comes to the fore in the pronouncements of Madame Gallet—"We live a rather lonely life, like all who have known better days do in this postwar period with its brutality and vulgarity" (*Monsieur Gallet décédé/Maigret Stonewalled*, 16)—and in her "smile of delight at humiliating the police who had had the effrontery to intrude on her" (9), whom, as her sister later reminds Maigret, are mere *fonctionnaires* in the service of the bourgeois state (90). The divisions within the petite bourgeoisie, and the attendant snobbery, are also to the fore in Sancerre. The vacationers must by definition be petit bourgeois, since urban workers did not win paid vacations until 1936. But this is once again a pale imitation of the bourgeois and aristocratic resorts of the Côte d'Azur and Deauville: "Everything was ordinary in Sancerre too; a cheap country holiday; a second-class hotel" (24). Nevertheless, there is a strict hierarchy for the hotels, with the Hôtel de la Loire at the top (according to its proprietor), followed by the Commerce and finally establishments such as the Pension Germain (20, 80).

Both the Hôtel de la Loire and Saint-Hilaire's chateau have electricity, but neither of them has a municipal water supply (22, 69), one more indication of the unevenness of France's economic progress in the 1920s. According to Berstein and Becker (1990, 347), less than one in five rural dwellings had running water by the end of the decade. The chateau is, naturally, one of the more impressive dwellings in Sancerre, but the garden path is overgrown with nettles (*Monsieur Gallet décédé/Maigret Stonewalled*, 49) and when the missing key to the rusty gate is found it, too, shows signs of decrepitude: "It was the key—an enormous key—of a kind only to be found now amongst antique dealers, and like the lock it was rusty" (85). Like the minor aristocracy, the chateau has seen better days.

The Citroën production line in 1934. In rejecting the practices of the classes which threaten his idea of France, Simenon marginalizes the representatives of these classes in his fiction. Hence the almost complete absence of those classes representing modernity. (Courtesy Bibliothèque nationale de France.)

Reading *Monsieur Gallet décédé* through the perspective of social class and social change, relations within the petite bourgeoisie emerge as a central theme. As indicated above, the petite bourgeoisie was far from being homogenous in the France of the 1920s. Zeldin's four-volume history of modern France is written essentially from a sociocultural point of view: his first volume is titled *Ambition et amour* (2003) and the notion of "ambition" provides a useful tool for examining the relations between the different petit bourgeois characters encountered in *Monsieur Gallet décédé*.

> The ambitions of those people who never became rich, who founded neither lasting family dynasties nor companies and who occupied middling or lower positions within the business world, have scarcely attracted the attention of historians. However, a society is characterized to a considerable degree by the form taken by the ambitions of such men and by the manner in which these ambitions are either achieved or frustrated [Zeldin, 2003, 141].

Although Zeldin does not define class in a Marxist manner, it is clear that he is talking here about the petite bourgeoisie; and ambition (or lack of it) is a constant theme structuring the relations between the novel's petit bourgeois characters and driving forward the events of the narrative. On one side stand the ambitious petit bourgeois characters: Saint-Hilaire, that is, the "real" Emile Gallet, the Préjean family, Eléonore Boursang, and Monsieur Tardivon, the proprietor of the *Hôtel de la Loire*. On the other side is Gallet (that is, the "real" Comte de Saint-Hilaire) who, despite his aristocratic origins, has lived as a traveling salesman of cheap silverware before becoming a small-time swindler and whose public persona is the epitome of the complacent petit bourgeois.

The faux Saint-Hilaire is the son of a horse trader from Nantes (*Monsieur Gallet décédé/Maigret Stonewalled*, 123): he had been working as a solicitor's clerk in Saigon in the early years of the century (99–100), having left metropolitan France to seek adventure and fortune, as did many ambitious young petit bourgeois who felt they had few prospects within the comparatively rigid class system of prewar France. Hearing of a dying uncle of Saint-Hilaire who has a fortune to leave, and learning that Saint-Hilaire is the last of the family line, Gallet tracks him down with considerable determination (122). On finding the "real" Saint-Hilaire, he acts with opportunism. Rather than offering to share the fortune, Gallet "invests" the small inheritance his father has left him in buying Saint-Hilaire's name and identity (123). The purchase of titles, by one means or another, has a long history in bourgeois and pre-capitalist society and the transaction (and effective swindling by Gallet of the "real" Saint-Hilaire) is presented by its perpetrator as no more than an astute piece of business: "A businessman does the same when he buys shares at two hundred francs knowing that he will be able to sell at five times that price a month later, doesn't he?" (123). The irony of this is magnified by the fact that the French word *titre* translates both the English notions of "title of nobility" and "stocks and shares." Having made the shrewd initial investment, the "new" Saint-Hilaire has worked hard to realize the profits of his initial speculative outlay: "I was working too. I looked for good investments, and I put down all the land you can see above the estate to vines" (124). From the perspective of capitalist ideology he has behaved as a sharp businessman rather than a criminal in either a legal or moral sense.

Just as Saint-Hilaire (the "real" Gallet) has sought his fortune and social advancement using the various means open to an ambitious petit bourgeois of the period (the colonies, speculation, hard work), so, too, the Préjean family, the in-laws of Gallet (the "real" Saint-Hilaire), use every means at their disposal to make the transition from the petite bourgeoisie to a higher social position. Préjean père had tied himself to the Royalist cause as secretary to the last Bourbon prince and editor of a legitimist newspaper (35). In the early unstable years of the Third Republic this may have seemed a good move for an ambitious young man. However, with the consolidation of the bourgeois republic and the economic acceleration from 1895, the possibilities of a monarchist restoration dimmed (hence the pitiful fortunes of Préjean's newspaper, *Le Soleil*, 35, 83, 87) and Préjean is obliged to look elsewhere for the social advancement of his daughters.

The Gallets had married in 1902 (31) and although at this time 37 percent of the adult female population were in paid employment, these were essentially working-class women in domestic service, industry or shop work (Zeldin, 2003, chapter XIII). For a woman of the petite or moyenne bourgeoisie, the most realistic possibility of social advancement was through marriage: "For the great majority of the bourgeoisie," wrote Paul Bureau in 1927, "marriage was the most important financial operation of their life" (cited in Zeldin, 424). One Préjean sister, Françoise, is married to an ambitious tanner who becomes "director of one of the biggest tanneries in the Vosges" (*Monsieur Gallet décédé/Maigret Stonewalled*, 88) and a rising politician (90). A second sister marries a social climber "who will one day be principal private secretary to a minister of state" (87).

Here can be found the reason for the opposition of the whole Préjean family to Aurore's marriage to Gallet. "I have not seen them [my family] since my marriage," she explains to Maigret (35). Françoise is vitriolic on the subject:

> With the name of Aurore Préjean ... one doesn't marry an Emile Gallet! ... a commercial traveller! ... but for you, a sister of mine, with the same education as me and with our mother's looks, to have chosen this nobody... [87].

For the ambitious petit bourgeois, money, whatever its origins, was the driving force and the key to social advancement. Hence Françoise's angry response when Maigret refers to her husband as a "tanner": "'A tannery owner,' corrected Françoise dryly" (88). In this she is simply reflecting the ideology of her class at the time. As Becker and Berstein explain:

> For all that, around 1925, the theme of the *nouveaux riches* began to lose its sharpness and the *parvenus*, who had been somewhat disdained by "good society," were easily integrated, since, after all, their wealth guaranteed their bourgeois lifestyle and where money is concerned the passage of time brings acceptance [1990, 361].

Henry Gallet and his mistress, Eléonore Boursang, also demonstrate ambition in business. At the same time as they are blackmailing Gallet, they use information gained from Henry's employment in a bank to speculate on the stock exchange (*Monsieur Gallet décédé/Maigret Stonewalled*, 61–62). The economic inflation of the 1920s and the rapid rises in share values made stock market speculation a common choice for anyone seeking quick profits (Braudel and Labrousse, 1979–1980, 875). There is an interesting parallel here with Saint-Hilaire. Both he and Henry/Eléonore obtain their initial "seed capital" from Gallet, which they then seek to enlarge using the means to hand. Eléonore is sharp enough in business matters to pay the minimum possible to the newspaper seller, Monsieur Jacob, whom they use as an intermediary in their blackmail of Gallet. This young petit bourgeois woman, the daughter of an accountant in a textile mill (*Monsieur Gallet décédé/Maigret Stonewalled*, 60), widowed at the age of 21, shows drive and determination, seeking to fulfill her ambitions with a complete lack of sentimentality: "And their [Eléonore and Henry's] relationship was regulated, like two partners in a business deal!" (62).

In sharp contrast to these characters is the figure of Monsieur Gallet himself, born Tiburce de Saint-Hilaire, who, despite his aristocratic origins, has effectively lived the life of a petit bourgeois from boyhood due to the economic difficulties of his family (122–123, 128). Gallet has been dead from the beginning of the novel, so we cannot observe him directly. Nevertheless, Maigret gradually pieces together a portrait of the man from testimonies he obtains from the other characters and his interpretation of this information. The contrast with the ambitions of the other petit bourgeois is striking.

All of the other characters are agreed on Gallet's mediocrity. Maigret himself sets the ball rolling on this theme (24) and Gallet's lack of ambition seems to be his defining characteristic for his family (his wife, his son and the Préjeans) and the faux Saint-Hilare:

> "He [Henry] rather disapproved of his [Gallet's] lack of ambition" [Eléonore Boursang, 63].

"I always hoped that he [Gallet] would try something ... I encouraged him to" [Madame Gallet, 87].

"an inferior sort of person, incapable of effort" [Françoise Préjean, 88].

"He made out that he was travelling as a representative for a firm, whereas, in fact, the only profession he was following was that of cadging on other people" [Saint-Hilaire, 124].

Gallet's mediocrity and lack of ambition are linked and explained as Maigret uncovers his origins as part of the declining aristocratic country gentry:

He was born under an evil star, his family was going downhill [129].

This man who spent his childhood without having a single farthing for pocket money.... He trails hopelessly from one job to another.... He has nothing he can pawn, but he has this name, which, one fine day somebody offers to buy from him. It's still a miserable existence, but with the name Gallet, he is one up— he is ordinary. And he's got enough to keep body and soul together [128].

Like many of the small-scale aristocracy in the late nineteenth and early twentieth century, who failed to adapt to the realities of a capitalist economy and who continued to follow an essentially pre-capitalist model of production, the Saint-Hilaire family had fallen on hard times. Even the uncle whose legacy the "real" Gallet dishonestly obtained had been obliged to seek his fortune in the colonies. Braudel and Labrousse (1979–1980, 51) contrast the *aristocratie nobiliaire* who were unable to adapt from the economic model of the Ancien Régime with the *aristocratie d'argent*, who had fully integrated into the capitalist model of the Third Republic. Though the Saint-Hilaires were in the former group, times were so hard for them that entry into the petite bourgeoisie paradoxically represented an improvement in material fortunes.

If *Monsieur Gallet décédé* is read in the manner suggested above, it emerges as a narrative which is critically informed by its historical context, that is, the development of French society in the early years of the twentieth century. The novel's twin themes of social class and social change can be summarized in two images: the old, rusty antiquated key to the chateau's back gate, as a symbol of the fallen rural gentry (85), and the new housing development in Saint-Fargeau, as a symbol of petit bourgeois aspiration in postwar France; the transition from an old world to a new one within which ambition is a key factor in the fate of individuals.

Le Chien jaune: Notables *and* Petites Gens; *Class Conflict in a Provincial Town*

Le Chien jaune was the fourth story published in the series, although it was probably the sixth in order of composition. The novel was written in

March 1931 at La Michaudière (Seine-et-Oise) and published later in the same year (Eskin, 1987, 280). Since its initial publication, *Le Chien jaune* has been highly regarded by the public and critics alike: it was produced in 1932 as the second film involving Maigret, directed by Jean Tarride and starring Abel Tarride as Maigret; Marcel Aymé wrote a preface for the 1962 edition; and Régis Boyer wrote a highly favorable monograph on the text (Boyer, 1973).

In *Le Chien jaune* Maigret, assigned for the past month to Rennes in Brittany, is called to Concarneau, where the town's biggest wine dealer has been shot and wounded after leaving his drinking partners in the Hôtel de l'Amiral. Circumstances make it appear that it was chance that made him the victim. When Maigret arrives he meets the other members of the group who drink in the hotel. Ernest Michoux, a non-practicing doctor and property developer, notices powder in the drinks, which turns out to be strychnine. The next day, Jean Servières, one of the group, disappears and his blood-stained automobile is found abandoned. Journalists descend on Concarneau, and subsequently a giant vagrant is arrested but escapes. Apparently the yellow dog of the title, which has been seen around the area since the shooting, is his. Maigret arranges with his assistant, Leroy, to watch a room across the street, where they see the escaped man meet with Emma, a waitress at the hotel. Meanwhile Maigret has Michoux arrested, apparently to protect him, Yves Le Pommeret, another member of the Hôtel de l'Amiral clique, having been found poisoned in his home.

Then there is another shooting, and a customs officer is wounded. The vanished Servières is found in Paris and brought back to Concarneau, where Maigret arranges a confrontation of all the main characters: Dr. Michoux, Servières, Michoux's mother, the vagrant Léon Le Glérec, Emma and the mayor of Concarneau. The story goes back five or six years to when Le Glérec had started making payments on his boat and had planned to marry Emma. Knowing of his need for money, Michoux, Servières and Le Pommeret approached Le Glérec to carry cocaine to America, but on arrival in the U.S. Le Glérec was immediately arrested. Le Glérec learned in prison that they had set him up in order to receive a bounty on smugglers, and when finally released he had vowed to have them imprisoned, even if it was for killing him. He revealed himself to the doctor, who had tricked Emma into writing Le Glérec a note to meet her at the doorway where the wine merchant was shot by mistake. Michoux had poisoned Le Pommeret when the latter had considered giving himself up to the police, and Michoux's mother had shot the customs officer to make her son, in jail, appear innocent. Le Glérec and Emma set off to restart their lives while the guilty Michoux faces a 20-year prison term.

Although the passage of time in *Le Chien jaune* is scrupulously recorded—indeed, the novel starts with the words "Friday, 7 November" (*Le Chien jaune/The Yellow Dog*, 1)—no year is given for the story. However, it seems reasonable to assume that the events are set in 1930 since in that year, as in the text, 7 November was a Friday. The international context was one in which the economic boom of the 1920s had been brought to an end by the Wall Street crash of 1929, which ushered in a period of recession. This downturn had a delayed impact on the French economy, which did not begin its slide into depression until 1931 (Dard, 1999, 15–16) and consequently much of the French public looked on what was happening elsewhere in the world as if they were detached spectators (Dard, 11). The prohibition of the manufacture, transportation and sale of alcohol in the United States in 1920, which was not repealed until 1933, had led to a massive increase in organized crime across that country as a profitable, frequently violent, black market for alcohol flourished and powerful gangs often corrupted law enforcement agencies. In *Le Chien jaune* the impact of this development reaches beyond the United States to a small provincial French town (*Le Chien jaune/The Yellow Dog*, 84, 112, 114, 116).

Although the international recession was delayed in France, the boom of the 1920s had not been without negative effects for many people. Inflation was rampant from 1914 to 1928 with the purchasing power of the franc falling by 415 percent (Braudel and Labrousse, 1979–1980, 646). This eventually led to the devaluation of the franc and the institution of the "gold exchange standard" by the Poincaré administration in June 1928. This erosion of the value of savings and its implications for those on a fixed income caused particular difficulties for French citizens such as Le Pommeret in *Le Chien jaune* whose income derived principally from inheritances, savings or fixed-return investments (Braudel and Labrousse, 43). As Zeldin (2003, vol. 1, 98) says of the *rentier* class who had prospered in the pre-war period: "A large proportion of them were more idle than they were rich." Increasingly, economic advancement was seen to be a function of speculation, "new" money rather than "old" (Braudel and Labrousse, 55; Abad, 1993, 18).

This speculation sometimes took the form of playing the stock exchange, as in the activities of Henry Gallet and Eléonore Boursang in *Monsieur Gallet décédé*, or of property speculation. This latter is also present in *Monsieur Gallet*, in the housing development at Saint-Fargeau, and it constitutes the primary economic activity of Doctor Michoux in *Le Chien jaune*. Significantly, the mayor of Concarneau, who appears as a representative par excellence of "old money," is also heavily involved in Michoux's property development scheme (*Le Chien jaune/The Yellow Dog*, 94). While in a period of economic boom such activities were potentially lucrative, even Michoux is forced to admit that there is "nothing very impressive" about it all (64).

A key feature of France's economy and society in the inter-war period was the deep inequality between "haves" and "have-nots." Abbad (1993, 17) provides the following breakdown of annual incomes:

Proportion of the population	Annual revenue
1.84%	More than 1 million francs
11.36%	100,000–1 million francs
11.35%	50,000–100,000 francs
59.83%	10,000–50,000 francs
15.62%	Less than 10,000 francs

Considering accumulated wealth, rather than income, Zeldin (2003, vol. 1, 96) calculates: "In 1933, 1,512 people who died left more than a million francs—that is to say, 30 percent of total legacies.... On the other hand, 53.6 percent of people who died left nothing at all."

Between 1921 and 1935 the population of France's cities and towns increased by 3.5 million inhabitants, a rise of 22 percent, with the urban population becoming a majority for the first time in 1931. Nevertheless, in 1931 only 17 cities possessed more than 100,000 residents. The majority of urban dwellers lived in towns of between 5,000 and 20,000 inhabitants (Abbad, 1993, 10). In many ways, Concarneau was a typical French town of the 1920s in its size and composition.

The economy, too, presented a dichotomy between rapidly expanding sectors such as automobile manufacture, aircraft production, steel, aluminum and chemicals, often concentrated in or around the largest cities such as Paris, Lyon, Marseille and Toulouse, and other, more traditional industries, often in smaller towns, where production methods had barely progressed from the pre-war period. This has led historians to talk about a "two-speed development" (Montero, 2001, 53), economic and social "dualism" (Becker and Berstein, 1990, 339) and "a mixture of archaism and modernity" (Abbad, 1993, 85).

The political life of most small towns reflected their economic and social situation. In many areas the main political force was the Radical Party, characterized by Agulhon, Nouschi and Schor (1993, 54) as:

> The most typically French of all the parties. "Little people" in the countryside and the towns, above all the small towns, neither millionaires nor proletarians, they typified in a general sense the persistence of individualism in the French economy: from an American perspective, they represented all that was most outdated in France.

Montero describes the Radicals as "the traditional representatives of small property owners" [2001, 42].

If there was nothing particularly "radical" about the Radicals, the situation in areas where a majority of the population were practicing Catholics (such as Brittany) was even more dominated by conservatism, with most small-town politics controlled by the various conservative forces who backed the right-wing administrations from 1919 to 1924 and 1928 to 1932 (Agulhon et al., 1993, 73). Whatever the political complexion of local politics, the dominant force in France's provincial towns was usually the *notables*: local businessmen, landowners or members of the professions who, through their economic standing, social networks and relationships of family or marriage, existed as a kind of separate group within society, living apart from and above the popular masses and governing as if by right.

The specific geographical setting of *Le Chien jaune* is established from the very first sentence of the novel: "Friday 7 November. Concarneau is empty" (*Le Chien jaune/The Yellow Dog*, 1). How important is the fact that the story is set in a small Breton seaport? To what extent is this setting central to the portrayal of the social context of the crime and its resolution? In the 1920s Concarneau was primarily a fishing port whose hinterland produced cauliflowers and artichokes for domestic consumption and export. The town was also a popular destination for vacationers from the Paris region during the summer months. Today the population of around 25,000 has increased little in the last eighty years and the principal economic activities remain the same. The *département* of Finisterre, where Concarneau is located, is the most western in metropolitan France, with its largest town the naval base of Brest; Servière's newspaper is the *Phare de Brest*.

Brittany has traditionally been known in France for its alleged economic and social backwardness, political and religious conservatism, alcoholism and its wet and windy climate (Aplin, 1993, 208–209). This weather is present from the opening of Simenon's narrative—"A south-westerly gale is slamming the boats together in the harbor" (*Le Chien jaune/The Yellow Dog*, 1)— but this may be thought of as providing a combination of local color and as a literary device metaphorically suggesting the murky state of affairs in the town; as the case becomes clearer, so the weather also clears. However, other specific references to the Breton context seem to highlight the text's desire to present a setting that represents all that is most backward-looking in French provincial life in the period. The streets are unpaved (42) and life can often be hard, as shown in the deaths at sea of Emma's father and brother (16). The potent mixture of religion and alcohol as a means of perpetuating the ideological subordination of working people is suggested in Léon's plans for the 'baptism' of the *Belle Emma*: "The Quimper priest promised he would christen her [the boat] next week.... Everyone will be drunk" [100–101]. Emma's pitifully few possessions include her rosary, communion medal and a small gold crucifix (100). The descriptions of the traditional costumes of the women on market day or other special occasions (7, 50, 75 and 99) suggest a society rooted in the past.

Concarneau was, and remains, an important fishing port and the inter-war period saw an expansion and modernization of the industry. But, according to Braudel and Labrousse (1979–1980, 845), this was centered on Boulogne-sur-Mer, in the Pas-de-Calais, and Lorient, in the Breton *département* of Morbihan, adjoining Finisterre. The reference to unemployment in the fish-processing industry in Concarneau (*Le Chien jaune/The Yellow Dog*, 55) and the difficulties faced by Léon as a small independent boat owner transporting vegetables to Britain (112–113) reflect the difficulties faced by working people in the region. Set against these difficulties is the privileged position of the *notables*, meeting at the Hôtel de l'Amiral, "the best in town" (5) which "was like the centre of town" (56).

The text portrays the dull, inward-looking backwardness of a provincial town, recognized as such by several of the story's characters. According to Maigret: "We're taking a real plunge into small-town life" (69). "Everyone knows everyone else," says Leroy (21); Maigret notes that "there was certainly something dead about the town" (27); and Madame Servières observes that "there's not much going on here" (30). Thus, while we might conclude that there is little to distinguish Concarneau from hundreds of other French towns, its choice as the setting for the story does in fact bring together Simenon's perceptions and implicit criticisms of social relations in provincial France during the inter-war period. The representative typicality of Concarneau is important for Simenon, but its implied regional backwardness also serves his purpose admirably.

The characters of *Le Chien jaune* can be divided into three groups: the *notables*, the working people and the police. Part of the richness of Simenon's characterization lies in the way the reader frequently sees the same person from a range of descriptive angles—as described by the narrator, another character or themselves. In the case of the *notables*, what little information is given about Monsieur Mostaguen, the first victim, sets the tone for the rest of the Hôtel de l'Amiral clique. He is "Concarneau's biggest wine dealer" (*Le Chien jaune/The Yellow Dog*, 3), which marks him as an important figure locally but only as a big fish in a very small pool, given the smallness of Concarneau and the fact that it is not in a wine-producing area. His provincialism is emphasized by his Breton surname, while his fear of his wife (3) suggests that, for all their pretense, the *notables* of the Hôtel de l'Amiral are a slightly ridiculous group.

Ridiculous they may be, but they are not harmless. Doctor Michoux is referred to by all and sundry by his professional title although he has never practiced medicine and gains his livelihood from property speculation. We see Michoux in an unflattering light from the perspective of Maigret ("degenerate type," 33), and even his own description of himself is self-pitying and negative ("all those evenings at a café table with those other failures," 64). The only character with a good word for him is Servières (6) and this is as much an attempt to present himself as part of an important group as any real respect or affection for the doctor. Everything about Michoux suggests failure: his business affairs, his poor health, his cowardice and his divorce (33 and Chapter 6) all add up to a portrayal of provincial small-mindedness.

Le Pommeret represents a different kind of smallness—the small aristocracy. Historically, the aristocracy's position was based on its ownership of land and feudal control of the peasantry, but Le Pommeret has fallen so far that he does not even own his apartment (46) or employ a servant (33). The impact of the high inflation of the 1920s on small *rentiers*, described by Abbad (1993, 18), has hit Le Pommeret hard. In contrast, his brother has become a successful businessman in the local fish-canning industry (*Le Chien jaune/The Yellow Dog*, 33, 69). We are reminded of the "two aristocracies" of Braudel and Labrousse (1979–1980, 51), those who have adapted to modern capitalism and those who have failed to do so. Le Pommeret is described in negative terms by Maigret (*Le Chien jaune/The Yellow Dog*, 33), a local policeman (55) and his brother (69).

Servières is another mediocrity: Inspector Leroy's researches reveal a history of shady dealings and bankruptcies (68). In common with Michoux and Le Pommeret, Servières has failed in Paris before retreating to establish himself as a *notable* in small-town Concarneau (34, 68). Madame Michoux is an equally unattractive character. As a woman, she cannot be a *notable* in her own right, but she uses her position as the widow of a former deputy and a friend of the mayor's wife to advance her interests: "They say she has a lot of influence," as the local policeman puts it (59). When she is summoned by Maigret for the dénouement, she reacts with the outrage of one who sees herself and her social class as being above the law: "It's simply outrageous! When I think that my husband was a deputy" [110].

While the *notables* of the *Hôtel de l'Amiral* represent the mediocrity of the provincial bourgeoisie, the mayor of Concarneau is an altogether different matter. Significantly, we never learn his name—he is always "Monsieur le maire," a character defined by his political position in the town. Whereas Michoux, Le Pommeret and Servières are all failures, the mayor is a successful provincial bourgeois. Becker and Berstein offer the following criteria for membership of the haute bourgeoisie:

> The bourgeois way of life was defined by ... a comfortable spacious home ... servants ... a certain style of dress ... a family life ... based on stay-at-home wives ... consumption ... vacations, an automobile, leisure activities [1990, 361 ff].

The mayor's house is compared to both a feudal chateau and an English manor house (*Le Chien jaune/The Yellow Dog*, 87) and he has several servants (86–87). His appearance is "very well groomed" (41) and he wears a derby outdoors (42) and a silk-trimmed smoking jacket at home (92). Although the mayor is about 65 years old, he has a "trophy wife" about 25 years younger than himself (87). Furthermore, his lifestyle extends to a luxurious chauffeur-driven automobile (41, 86). The mayor is, indeed the most notable of the *notables*. He threatens Leroy and Maigret with his political connections in Paris (32, 52) and does not hesitate to meddle in the police inquiry, giving orders to the local police and gendarmerie with the air of one who expects to be obeyed without question as a function of his social class and political position (60, 66, 92).

At the opposite end of the social spectrum in Concarneau are Emma and Léon, the former a waitress, the latter a seaman. These two representatives of the popular classes are initially presented in contrasting manners: Emma as a victim of the *notables* and Léon as a threat to them, although it emerges that he, too, has previously been their victim. In keeping with her passivity, Emma is also rather nondescript physically: "She was anemic. Her flat chest was not formed to rouse desire" (16). Léon, in contrast, is a more active character, and the descriptions of him emphasize his size and animality—"a colossus" (51), "a bear" (66), "an attack dog" (112), "the brute" (113)—and we are treated to three descriptions of his animal-like eating habits (23, 58, 78). Yet Emma and Léon are also described in ways that emphasize their social existence within the political context of the Third Republic. The introduction of free and compulsory education in the pre-war period meant that by 1920 virtually all children, whatever their social origins, benefited from primary education up to the age of 12 and levels of illiteracy fell dramatically (Abbad, 1993, 52). So it comes as little surprise that both Emma and Léon can read and write competently (*Le Chien jaune/The Yellow Dog*, 100–101, 103). It should be noted, too, that although Emma and Léon represent the popular classes in *Le Chien jaune*, Léon is in fact an aspiring petit bourgeois. Even though he is forced into debt in order to purchase his boat, he sees his future as a self-employed "free man" rather than as a wage worker. Although Emma's status is altogether proletarian—she has no source of income other than the sale of her labor power—she works in a service sector of the economy rather than in one of the fish-processing factories where she would have found herself in contact with other workers, with the potential to seek collective, rather than individual, solutions to her conditions of economic and sexual exploitation by the clients of the *Hôtel de l'Amiral*.

The third social group portrayed in the novel are the various representatives of the republic's law-enforcement agencies: Maigret, Inspector Leroy and the local gendarmerie and police officers. The brigadier of the gendarmerie accepts orders from the mayor (66) and the lieutenant seems keen to pursue Léon on a spurious vagrancy charge even after the main case has been resolved (128). The local policeman comments caustically on class relations in Concarneau (55–56) but is nevertheless willing to follow orders from the town's elite. Leroy, as an inspector based in Rennes, is independent of the local politics of Concarneau, but is nevertheless intimidated by the mayor's threats (32).

This leaves Maigret. Bourgeois republican ideology would assert that as a highly placed *fonctionnaire*, Commissaire Maigret should stand above social class and act impartially as a servant of the republic. From early in the story, there is no doubt where Maigret's personal sympathies lie: "There was an instinctive rapport between the waitress and the superintendent," (32) and his own plebeian social origins are hinted at in his physical similarities to Léon: "big hands" (57, 95), "thick fingers" (92) and "broad shoulders"(70); the contrast between his pipe and the cigars of the *notables* (2, 87); his "awkward manner of a petit bourgeois visiting an aristocratic house" (88) when he visits the mayor's home; and the occasional vulgarity of his speech (91). Although he begins his interview with the mayor in the manner of a "proper civil servant reporting to his superior" (88), he quickly changes his tone and is unafraid to confront the mayor (91). The expected social niceties are followed insofar as the bourgeoisie are always addressed by their formal titles, whereas Léon is addressed by his first name in the final examination (111, 120) and Maigret addresses Emma in a familiar manner (using *tu* in the original French text) from the beginning (*Le Chien jaune*, 31). Nevertheless, in his inquiry Maigret remains scrupulously fair, not allowing his actions to be influenced either by personal sympathy or political pressure.

The overwhelming impression that Simenon's text creates is one of small-town parochialism. This is not just in connection with Concarneau but France as a whole. The contrast between France and the United States is striking. In the latter both society and crime are organized on a "modern" model, as profitable businesses, with the lines between the two often indistinct. Hence the "American from Brest," whom Léon meets again in Sing Sing, is simultaneously a criminal, a police informer and a successful businessman (*Le Chien jaune/The Yellow Dog*, 116). "Things go fast over there" (115), says Léon, referring to his arrest and trial within 24 hours, whereas Michoux's French trial and appeal drag on for 18 months (130). In contrast to the United States, the society of the Concarneau *notables* is backward and inward-looking. The ruling class band together but are inwardly divided by petty snobbishness. Hence the mayor's comment that Servières is "an unimportant newspaperman" (93), and the observation that "one couldn't, for example, receive his wife, a woman whose past is not entirely above reproach" (93). Madame Servières herself complains of this snobbishness to Maigret (97). For the bourgeoisie, family contacts and family history are important. The mayor's grandfather was formerly mayor himself (107); Le Pommeret's family contacts have allowed him to take the honorary title of Danish vice-consul and he relies on his brother to pay his debts (33–34); Michoux is the son of a former deputy and his mother continues to use her late husband's contacts right to the end of the narrative to try to overturn the conviction of her son (130).

For working people without the benefit of inherited wealth or family contacts, life is a struggle. Léon is drawn into the cocaine-smuggling affair by economic circumstances beyond his control—the rise in the exchange rate of the franc, interest rates and the decline in British demand for Breton fruit (112–113). Nor is there equality between rich and poor before the law: Léon is brought through the town in handcuffs (51) whereas Michoux receives preferential treatment while under arrest at the gendarmerie (60–61). Léon's account of life in Sing Sing (116–118) paints a similar picture of the U.S. penal system, where "there were rich prisoners who went off into town almost every night ... and they used the rest of us as their servants!" (116).

Michoux kills Le Pommeret because the latter is considering going to the police, but Le Pommeret only contemplates this course of action in the knowledge that "he belongs to a respectable local family" (124) and therefore is likely to receive a sympathetic hearing: "After all, what's the risk for him? A fine, a little stint in prison. If that!" (124). The local *agent de police* provides Maigret with a commentary on class divisions in Concarneau:

"Ordinary folks—workers, fishermen—aren't too upset.... In a way they're even kind of glad about what's happening...."
"Well in that case who's upset?"
"The middle class and the businessmen who rubbed shoulders with that bunch at the Admiral Café" [55–56].

And the mayor is equally aware of class divisions: "That's small-town life superintendent! You've got to resign yourself to these distinctions.... You don't know what it is to manage a community of fishermen and at the same time watch out for the sensibilities of the gentry—and of some middle-class elements besides" (93). Nevertheless, there is little evidence of the open class struggle between *les blancs* (the ruling class) and *les rouges* (their working class and peasant opponents) which *did* exist in Brittany according to P-J Hélias (1975) in his memoir of his Breton boyhood in the period of *Le Chien jaune*.

Finally, running like a thread through *Le Chien jaune* is the presentation of the position of women of different social strata in French society. Emma as a working-class woman is truly at the very bottom of Concarnois society.

She is essentially passive throughout, although she does have a moment of independent action when she attempts to poison the *notables*' aperitif (*Le Chien jaune/The Yellow Dog*, 9–11, 128). Emma is subject to sexual exploitation by the ruling-class males of the town, as are the young women workers of the fish-processing factories (16–17, 55, 119, 121). Servières' wife is shunned by Concarneau's polite social circles because of her humble social origins (34, 93, 97) and she has to tolerate her husband's extramarital escapades (96–97). All in all, the behavior of the Concarneau *notables* towards women is reminiscent of Marx's and Engels' denunciation of the hypocrisy of bourgeois men in these matters: "Our bourgeois, not content with having the wives and daughters of their proletarians at their disposal, not to speak of common prostitutes, take the greatest pleasure in seducing each other's wives" (2004, 28–29). Although Emma's relationship to Léon is as a subordinate, the allegedly greater affection and equality in working-class marriages than in those of the bourgeoisie (Zeldin, 2003, 439) holds out some hope for her future happiness. Indeed, the story ends on an implied note of conjugal contentment for the couple: "Léon Le Glérec fishes for herring in the North Sea ... and his wife is expecting a baby" (*Le Chien jaune/The Yellow Dog*, 130).

At the other end of the social scale, the relationship of the mayor and his wife (87) reflects Zeldin's observation that "the wife was usually much younger [than the husband]. It was therefore natural that he would expect his wife to be obedient and submissive" (Zeldin, 2003, 439). Madame Michoux is the most disagreeable of the female characters, and her manipulative and domineering character may reflect Simenon's view of the personality of his own mother (Assouline, 1997; Eskin, 1987). Nevertheless, even Madame Michoux is shackled by her gender: she can make her way only as a result of her late husband's position as a former *député* (*Le Chien jaune/The Yellow Dog*, 59, 64) and because of her relationship with the mayor's wife (93).

The central issues which emerge in *Le Chien jaune* are those of parochial small-mindedness and of the exploitation of the weak by the strong. But these themes do not exist in a void: rather they are realized in a concrete historical conjuncture, that of the impact of a changing world on a French provincial town caught between its past and the new modernity of the postwar period.

La Tête d'un homme: *Class, Nationality and "Race" in Interwar Paris*

La Tête d'un homme, the fifth Maigret novel, was written in the winter of 1930 at the Hôtel Aiglon on boulevard Raspail in the 14th arrondissement of Paris. The Montparnasse setting of much of the novel would have been directly visible to the author from the window of his room, and the hotel is only a stone's throw from the Boule Blanche nightclub where the Bal Anthropométrique, a crime-themed party to which Simenon invited everyone who was anyone in Parisian high society and bohemian circles, would be held to launch the Maigret series on the night of February 20–21, 1931. The novel was well received: according to Eskin (1987, 93) it "was voted the best detective story of 1931." The story was released as the third Maigret film in 1933, directed by Julien Duvivier and featuring Harry Baur in the leading role. A second, English-language, version was released in 1950, directed by Meredith Burgess and with Charles Laughton in the role of Maigret, although the title was altered to *The Man on the Eiffel Tower* and significant changes were made to the storyline.

In *La Tête d'un homme* Maigret has requested permission to let a prisoner in the Santé prison "escape." He is Joseph Heurtin, condemned to death for having killed a rich American, Mrs. Henderson, and her maid at Saint-Cloud. The evidence against Heurtin is strong but he had no motive and nothing was stolen. He has refused to say anything except that he has not killed the women. Maigret is convinced that Heurtin is either mad or innocent and that someone else is involved. The day after Heurtin's "escape" a newspaper receives a note alleging police connivance—obviously from someone who knows something about the murder. The paper on which the note is written is from La Coupole, a bar in Montparnasse, where Maigret encounters Jean Radek, a Czech medical student. Heurtin, who has managed to elude the police, seems to be waiting outside for Radek, who has himself arrested for not paying his check. Radek challenges Maigret to connect him to the murders. He shows Maigret banknotes which can be traced to William Crosby, Mrs. Henderson's nephew, who is a regular customer at La Coupole. Maigret goes back to Saint-Cloud, and finds Crosby in the murdered woman's house, where he commits suicide. Radek taunts Maigret, who continues to follow him everywhere. They return to La Citanguette, the bar where Heurtin slept on escaping from the Santé, and they see Mrs. Crosby go to Heurtin's room and tear up a mattress. They then follow her to Saint-Cloud, where she goes into the house, returning with a small package. Maigret brings Radek into the house, where the commissaire reveals Edna Reichberg, Crosby's mistress and his wife's friend, hidden in a wardrobe. Radek realizes he has been caught, and shoots at Maigret, but Maigret has substituted blanks for the bullets in his gun.

Radek confesses to Maigret and the latter recounts the truth of the case to Coméliau, the *juge d'instruction*. Radek had overheard Crosby say that he would pay 100,000 francs to anyone who would kill his aunt, and replied anonymously, getting the key to the house. He killed the two women and persuaded Heurtin to go there under the pretense of committing a burglary, tricking him into leaving tracks and fingerprints, that would eventually lead to his conviction. Once Heurtin escaped, Radek wrote to Crosby for the money and then had Crosby go to the house, hoping Maigret would find him there. Maigret intercepted letters from Radek to Mrs. Crosby and Edna Reichberg telling them to go to the house in Saint-Cloud. Radek, suffering from a terminal illness and embittered by his poverty, had organized the killings as a kind of revenge against the wealthy Crosby and society in general. Three months later Radek is executed at the Santé prison in the presence of Maigret.

Although the text of *La Tête d'un homme* makes it clear that the story is set in October (*La Tête d'un homme/A Battle of Nerves*, 8) and concludes the following January (139), no years are mentioned. However, given that the novel was written in the winter of 1930 and that much of the action takes place in La Coupole, we can deduce from the fact that this establishment, which is a real restaurant and bar, opened only in December 1927 (Baronian et al., "L'Univers de Maigret," 98) that the story must be set in 1928–1929 or 1929–1930.

At the end of the war, in November 1918, France found itself with a massive task of reconstruction. Large parts of the north and northeast of the country required rebuilding and the country had lost over ten percent of its economically active population to death or mutilation in the fighting (Abbad, 1993, 5–6). The combination of a favorable international economic situation with the need for reconstruction made the 1920s years of sustained economic growth: by 1929, France had emerged from the postwar decade as the fourth biggest industrial economy in the world, the third largest producer of steel after the United States and Germany and the leading European manufacturer of automobiles (Montero, 2001, 53). Although nationally economic progress was uneven, modernization was rapid in a number of key industries such as coal, chemicals, steel, aeronautics and vehicle production: the factory replaced the workshop and production was standardized, increasing the demand for production-line workers rather than craftsmen (Montero, 60). This phenomenon was particularly evident in the Paris region. According to Agulhon et al.:

> The city of Paris ... spread more and more towards its outskirts.... The city lost its traditional craftsmen but gained an increasing number of workers in the growing number of factories in the suburbs (for example, vehicle production, sheet metal work, chemicals, dye works, electricity production): this process had begun before 1914 and it was accentuated by the war. Among these workers were many foreigners (North Africans, Slavs, Armenians, Greeks, Jews) [1993, 176].

To take a single example of this industrial expansion, automobile production rose from 40,000 vehicles in 1920 to 254,000 in 1929 (Braudel and Labrousse, 1979–1980, 650).

During the 1920s the population of the major cities increased rapidly. The Paris region saw an increase of 35 percent between 1921 and 1931 (Montero, 2001, 57); in 1931 around half of the inhabitants of Bobigny, a suburb to the northeast of Paris, had been born outside the region (Abbad, 1993, 24). The drift from the countryside to the Paris region continued in the postwar period (Agulhon et al., 1993, 177) but, given the low French birthrate, this was not enough to meet the needs of the capital's industrial expansion, and immigration became increasingly important. In 1911, there were 1,160,000 foreigners in France (2.8 percent of the population); by 1931 the figure was 2,715,000, or 7.1 percent of the total (Braudel and Labrousse, 1979–1980, 613). Whereas immigration in the pre-war years had been essentially from countries bordering France (particularly Belgium and Italy), the pattern in the 1920s changed, as the following statistics for the division of foreign residents by nationality demonstrate:

Nationality	1921	1931
German	4.9%	2.6%
Belgian	22.8%	9.3%
Spanish	16.6%	13.0%
Italian	29.4%	29.8%
Polish	3.0%	18.7%
Portuguese	0.7%	1.8%
North African	2.5%	3.9%
Other	3.8%	5.6%

SOURCE: *INSEE*, 1990

Given that many immigrants from Central and Eastern Europe and North Africa were "undocumented," it may be that these figures underestimate their numbers. At an anecdotal level, the British writer George Orwell suggests in his account of his time in Paris in the 1920s (Orwell, 1933, reprint, 1961), that a significant proportion of the lowest-paid, lowest-status jobs were occupied by foreigners from these countries.

Economic growth in the United States, combined with a highly favorable exchange rate, also made Paris attractive to many Americans. Eskin (1987, 46) tells us: "The franc was so low that Americans ostentatiously lit their cigars with thousand franc notes." This echoes a reminiscence of Maigret's in *Les Mémoires de Maigret*: "The dollar was worth I don't know what fantastic sums. Americans used to light their cigars with thousand-franc notes"

(*Les Mémoires de Maigret/Maigret's Memoirs*, 1978, 20–21). Many wealthy young Americans came to Paris, often to pursue a social life that was not possible in prohibition-era USA. Writers and artists including Ernest Hemingway, Henry Miller, Gertrude Stein, Ezra Pound, F. Scott Fitzgerald and a host of others all lived in Paris for longer or shorter periods during the 1920s (Cronin, 1994, Hemingway,1966). Although not all of these figures were necessarily wealthy in American terms, they were keen to benefit from proximity to what was seen as the center of cultural modernity and where "whatever the dollar exchange rate, one franc bought two packs of Gauloises and three and a half francs a meal at a cheap restaurant" (Eskin, 1987, 46). This was at a time when "an average [French] white-collar employee might make about 1000 francs a month" (46).

The narrative of *La Tête d'un homme* unfolds entirely in Paris and the surrounding region. Maigret's travels are frequent and rapid, taking in the Santé prison, in the south of the city, where the story begins and ends; the Palais de Justice and the Hôtel George V in the city center; the southwestern suburbs of Issy-les-Moulineaux (proletarian) and Saint-Cloud and Auteuil (bourgeois); Montparnasse (south-central), famous for its nightclubs, restaurants and bars; and Heurtin's home village of Nandy, 35 kilometers to the southeast.

Simenon had been living in Paris on and off for eight years when he wrote *La Tête d'un homme* and the picture he paints in the novel is a broadly accurate one, contrasting as it does the different *quartiers* of the city, where "certain districts were home to great wealth while others were inhabited by a poverty-stricken proletarian mass" (Agulhon et al., 1993, 176). The author knew well the bars and nightclubs of Montparnasse (Baronian et al., 2004–2007, "Le Roman de Georges Simenon," 36; "L'Univers de Maigret," 97–98), where "French nightlife was fired by enthusiasm for the new rhythms of jazz [and] the *Revue nègre*, starring Josephine Baker" (with whom Simenon had a highly public affair) "was at the height of its popularity. Paris was the city of choice of the roaring twenties ... the centre of cultural cosmopolitanism" (Montero, 2001, 99). When Maigret goes to La Coupole he finds an establishment that seems culturally alien to him:

> Snatches of different languages broke in on all sides....
> People accosted each other without introduction. A German was speaking English with a Yankee, while a Norwegian was making use of at least three languages to make himself understood to a Spaniard [*La Tête d'un homme/A Battle of Nerves*, 48].

Alongside these wealthy cosmopolitans are other clients, who are drawn to the bar's atmosphere although they lack the financial means to participate in it:

> There was a girl who could hardly have been much more than twenty, dressed in a little coat and skirt that was well-cut but had certainly been pressed a hundred times.... And in the middle of those people drinking cocktails at ten francs a time she was drinking a glass of milk and eating a croissant. At one o' clock—so it was obviously her midday meal....
> No less striking was a man with a head of hair that was alone sufficient to attract attention. It was red, frizzy, and very long. He wore a dark suit, shiny and threadbare.... Had he as much as five francs in his pocket? [49].

The contrast between La Coupole and the La Citanguette bar in working-class Issy-les-Moulineaux, with its clientele of longshoremen and factory workers (35), where Heurtin initially hides after his escape, is striking: "The gates of the neighboring factory had been flung open to a stream of workmen.... The bar of the Citanguette was lit up by a single electric lamp" [33].

Just as La Coupole is contrasted with La Citanguette, so the area surrounding the latter bar is contrasted with the bourgeois suburb of Auteuil, across the river from where Maigret watches the drama unfold through binoculars:

> Blocks of luxury flats looked down on him as he walked along the quay, while on the other side the scene was typical of Paris suburbs—factories, waste spaces, wharves with stacks of goods of every description.
> Even from that distance it was easy to spot the Citanguette, for it stood all by itself in the middle of a stretch of land littered with gear of all sorts: piles of bricks, rolls of roofing felt, scrapped cars, and even railway lines [19].
> The smart flats of Auteuil formed the horizon of the other bank of the Seine [39].

Housing conditions are also a function of social class: Heurtin lived in his single room in rue Monsieur-le-Prince (28) while "the examining magistrate, Monsieur Coméliau, sat at the head of a table laid for twenty" (41). The contrast between bourgeois and popular Paris is just as strong further out from the center. The Henderson villa in Saint-Cloud "was a substantial ... building flanked by a turret and surrounded by a good-sized rambling garden" (85), while Heurtin's family home in Nandy has "the beams showing in the ceiling, the wallpaper peeling off here and there" (80). Instead of a garden, there is a manure heap (84).

A central theme of *La Tête d'un homme* is that of division based on social class. This division runs not only between native-born French and foreigners but, more importantly, within the two groups. Among the native-born French, the three principal characters are Coméliau, Heurtin and Maigret, representing the upper echelons of the bourgeoisie, the proletariat and the petite bourgeoisie respectively. Among the foreigners, the Crosbys represent wealth, the unnamed Algerian and Polish workers in the Citanguette are in France only to sell their labour power and Radek is a déclassé element, proletarian in origin (65, 123), a former brilliant student of medicine (63, 124) but penniless (124, 127).

Although the *juge d'instruction* Coméliau had already appeared very briefly in the Fayard Maigret series in *Pietr-le-Letton*, his role was a very minor one. However, in *La Tête d'un homme* the conflict between Coméliau and Maigret is central to the narrative. We see the two men together at the beginning of the story, where they are immediately contrasted: "Maigret ... his hands stuffed in his overcoat pockets [was] so still that he seemed a lifeless mass. [Coméliau] had arrived at one o'clock from some reception or other. He was in evening dress, his thin moustache carefully brushed up" (9). The difference between the two men extends far beyond their physical appearance. While Maigret seeks the truth, Coméliau would be satisfied with any likely suspect being found guilty and executed if scandal can be avoided and the judicial system *appears* to be functioning effectively:

> MAIGRET: "Things are going splendidly, Monsieur Coméliau!"
> COMÉLIAU: "You think so? And suppose all the other papers reprint this stuff?"
> MAIGRET: "That'll make a scandal."
> COMÉLIAU: "You see..."
> MAIGRET: "Is a man's head worth a scandal?" [24].

When Crosby commits suicide, the main thing that worries Coméliau is the "complication" of the case: "By the look on Monsieur Coméliau's face you might have thought he doubted Maigret's story. But really it only expressed his abiding horror of complications of any kind" (91). Fabre succinctly summarizes the difference between Coméliau and Maigret: "The equation is evident: bourgeoisie (= Manichean rigidity) versus plebeians (= understanding and compassion). Possessed only by the poor, who alone are capable of understanding, compassion is not possible for the wealthy" [1981, 57].

La Tête d'un homme gives the reader a first glimpse of the conflict between the petit bourgeois Maigret and the haut bourgeois Coméliau that will be a recurrent feature in the postwar Maigret novels:

> Judge Coméliau's voice was curt, dry, deliberately impersonal... [*Maigret et son mort/Maigret's Special Murder*, 319].
>
> It all went back to the question of social classes. The magistrate had remained a man of an unchanging background in a changing world.... He was the typical product of his society, the slave of its ways, of its rules of conduct, even of its language. One would have thought that his daily experiences in the Palais de Justice would have given him a different idea of human nature, but that was not so, and he was invariably influenced by the point of view held by his class [*Une Confidence de Maigret/Maigret has doubts*, 80–81].

And, most explicitly:

> His [Maigret's] differences with certain judges, particularly Judge Coméliau, who for over twenty years had been as it were his private enemy, were a legend at the Quai des Orfèvres.... The people in the Parquet—attorneys, deputies and examining magistrates—nearly all belonged to the middle, if not the upper, strata of the bourgeoisie. Their way of life ... scarcely ever brought them into contact, except in their chambers, with those whom they had to prosecute in the name of society. Hence their well-nigh congenital incomprehension of certain problems [*Les Scrupules de Maigret/Maigret has scruples*, 72–73].

The theme, developed by Simenon in *Le Port des brumes*, of Maigret as "just a man—without the 'guinea stamp'" (*Le Port des brumes/Maigret and the Death of a Harbor-Master*, 77), contrasted to the haut bourgeois Grandmaison, is prefigured in the relation between Maigret and Coméliau:

> Thin, nervous, exasperated, the examining magistrate paced up and down his room. Sometimes his voice rose almost to a shout....
> Maigret stood there, steadily, towering above the angry little man.
> The latter, after a final jibe, looked into the inspector's face. But he quickly turned his head away; for after all Maigret was a man of forty-five who for over twenty years had been in the police, handling all sorts of cases, many of them extremely delicate.
> And then.... Well, he was a man! [*La Tête d'un homme/A Battle of Nerves*, 41–42].

If the social class of Maigret and Coméliau is clearly defined by the narrator, Joseph Heurtin is described by Maigret as "déclassé" in the original French text (*La Tête d'un homme*, 231), although the English translation does not use this sociological term (*A Battle of Nerves*, 128). In fact, this characterization is not accurate: Heurtin's experience is actually typical of many young Frenchmen from the villages and small towns surrounding Paris in the 1920s who came to the capital, found employment as wage workers and therefore constituted a fraction of the proletariat. The son of a waiter and laundress who have managed to become proprietors of a small village inn, he is drawn to Paris along with thousands of others during the economic expansion of the postwar period, because provincial life has little to offer a young man of humble origins, only to find that the streets are not paved with gold. His lack of financial means renders him unable to penetrate the bright world of establishments like La Coupole, full of wealthy foreigners, symbolized by his being chased away from its terrace (58), an "outsider" in the capital city of his own country. "He's a day-dreamer, devours cheap novels, goes to the films and pictures himself playing the hero in all sorts of marvelous adventures.... But instead of that he's carrying round bunches of flowers for six hundred francs a month" (128). Isolated from family, friends or the workmates he would have found in one of the new factories of the city, he is easily manipulated by Radek. Maigret describes Heurtin as "one of Radek's victims" (132), but he is also a victim of an expanding capitalist economy which sucks in labor but is unable to provide for the social or spiritual needs of those who create its profits.

Just as the native French characters can be divided into three groups—the haut bourgeois Coméliau, the proletarian Heurtin and the petit bourgeois Maigret—a similar division can be made of the foreign-born characters in *La Tête d'un homme*. Wealth and power are represented by the Crosbys and Crosby's aunt Mrs. Henderson. For all of his wealth, William Crosby is a moral degenerate, ready to pay for the murder of his aunt so he can inherit her money in order to divorce his wife and marry his mistress, the daughter of a wealthy Swedish industrialist (105). Maigret admits that Radek has understood Crosby's character better than he:

> Looking at Crosby ... I'd seen no more than a spoilt boy myself, a nice-mannered, frivolous man about town. Radek had seen another side altogether.
>
> He sketched for me a happy-go-lucky Crosby, beloved by women, by everybody, and enjoying all the good things of life—but also a Crosby ready to put his hand to any dirty meanness to satisfy his thirst for pleasure.... A Crosby who could let his wife live on terms of closest friendship with his mistress, Edna Reichberg. While all the time he was conspiring with Edna to get a divorce and marry her. A Crosby who was not above forging his relation's signatures, and who finally in a careless moment dropped the mask altogether [125].

At the other end of the scale from the Crosbys are the foreign workers, whom Maigret encounters at La Citanguette, and for whom he shows none of his celebrated sympathy for *les petites gens*:

> Maigret ... turned to an Arab sitting on the bench....
> "So you've got a job now?"
> "At Citroën's, yes...."
> "For how much longer are you forbidden to be in the district?"
> And Maigret made a sign to one of the policemen which meant: "Off with him!"
> "Inspector," ... whined the Arab as he was led towards the door, "let me explain ... I haven't done anything...."
> But Maigret took no notice. There was a Pole whose papers were not in order.
> "Off with him!" [40].

Unlike the wealthy foreign habitués of La Coupole, these non–French residents who have come to France to work are treated with callous contempt, in contrast to Crosby, who has inherited his fortune and come to Paris to amuse himself. In the original French, Maigret *tutoies* the Algerian auto worker (in this context a sign of disrespect), while the latter addresses the policeman with a respectful "vous," and the narrator employs the abusive expression "sidi" to refer to the Arab (*La Tête d'un homme*, 153) which had the derogatory weight that "shine" or "wop" would have had in contemporary American English. This scene has a ring of truth in its depiction of French attitudes to foreign-born workers in the period. As Baronian et al. observe:

> In France, the years 1920–1930 were characterized by a large wave of immigration, required for the reconstruction of the country, and an equally strong racist response. There was a multiplication of exacting document checks, administrative requirements and round-ups of foreigners.... A quarter of the victims of police detentions between 1926 and 1928 were foreigners, above all those from North Africa, Russia and Poland [2004–2007, "L'Univers de Maigret," 126].

Instilling a sense of insecurity and fear was a method regularly practiced by capitalist employers and their representatives in the state apparatus, to ensure the docility of non-native labor. These same workers would be expelled from their jobs and the country itself following the onset of the economic recession in 1930 in an attempt to limit the growth of unemployment among native-born French workers (Dard, 1999, 23).

Between the wealthy clientele of La Coupole and the Algerian and Polish workers who frequent La Citanguette stands the figure of Radek. Proletarian in origin, the son of a servant, he has, however, come to Paris to study medicine rather than to work in a factory. As poor as the workers of La Citanguette in financial terms, he has, nevertheless, an academic and cultural level the equal of any bourgeois intellectual. Unlike Heurtin, Radek is a genuine déclassé. Central to the portrait of Radek is the notion of his cosmopolitan rootlessness:

> [Maigret] took the Czech's passport ... nearly every page of which was covered with visas and the stamps of frontier officials.
> Johann Radek ... born at Brno of unknown father. From the rubber stamps, it could be seen that he had resided in Berlin, Mainz, Bonn, Turin, and Hamburg [65].

Much is made of Radek's red hair (*La Tête d'un Homme/A Battle of Nerves*, 49, 52, 72) and, although there is never any explicit statement, this seems to be a reference to Radek's Jewishness, as Jews were often associated with this trait in the popular imagination in France at the time (Orwell, 1961, 36). Furthermore, it is known that "the character was inspired by Simenon's friend Ilya Ehrenbourg, a Jew from Kiev who, like the author, was a regular customer at La Coupole" (Assouline, 1997, 110). Anti-Semitism was a powerful sentiment in inter-war France, as it had been prior to the war (Becker and Berstein, 1990, 164) and even "respectable" authors such as François Mauriac

Immigrant workers in Le Havre, 1931. For Maigret, all the foreign characters in *La Tête d'un homme* represent a symptom of the disorder and social changes provoked by postwar developments, two aspects of contemporary life that he finds difficult to understand and accept. (Courtesy Agence Roger-Viollet.)

were not averse to stereotypical characterizations of Jews: for example, in *Thérèse Desqueroux* (1927), he describes Jean Azévédo as having "the soft velvety eyes of his race" (Mauriac, 1989, 78). Jean Giraudoux extended the sentiment of rejection to all foreigners when he spoke about [the intrusion in France] "under cover of all sorts of revolutions, ideological movements and persecutions, of every kind of alien, misfit, money grabber and cripple" ("Pleins pouvoirs," cited in Borne and Dubief, 1989, 224).

Radek is perceived by Maigret as an agent of disorder in society, and the commissaire twice tells Coméliau that twenty years previously he (Radek) would have been an anarchist (*La Tête d'un homme/A Battle of Nerves*, 124, 127). This says as much about Maigret and his views as it does about Radek: on the one hand, there is the petit bourgeois fear of social change, on the other there is an implied anti–Semitism—in the view of many social conservatives at the time there existed a link between Jewishness and revolutionary politics. This was more than just a French phenomenon: Emma Goldman in the United

States, Rosa Luxemburg and Leo Jögiches in Germany, Leon Trotsky and Karl Radek in Russia, not to mention Marx himself, were all held up as examples of the link between Jewishness, rootless cosmopolitanism and a revolutionary threat to the existing social order and its values.

In *Pietr-le-Letton*, Juge Coméliau is exasperated by the influx of foreign nationals: "What the devil are all these foreigners doing in France?" (*Pietr-le-Letton/Maigret and the Enigmatic Lett*, 150) For Maigret, with his deep sense of "Frenchness" and "tradition," all the foreign characters in *La Tête d'un homme*—rich or poor—represent a symptom of the disorder and social changes provoked by postwar developments, two aspects of contemporary life that he finds difficult to understand and accept. Maigret is as disconcerted by the apparently completely opposed worlds of La Coupole and *La Cintanguette* as he had been by the wealthy Americans of the Hôtel Majestic and the Jewish ghetto of the Sentier in *Pietr-le-Letton*. In *La Tête d'un homme* the commissaire finds himself confronted by developments in contemporary French society which challenge many of his deepest-held beliefs concerning national identity. This disorientation in the face of change is a theme that will reappear in different forms and settings throughout the Maigret series.

CHAPTER 2

The Fayard Maigret Novels: Narratives, Contexts, Settings and Themes, 1932

L'Ombre chinoise: *Social Mobility in the Postwar Period; a Divided Bourgeoisie*

L'Ombre chinoise, the title of which refers to a projected backlit shadow, was written in December 1931 in Antibes and published in February 1932 as the twelfth Maigret novel (Eskin, 1987, 280). The critic René Lalou, writing in *Les Nouvelles Littéraires* immediately after publication, considered it to be perhaps the best Maigret story to date:

> His originality was obvious from the beginning: he didn't try to dazzle us by sensational turns of events or demonstrations of reasoning; on the contrary, he strove to create dense and dark ambiances, where the murder, the investigation and the punishment were equally lacking in lustre. *L'Ombre chinoise* seems to me not only the most characteristic evidence of this attempt to renew a literary genre; it is also an almost complete success [cited in Baronian et al., 2004–2007, "Le film dans le texte," 14].

In *L'Ombre chinoise* Maigret is called to the place des Vosges in central Paris, where Raymond Couchet, a businessman, has been found shot dead at his desk. Behind him is the empty safe, unlocked but unreachable with him in his chair. Maigret wonders if the robbery and murder are two separate crimes. He soon becomes convinced that the answer lies among the residents of the building, who include Couchet's former wife, Juliette Martin, and her civil servant husband, Edgar. Couchet's mistress, Nine Moinard, lives in the

Hôtel Pigalle, and in the next room lives Couchet's son, Roger, a young wastrel. Madame Martin comes to Maigret's office, and Maigret visits her home to return a forgotten umbrella, where he discovers that the window overlooks Couchet's office. Both Madame and Monsieur Martin had been seen in the courtyard the night of the crime. Couchet's will is found, leaving a third of his fortune to his wife, his ex-wife, and his mistress respectively. Roger commits suicide, and Maigret's suspicions concerning the robbery and murder of Couchet focus on the Martins. Monsieur Martin catches a train for Belgium, with Maigret in pursuit, and they return to the apartment in the place des Vosges for a final confrontation. It is revealed that Martin's wife had nagged him into robbing the safe while Couchet was absent from the scene, but Martin left his glove on the desk. She had gone to the office with a revolver to retrieve the glove, she was caught by Couchet, who threatened to call the police, and she had shot him. Her husband, feeling guilty after his theft, tossed the money into the Seine, and did not realize his wife was the murderer until later. His escape to Belgium had been to establish her innocence, so that she could inherit. Apprehended, she is diagnosed as insane and is removed to a lunatic asylum.

L'Ombre chinoise has a setting that is contemporary to its composition and publication, that is, the beginning of the 1930s. However, it is not the economic depression of this decade which is crucial to the story but past events rooted in the development of France's economy and society in the first thirty years of the century which have formed the psychology of the characters. The origins of the murder stretch back to the marriage of Couchet and his first wife (the future Madame Martin), their divorce, Madame Martin's second marriage to a civil servant and Couchet's business success, wealth and subsequent remarriage. The study of the context of *L'Ombre chinoise* must therefore reach back to the period before the Great War, the war itself and, particularly, the period of Couchet's rise to fortune in the 1920s.

The years from 1904 to 1913 saw a general acceleration of the French economy (Braudel and Labrousse, 1979–1980, 16). However, this seems to have been part of a general upswing in the capitalist economic cycle, starting in 1895, just as the years 1880–1895 had seen a downswing, rather than signifying any underlying changes in the nature of French capitalism. Economic activity took place in broadly the same context as before, with a limited number of opportunities for new entrepreneurs to flourish on anything other than a comparatively modest scale. Shopkeeping was a favored way for enterprising individuals to seek economic advancement, but the failure rate was high. According to Zeldin (2003, 171), "Almost 40% of small businesses ended in bankruptcy." Braudel and Labrousse insist that "common sense is not wrong in perceiving 1914 as a dividing line" (1979–1980, 12).

Certain sectors of industry, such as coal, steel and chemicals were forced to modernize by the demands of the war, new sectors such as vehicle production and aeronautics received a massive stimulus from military orders, and the development of aircraft manufacture led to increased demand for aluminum.

> The war created the *nouveaux riches*—middlemen and small industrialists who became magnates as a result of war contracts, such as Citroën (shells), Boussac (textiles), Loucheur (poison gas), Berliet (heavy goods vehicles) [Montero, 2001, 61].

In the postwar period, the combination of reconstruction and a highly favorable international economic climate saw a continuation of the expansion and concentration of certain sectors which had profited from the war, such as vehicle manufacture (Peugeot, Renault, Citroën), chemicals (Rhône-Poulenc, Saint-Gobain), steel (Wendel) and aluminum (Pechiney). At the same time, new patterns of mass consumption, such as electrical consumer goods, began to emerge based on the prolonged expansion. Credit became easier to obtain and chain stores such as Casino, Uniprix and Monoprix all developed rapidly in the 1920s (Montero, 2001, 53–55). The failure of certain "traditional" sectors of the French bourgeoisie to respond to changing conditions left an opening for "new" entrepreneurs to prosper in the changed situation. According to Braudel and Labrousse (1979–1980, 874): "The postwar period consolidated the position of the *nouveaux riches* and multiplied new openings.... The prosperity of small businesses brought about modest but significant new fortunes."

This, then, is the historical context of the financial and social ascent of Raymond Couchet in *L'Ombre chinoise* and the framework within which his two families—his first wife, now Madame Martin, and son, and his new family, the traditional haut bourgeois Dormoys—must be understood.

As in *La Tête d'un homme*, but unusually for the Fayard Maigret series, the whole of the action of *L'Ombre chinoise* takes place in Paris. Apart from a brief episode in Maigret's office, the action unfolds in the place des Vosges, where Couchet has his business and where the Martins live, Pigalle, where Nine and Roger Couchet live, and Couchet's home in boulevard Haussman. Boulevard Haussman, in the eighth and ninth arrondissements of Paris, was one of the *grands boulevards* constructed during and after the redevelopment of Paris by the Prefect Baron Haussman during the Second Empire, from 1852 to 1870. It was, and still is, a highly prestigious address: "a handsome late-nineteenth-century apartment, like most of those along the Boulevard Haussman. Spacious rooms. Ceilings and doors somewhat over-ornate" (*L'Ombre chinoise/Maigret Mystified*, 63). Although technically also in the ninth arrondissement (on the boundary with the eighteenth), Pigalle might as well have been in another world. Whereas the butte de Montmartre, to the north, had been an artistic center in the late nineteenth and early twentieth centuries, Pigalle was known for its cheap hotels, nightclubs and brothels. The very address is enough to disgust Colonel Dormoy: "I don't need to know her! Her address, rue Pigalle, is quite enough to tell me" (87); and Nine is pleased to report that the hotel into which she moves is *"fairly* clean" (my emphasis) (97).

If boulevard Haussman and Pigalle were home to two contrasting strata of Parisian society in the interwar period, all types of Parisians could be found in the place des Vosges. Incidentally, there is no number 61, where the action purportedly takes place, as there are only 36 buildings on the *place* (*Michelin*, 1982, 80). Inaugurated in 1612, the place des Vosges is considered by many today to be one of the most exclusive addresses in Paris (Ardagh, 1988, 277). However, in the interwar period, due in part to rent-control legislation, the place des Vosges included residents from the very wealthy to the poor, from the aristocratic Saint-Marc to old Mathilde and her sister. When Maigret is questioning Mathilde, she launches into a diatribe against her landlord:

> "You'd do better to ask the landlord to fix me up with gas..."
> "Gas?"
> "They've got it in the rest of the house. But because he's not entitled to raise my rent he won't let me have it" [*L'Ombre chinoise/Maigret Mystified*, 77].

Simenon and his first wife, Tigy, had lived in the place des Vosges, at number 21: first from mid–1924 in a two-room first-floor flat with no bathroom, overlooking a rear courtyard; then, from summer 1926, in a more spacious apartment in the same building (Assouline, 1997, Chapter 5). Therefore, it can be assumed that the descriptions of the residents and their homes are rooted in firsthand experience. Simenon makes much of the contrasts within the same building. On the one hand, the Saint-Marcs' apartment overlooks the *place*, where gardeners water the lawns and flowerbeds (*L'Ombre chinoise/Maigret Mystified*, 79). On the other hand, the Martins' apartment overlooks the rear courtyard (56). Much is also made of the contrast between the first and second floors of the building:

> As far as the first floor, the house had been redecorated, the walls were freshly painted and the staircase varnished. On reaching the second floor one was in a different world, with dirty walls and worn floorboards. The doors of the apartments were painted an ugly brown [54].

In choosing a location where he could place cheek by jowl several of the social classes making up the population of Paris, Simenon could not have done better than 61 place des Vosges.

The central characters in *L'Ombre chinoise* (with the exception of Nine Moinard) all belong to the bourgeoisie. However, within the bourgeoisie there were numerous subdivisions. Braudel and Labrousse (1979–1980, 51–55) describe six distinct groups, ranging from semi-aristocratic layers to a *bourgeoisie populaire*. The first eight chapters of Zeldin's encyclopedic work are all devoted to the bourgeoisie, and he concludes:

> The picture that these chapters on the bourgeoisie have tried to paint doesn't support the image ... of a unified, coherent and conscious class. Rather, its main characteristics appear to be internal conflicts and contradictory interests [Zeldin, 2003, 201].

L'Ombre chinoise can be read as a study of the "internal conflicts" and "contradictory interests" of the "traditional" haute bourgeoisie (represented by the Dormoy family and the Saint-Marcs), the nouveau-riche Couchet and the petit bourgeois Martins. It could, of course, be argued that the Martins are not petit bourgeois in the "classical" Marxist meaning of small property owners. I am using the term here in the sense of what Poulantzas (1974) calls the nouvelle petite bourgeoisie, a grouping which includes civil servants such as Martin, whose primary function within society is to maintain the functioning of the capitalist state apparatus and who derive from this role certain privileges relative to other wage workers.

Among the bourgeois characters in *L'Ombre chinoise*, only Couchet has contact in "both directions": he is a sort of intermediary between the haute bourgeoisie (which he has entered, as a result of his business success) and the petite bourgeoisie (from which he originated). The only contact between the world of the Dormoys and the Martins is their common link with Couchet. In what follows, I will consider the relationship between, on the one hand, Couchet and the Dormoys and, on the other hand, between Couchet and the Martins.

Couchet's story is one of "rags to riches":

> A full-blooded, powerful, vulgar fellow, risen from nothing, who had spent thirty years of his life trying to make his fortune and having a rough time...
> He'd grown rich ... gained access to a world into which he had never been admitted [*L'Ombre chinoise/Maigret Mystified*, 67].

Just how successful and how rich is Couchet? We learn that his business has another set of premises at Pantin, in the eastern suburbs of Paris, that it employs a significant number of staff and that the company's product, Doctor Rivière's Serums, is famous throughout the world (19). Interestingly, work in Couchet's business seems to be organized on the then modern American production-line method:

> A row of women in white overalls could be seen at a long table, busily packing up glass tubes.

> Each had her job. The first picked the unwrapped tubes out of a basket and the ninth handed over to an assistant perfect parcels, neatly wrapped and labelled, all ready to be delivered to chemists' shops [56–57].

If the bottom line for measuring business success is hard cash, then Couchet has definitely been highly successful. His estate is valued at five million francs (128) which, at the then exchange rate of 25 francs to the U.S. dollar, would have been worth $200,000. Assuming an average annual inflation rate of 5 percent from 1931 to the present, this sum would equate to $6.5 million or £4.25 million at 2010 values. According to Zeldin (2003, 96) in 1933 only 1,512 people died leaving estates of over one million francs, so it can be said with certainty that Couchet had risen to the very pinnacle of wealth.

Yet for all of his fortune, Couchet retains vestiges of his humble origins. When Maigret visits his bedroom in the boulevard Haussman apartment, he discovers a number of markedly contrasting features:

> Certainly the furniture was antique, as in the rest of the apartment. There were a few objects of value. But side by side with them were things that revealed the man's simple tastes.
> In front of the window, a table had done service as a desk. There were Turkish cigarettes, but also a whole row of those cherry-wood pipes that cost next to nothing.... A crimson dressing gown, the most dazzling he could find! And then, at the foot of the bed, a pair of old slippers with worn-out soles [*L'Ombre chinoise/Maigret Mystified*, 85–86].

It is this perceived vulgarity of the nouveau riche that provokes the snobbery of the Dormoys, despite Couchet's wealth. The difference in social origins is recognized by Madame Couchet who, when asked by Maigret if her husband saw much of her family, responds: "Very little! ... They hadn't the same mentality, you see ... nor the same tastes" (67). As Couchet's body lies awaiting his funeral, the Dormoys treat his sister with disdain:

> [Maigret] was well aware that they were not particularly anxious for members of the Couchet family to turn up looking like peasants or *petits-bourgeois*.
> There were the husband's relatives and there were the Dormoy relatives.
> The Dormoy relatives were all tact and elegance.... So far the Couchet relatives were only represented by that homely matron, whose silk bodice was too tight under the arms [64].

Although Becker and Berstein (1990, 361) suggest that, "around 1925, the theme of the *nouveaux riches* began to lose its sharpness and the parvenus, who had been somewhat disdained by 'good society,' were easily integrated," they add that "nevertheless, public opinion remained suspicious of wealth that had been too rapidly acquired." Monsieur and Madame de Saint-Marc (note the aristocratic "de") originate in the same traditional haut bourgeois circles as the Dormoys. Indeed, Madame de Saint-Marc had gone to school with the second Madame Couchet (*L'Ombre chinoise/Maigret Mystified*, 79). Questioned by Maigret as to whether he knew Couchet, Saint-Marc's reply is redolent of the disdain of old wealth for new money:

> I scarcely knew the man Couchet ... I caught sight of him once or twice as I went through the courtyard.... He belonged to one of the clubs I go to occasionally, the Haussmann. But I don't think he often set foot in it.... I believe he was rather a common person, wasn't he? [78–79].

For Couchet, his second marriage is proof that he has "arrived," that "from now on nothing was beyond his reach" (67). But why did the Dormoys agree to a marriage linking their established wealth to a parvenu? We are not told explicitly, but there may be a hint in an exchange between Maigret and Madame Couchet. The former begins by asking if Couchet was already wealthy at the time of the marriage, and the dialogue continues:

> "Yes... Less so than at present, but he was beginning to get on..."
> "A love match?"
> A veiled smile.
> "You might call it that" [65].

The rapid inflation of the 1920s had diminished the financial situation of a number of haut bourgeois families whose wealth was based on inherited property rather than current revenue (Braudel and Labrousse, 1979–1980, 51ff). In economic terms, which according to Zeldin (2003, 424), was how the bourgeoisie essentially viewed wedlock, a marriage to the nouveau riche Couchet, while socially undesirable, would at least bring financial security, "since, after all, their wealth guaranteed their bourgeois lifestyle and where money is concerned the passage of time brings acceptance" (Becker and Berstein, 1990, 361).

Couchet's wealth and second marriage link him to the haute bourgeoisie, but his social origins, his early jobs and his first marriage are all within a petit bourgeois milieu. The daughter of a provincial confectioner (*L'Ombre chinoise/Maigret Mystified*, 44)—the petite bourgeoisie traditionnelle in Poulantzas's terminology (1974)—Juliette, the first Madame Couchet (later Madame Martin), is highly ambitious. At first she supports Couchet's attempts to get rich, but rapidly becomes disillusioned as he encounters one setback after another. As she bitterly recounts to Maigret: "In those days Couchet was a traveller.... Whatever money he made he frittered away on absurd projects.... He claimed he was going to get rich.... He changed his job three times a year" (*L'Ombre chinoise/Maigret Mystified*, 44). For Juliette, the future lies with the nouvelle petite bourgeoisie, specifically the civil service: "I used to tell him to look for a respectable situation, something that would bring in a pension.... In the Civil Service, for instance!" (44). As Couchet pursues yet more "get rich quick" schemes, Juliette takes her position to its logical conclusion, asks for a divorce on grounds of incompatibility, and marries a neighbor, Monsieur Martin, himself a civil servant (45).

However, Juliette's project is doomed to failure: "Martin's got no initiative, he doesn't know how to put himself forward, he lets less intelligent colleagues cut the ground from under his feet" (63–64). In his appearance:

> From his shoes to his tie, fixed to a celluloid collar, Monsieur Martin was the caricaturists' prototype of the petty official. A neat, respectable functionary with well-waxed moustaches, not a speck of dust on his clothes, who would undoubtedly think it below his dignity to go out without gloves on his hands [34].

Psychologically, too, Martin seems to be the prototypical mediocre civil servant, obsessed by the length of his service and loyal to his superiors to the point of servility. As his wife descends into madness, his immediate response is to worry that he hasn't had time to let his boss know of his absence from work at a time when the office is particularly busy (73); and he reacts similarly to the news of his stepson's suicide (103).

The irony of the situation is not lost on the second Madame Couchet: "She [Madame Martin] left Raymond because he wasn't making enough money.... Then, to meet him again, a rich man ... while she herself was the wife of a petty official!" (66). However, from a material point of view, Juliette is not simply a victim of her own poor judgment but also of social forces beyond her control. The rigid economic and social structures of prewar France made financial success and social advancement difficult for an entrepreneur with humble origins such as Couchet. The "opening up" of society resulting from the prolonged postwar boom changed this situation. In contrast, the economic prospects and social status of civil servants suffered a decline during the interwar period. Salaries barely kept pace with the rapid inflation of the 1920s (Zeldin, 2003, 191), a large number of posts were reserved for war veterans or their widows (192) and the massive expansion of the civil service removed any social cachet that a post in the administration may once have had:

> In 1945, there were twice as many civil service jobs as in 1914, of which, of course, the greater part were low-ranking. The image of the civil servant changed with the dull drab nature of his existence coming to the fore.... Joining the civil service meant abandoning life, seeking security before all else to the detriment of riches and hope [193].

The insults hurled at Martin by his wife reflect her frustration but also her inability to understand how individual lives are constrained and shaped by social forces:

"A man ought not to deceive a woman by leading her to believe he's going to get promotion when it isn't true...
"Taking a woman away from a man like Couchet, who's capable of making millions!..."
"You officials are poor-spirited creatures.... A man has got to work on his own, to enjoy taking risks, to have some initiative, if he wants to get anywhere" [*L'Ombre chinoise/Maigret Mystified*, 109–110].

Of the remaining central characters, Roger Couchet's position is most unusual. Brought up by his mother and Monsieur Martin in petit bourgeois circumstances, he has at the age of 17 met his now wealthy father, whose generous handouts offer an easier life than the job in a bank that Martin has found for him (45). Roger gives up work and moves from the middle-class apartment in the place des Vosges to a furnished room in Pigalle, where he passes his days taking drugs and regularly changing girlfriends (30, 31, 32). Roger's lifestyle separates him from his petit bourgeois origins, yet the fact that he is not obliged to work means that he is not part of the working class. In short he is a déclassé element, not properly integrated into any social class, and representing, in the narrator's phrase, "the quintessence of a defeated world" (91).

The mistresses of Couchet père and fils, Nine and Céline, face a life typical of that experienced by tens of thousands of working-class women in the interwar period. In 1931, 37 percent of the total female population was in paid employment, compared to 68 percent of the male population. These figures had changed little since 1906, when the proportions were 38.9 percent and 68.2 percent respectively (Zeldin, 2003, 509). However, these figures did not mean that women enjoyed any great degree of financial independence. Women's employment tended to be concentrated in poorly paid sectors, and the principle of equal wages for equal work was virtually unknown. The working class in general benefited less from the prosperity of the 1920s than any other class (Becker and Berstein, 1990, 353) and, furthermore, in 1921 the salaries of women working in industry were 31 percent less than those of men. Posts for women in the public sector were limited in order to reduce male unemployment and create jobs for returning disabled war veterans (Zeldin, 2003, 521).

Marriage was one way in which women could achieve some degree of economic security, but this was not always possible given the imbalance between the number of men and women in the population ensuing from the Great War. In 1921 there were 1,245 women for every 1,000 men between the ages of 20 and 39. Prostitution was already widespread in the early years of the twentieth century and was seen by many young, unmarried, working-class women as a way of supplementing their pitifully low wages (Palet, ed.,

2006, 9). With the shortage of potential husbands in the postwar period, the trend intensified. Some single women attached themselves to wealthy men, such as Couchet, as kept mistresses; others, less lucky, worked as prostitutes in *maisons closes*, sometimes referred to as *maisons de tolérance*, one of which is regularly visited by Ducrau in *L'Ecluse numéro 1/The lock at Charenton* (44); others still plied their trade as independent, but state-registered, prostitutes. The latter, known as *encartées*, were obliged to follow certain rules laid down by the Préfecture, including a health check for venereal disease every fifteen days. "Authorized" prostitution was regulated by the Brigade des Moeurs (Palet, 12–13) and this is the background to Maigret's telephone call to the Vice Squad to check on Céline:

> Céline ... was well known there. She had her card. She came fairly regularly for inspection.
> "She's not a bad girl!" the sergeant said. "She usually sticks to one or two regular boyfriends. It's only when she falls back on street walking again that we pick her up" [*L'Ombre chinoise/Maigret Mystified*, 50].

The poverty and precariousness in which Nine lives can be seen following the death of Couchet. She is forced to take a job as an "exotic dancer" (39, 61), pawn her handful of jewelry (68) and move to a cheaper room (89, 94), carrying all of her worldly possessions in a single suitcase (93). Maigret is under no illusion, and neither is Nine, that even though she is named as a one-third beneficiary of Couchet's estate, as a working-class woman, she is unlikely to see the benefits:

> "When you're rich, you'll be able to..."
> She gave a tearful smile.
> "You know I shan't ever be rich. I'm not that type..."
> The strange thing was that Maigret had exactly the same feeling! Nine didn't look the type who would ever be rich! [97].

And, at the end of the story, Maigret realizes that they are right. Madame Martin and Madame Couchet have already commenced legal proceedings to exclude Nine from Couchet's will. Even with Madame Martin removed from the equation, as a result of her crime:

> "She'll [Nine] get nothing! Not a penny..." he murmured beneath his breath. "The will is sure to be declared invalid. And it's Mme Couchet, née Dormoy..." Madame Couchet would get it all! All those millions [138].

While the focus of *L'Ombre chinoise* is on relations, conflicts and contradictions within the bourgeoisie—old and new, haute and petite—we are left with the realization that the *petites gens*, those such as Nine, at the very bottom of the social class ladder, will always face an uphill battle in the France of the period. For all of his sympathy for Nine, Maigret's disappointment in respect of her likely fate remains at the level of private sentiment. He may feel a certain disillusionment with contemporary bourgeois society, but the combination of his objective position as a senior police *fonctionnaire* and the limitations of his social perspective restrict his role to that of an observer of a society in mutation rather than an active participant in the process of social change.

L'Affaire Saint-Fiacre: *What Future for the Rural Aristocracy in a Changing France?*

L'Affaire Saint-Fiacre was written in January 1932 in Antibes and was published later in the same year as the thirteenth novel in the series. It has remained one of the most popular Maigret stories and was produced as a film in 1959, directed by Jean Delannoy and starring Jean Gabin as the commissaire (Eskin, 1987, 280, 288).

Maigret had originally been conceived by Simenon as little more than a silhouette, the vague outline of a large, strong man, who "it seemed to me, would do reasonably well as a police inspector." As the series progressed, he gradually endowed the character with more details: "a pipe, a derby, a heavy overcoat with velvet lapels ... an old cast-iron stove for his office" (cited in Eskin, 74). In the early novels Simenon also gave Maigret a wife and colleagues and hinted at his plebeian origins. In *L'Affaire Saint-Fiacre*, Maigret's past is firmly situated in the history of rural French society in the pre– and post–Great War periods, and this coming together of social and personal histories (the real context and the fictional character) shapes the storyline. According to Dubois:

> *L'Affaire Saint-Fiacre* is undoubtedly the key text of the [Fayard] series. In it the author gives his hero a past, as Maigret conducts the inquiry in his childhood surroundings, where his father worked and where he himself grew up. Memories weigh heavily on the inquiry, shackling Maigret to a certain degree and giving the story an explicitly retrospective and biographical dimension [Dubois, 1992, 173].

In *L'Affaire Saint-Fiacre* Maigret goes to Saint-Fiacre, his home village, after coming across a note that had been received by the Moulins police and sent to Paris warning that a crime would be committed during the first Mass on All Souls' Day. And in fact, before Maigret's eyes, the old Comtesse de Saint-Fiacre dies during the Mass, but of heart failure. Maigret locates her missal, in which a fake newspaper story about her son's suicide had been planted. Her son Maurice de Saint-Fiacre appears with his mistress. He is in debt, as usual, and has come to borrow more money from his mother. His mother's secretary and lover, Jean Métayer, is quick to protest his innocence. The steward, Gautier, who lives in the tied house that had been Maigret's boyhood home when his father was the estate steward, tells Maigret that the countess had been in deep financial difficulty. His son, Emile Gautier, works in the bank in Moulins, where Maigret verifies the finances of the estate. Maurice organizes a dinner to which all concerned are invited, including the priest, Dr. Bouchardon and Métayer's lawyer. During the dinner Maurice promises that the murderer will be dead by midnight, and as 12 o'clock strikes, Emile shoots him. But the gun contains blanks, and Maurice is quick to show that it was the steward and his son who had engineered the countess's death, which, however, is unpunishable as a legal crime. The count administers a severe beating to Emile and expels the steward's family from the estate.

Although there are no overt references, we can assume that *L'Affaire Saint-Fiacre* has a contemporary historical setting. Following the references to the characters' ages—Maigret is forty-two (*L'Affaire Saint-Fiacre/Maigret Goes Home*, 15) and the countess is into her sixties (9) and the statement that "when he had last seen her she was twenty-five or twenty-six" (9)—this would place Maigret's childhood memories in the 1890s, his absence from the village had lasted about 35 years and the count of Saint-Fiacre would have died during the war (20). If we take the context of the story to include its historical background, this requires us, then, to consider the changing situation in rural France from around 1890 to 1932.

Over this four-decade period, "the proportion of the national population made up of rural dwellers fell from 45% in 1891 ... to 32.5% in 1931" (Zeldin, 2003, 259). Nevertheless, "In spite of this spectacular fall, there were still many more peasants in France than in most other West European countries" (259). As the cultivated land surface area fell by 19 percent over the same period, in conjunction with the declining population engaged in agriculture, this means that the gains in agricultural productivity were quite spectacular (Abbad, 1993, 104; Braudel and Labrousse, 1979–1980, 31–36).

However, these gains were unequally shared. Essentially, productivity increased on larger farms and in the northern regions of France. Consequently, the relative prosperity of agriculture in the postwar period, based on rising prices from 1920 to 1926 (Braudel and Labrousse, 1979–1980, 834) did not extend to all rural communities. On smaller holdings, particularly in the south and center of the country—and the Allier *département*, the location of Saint-Fiacre, is almost the exact geographical center of France—progress was much less evident (Abbad, 114). Becker and Berstein (1990, 334–335) place the Allier in the "third quartile" of productivity: "more advanced than the South West and the Massif Central but below the national average" (335).

The Saint-Fiacre estate had once been enormous, but by the time of the story it had been drastically reduced by successive land sales ("the farms being sold one after another," *L'Affaire Saint-Fiacre/Maigret Goes Home*, 64) and farming methods were not particularly advanced ("a cart full of manure went slowly by," 64).

High inflation during the war and in the immediate postwar period had also taken its toll on less economically progressive sectors of the landed aristocracy. Suddenly, annual revenues became more important than inherited property ownership: "The inflationary conjuncture disturbed the structure of property and wealth. In fact, by reducing the value of the franc by 4/5, the war and postwar periods ... brought about readjustments in social class that were occasionally quite brutal" (Abbad, 1993, 18). These economic effects coincide absolutely with the suggestion that the fortunes of the Saint-Fiacres had gone into decline with the death of the old count around the time of the war (*L'Affaire Saint-Fiacre/Maigret Goes Home*, 21, 24–25, 46). Indeed, the family fortune is so precarious that Maurice is unable to raise the money to pay his debts and has even had to turn to a Jewish money-lender ("a certain Monsieur Wolf," 92).

The postwar boom saw a frenzy of financial speculation, in which social classes not accustomed to "modern" business attempted to recoup flagging family fortunes:

> After the war, stock market speculation seemed to acquire a new importance for the owners of longstanding fortunes tempted by the prospect of rapid and substantial profits. Many families ... abandoned their traditional caution, which had primarily sought to conserve the family heritage, and looked to increase their wealth, conducting their business affairs as if they were financial capitalists [Braudel and Labrousse, 1979–1989, 875].

This appears to have been the route taken by Maurice de Saint-Fiacre (*L'Affaire Saint-Fiacre/Maigret Goes Home*, 28) and Jean Métayer (33–34) and had been the cause of the financial ruin of Métayer's family ("My parents had just been ruined by the crash of a little bank in Lyons," 19).

At the same time, the economic and social turbulence of the war and immediate postwar period had led to new possibilities for social mobility, represented in the rise of Maigret himself from humble origins to a high-ranking post in the Police Judiciaire, the social advancement of Docteur Bouchardon ("a peasant and the son of peasants," 14) and the ambitions of Emile Gautier:

> Not so much a resemblance of details as a resemblance of race. The same peasant origins: clear-cut features and big bones.
> The same degree of evolution, more or less, revealed by a skin which was rather better cared-for than that of the farm workers, by intelligent eyes, and by a self-assurance which was that of an "educated man" [86].

It is curious that Saint-Fiacre seems to have no war invalids, given that in postwar France there were 1,100,000 ex-combatants formally classified as *invalides* (Becker and Berstein, 1990, 165). Nevertheless, the fact that Marie Tatin has been unable to find a husband reflects the radical imbalance between the genders after the war: 1,000 men between the ages of 20 and 39 to 1,245 women of the same age range in 1921. "Thus thousands of French women would never marry because their potential husbands had died on the battlefields" (Agulhon et al., 1993, 173).

In *L'Affaire Saint-Fiacre* the fictional Saint-Fiacre can be reliably identified with the village of Paray-le-Frésil, site of the chateau of the marquis de Tracy, for whom Simenon worked as private secretary from 1923 to 1924, the period from which dated his fascination with the landed aristocracy and chateau life (Assouline, Chapter 4; Eskin, Chapter 5). Paray-le-Frésil/Saint-Fiacre is situated 320 kilometers south of Paris, 25 kilometers from Moulins (*L'Affaire Saint-Fiacre/Maigret Goes Home*, 103), the *chef-lieu* of the Allier *département*, and had a population of about 400 inhabitants in the 1930s (De Croock). The Allier is currently in the Auvergne administrative region and, although it is not as isolated as the *départements* of the Massif Central, it is a rural area that saw a steady population decline throughout the twentieth century (Aplin, 1993, 14).

Within the text, it appears that superficially little has altered in Saint-Fiacre since Maigret's childhood: "And he [Maigret] looked around him at this unchangeable scene in which not a single detail had altered in thirty years" (*L'Affaire Saint-Fiacre/Maigret Goes Home*, 17). The image is of an unchanged and unchanging *France profonde*. As the taxi driver remarks, when he drives Maigret from the village to Moulins: "This is real country for you!" (84).

Rural participation in the postwar prosperity was relative (Montero, 59). Although by 1932 82 percent of communes enjoyed household electricity (Abbad, 1993, 22), Saint-Fiacre has no electrical connection (*L'Affaire Saint-Fiacre/Maigret Goes Home*, 5, 7,104) and the chateau is reliant on its own private generator for electricity (104). Fewer than one in five peasant homes had a municipal water supply (Becker and Berstein, 1990, 347) and the village inn, of which there is only one (*L'Affaire Saint-Fiacre/Maigret Goes Home*, 52), seems to be in the same situation (6). Food is basic: "Coarse grey bread. A smell of coffee with chicory" (7). Compounding the isolation of the village, there is only one bus a day to Moulins (84). Simenon makes much of the contrast between Marie Tatin's village inn ("lit by oil lamps," 7) and the Café de Paris in Moulins with its telephone, electricity, billiards, cocktails and even a small orchestra (Chapter 7).

Nevertheless, a close reading reveals that social change is coming slowly even in the rural backwater of Saint-Fiacre. Montero (2001, 59) notes that in the immediate postwar period, rural life experienced a "decline in traditional village structures" and Becker and Berstein comment that "Communal religious activities ... tended to diminish.... Processions became less common, the elderly and children made up a majority of the faithful" (1990, 349). Sure enough, in Saint-Fiacre for first Mass on the important Catholic festival of Toussaint: "How many people were there in that ghostly gathering of half-asleep people? Fifteen at the most. There were only three men: the sacristan, the bell-ringer, and Maigret" [*L'Affaire Saint-Fiacre/Maigret Goes Home*, 8].

Furthermore, while the peasantry may only have participated to a limited degree in postwar prosperity, other sections of the rural population were being drawn into the new consumerist lifestyle of the 1920s:

> The entry of urban France into the consumer age aroused aspirations among rural dwellers for a similar lifestyle, whether this was in clothing, furniture purchased from "Galerie Barbès," the acquisition of record players, radios and motorcycles. These desires were encouraged by newspapers and radio broadcasts. But these aspirations stood in contradiction to a rural economy geared to self-sufficiency, leaving little surplus disposal income for these kinds of purchases.... The solution to this contradiction was found in an exodus of young rural dwellers to the urban centers, where salaried employment opened up access to modern consumerism [Becker and Berstein, 1990, 349].

This almost reads like a description of the lifestyle and ambitions of the Gautiers, father and son. In Maigret's former family home, where the Gautiers now live, "the armchair in which Maigret was sitting was new, like the mantelpiece, and must have come from a Paris furniture shop. There was a gramophone on the sideboard" (*L'Affaire Saint-Fiacre/Maigret Goes Home*, 82). Emile Gautier works in a bank, owns a motorcycle (51), looks "smarter than most of the inhabitants of Saint-Fiacre" (51) and spends his leisure time playing billiards and consuming "modern" drinks at the *Café de Paris* in Moulins (95). In short, in the eyes of Marie Tatin, "He's practically a townsman" (51).

In *L'Affaire Saint-Fiacre* the reactions of the characters to the combination of continuity and change in rural France emerge as a central theme in the novel and this in turn informs the development of the narrative. The Saint-Fiacre family belongs to what Braudel and Labrousse characterize as "the aristocracy of nobility ... often rural ... which preserved the traditions of the *Ancien Régime*" (1979–1980, 51). This backward-looking quality is reflected in the character of the countess—even her automobile is "an old model" (*L'Affaire Saint-Fiacre/Maigret Goes Home*, 14)—and the dilapidated state of the chateau (19, 20). Property and wealth are seen as belonging to the dynastic family rather than any single individual (77). The words "respect" (23, 27) and "fitting"/"dignified" (65, 66, 76) are never far from the lips of Maurice de Saint-Fiacre, and these values are contrasted with the perceived "confusion" (*désordre* in the original French) of the current situation (48, 52, 77), in which the narrator, observing the scene through the eyes of Maigret, tells us "The confusion was growing. Not a material, reparable confusion, but a moral confusion which seemed to be contagious" (48).

Not only do the Saint-Fiacres have a backward-looking worldview in a general sense, but Maurice literally looks back to the "good old days": "Before, yes! When my father was alive" (64), and "There was a time when people held their breath when they came into this room, because my father, *the master*, was working here" (76). Maigret, who emerges as a sympathizer with the Saint-Fiacre family and what they represent, empathizes with these nostalgic reflections: "Maigret knew that as well as anybody else" (64), and "Maigret remembered that too!" (76).

Maigret, faced with the downfall not just of an aristocratic family to whom he feels an attachment dating from his childhood, senses also a change in the whole fabric of rural society. His speech (and that of the narrator describing his feelings) is peppered with words such as "indignation" (16), "disgust" (51), "furious" (31), "horrible" (117) and "sacrilege" (16, 117). The strength of the vocabulary reflects Maigret's depth of feeling about the perceived collapse of an ordered world based on values to which he feels strongly attached. It is as if his childhood is being devalued by the developments and events to which he is a witness.

Vestiges of this world still exist, as in the church where "there was a row of stalls reserved for people from the château" (9), and in the deference showed by the peasants when Maurice enters the village inn: "The four peasants who were drinking there suddenly felt as if they were no longer at home. They greeted the count with a respect mingled with fear" (27). However, symbolically, even though Maigret recognizes many of the villagers (7, 15), "nobody recognised him" (15). Perhaps Maigret realizes that this is not just because he has changed physically—"He was forty-two. He had put on weight" (21)—but because the world too has changed. If people from the past cannot be recognized in the literal sense, then, the text seems to suggest, will the values of the past also be no longer recognized?

Maigret seems to have little difficulty understanding those aspects of rural society and attitudes which are unchanged, whether it be Marie Tatin, with her mixture of simplicity and deference to the aristocracy, or the choirboy's mother who combines cunning and avarice, all of which are almost stereotypical peasant characteristics in the French context. The problem comes when he tries to address the changes that have taken place, in particular with regard to the Gautiers, father and son. These characters reflect back to the commissaire an image of a chateau steward and his ambitious son, an image which, despite its superficial resemblance to the Maigrets father and son, has fundamentally changed. Maigret's father "had been the steward of the château for thirty years" (7). While feigning loyalty (81–82), Gautier has used his position to swindle his employers (114). Maigret fils, while he has physically moved away from the chateau, retains a commitment to its values and a respectful view of his family's "masters" (15, 16, 23, 95). Emile Gautier, in contrast, wishes not only physically to leave the village environment to live in the "modern world" but has, concomitantly, also rejected the values of the "old world." Where Maigret had regarded the countess with a quasi-mystical reverence, "a young woman who, for the country boy he had been, had personified all that was feminine, graceful and noble" (15), the young Gautier has committed the ultimate *lèse-majesté* by sleeping with her (128).

It is this inability to comprehend social changes which challenge the very origins of his own being and beliefs that paralyzes Maigret throughout the inquiry. Maurice de Saint-Fiacre effectively resolves the case, and Maigret's only real contribution is to discover how the Gautiers had intended to throw suspicion on Jean Métayer for the death of the countess: "He was thinking that his part in this case had been limited to finding the last link, a tiny link which completed the chain" (137). In a sense, *L'Affaire Saint-Fiacre* can be seen as the reversed image of a typical Maigret inquiry. Usually the commissaire enters an environment with which he is unfamiliar such as the canal boats of *Le Charretier de la Providence/Maigret Meets a Milord* (1931), the port of Ouistreham in *Le Port des brumes* (1932), the Fécamp fishing community in *Au Rendez-Vous des Terre-Neuvas/The Sailors' Rendezvous* (1931), the Flemish shop of *Chez les Flamands* (1932), and so on. He gradually orients himself and, by coming to understand the environment in which the crime has occurred, he is able to solve the case. However, in *L'Affaire Saint-Fiacre* the opposite process is at work. Maigret enters a community with which he believes he is familiar yet he is unable to move towards an understanding of what has happened. At the dinner presided over by Maurice de Saint-Fiacre (Chapter 9), as the problem moves towards its dénouement:

> Never in his whole career had Maigret felt so uncomfortable. And it was probably the first time he had had the impression of being incapable of dealing with the situation. Events were leaving him behind. Now and then he thought he understood, and the next moment a phrase of Saint-Fiacre's would call everything in question again [119].

So it is not Maigret, the representative of the bourgeois police, who unravels the problem, but the aristocrat Maurice, who acts as detective, judge, jury and punisher of the upstart Gautiers: "Maurice de Saint-Fiacre was in command of the situation, and he was adequate to his task" (128); "Maurice de Saint-Fiacre dominated the company" (130); Emile is savagely beaten (128–133) and father and son are physically thrown out of the chateau ("Saint-Fiacre ... literally threw the body down the steps and shut the door," 133). As Maurice explains, this is not the "the justice of the courts" (129), bourgeois justice with its apparatus of courts and lawyers, requirements of due process and proofs, and juries of the accused's peers. Rather it is the "justice" of the Ancien Régime, dispensed by the feudal lord.

The narrative poses the question whether, in Maurice's eyes, Emile's greatest crime is not his role in the death of the countess but rather that he had slept with her (128). That his mother could employ bourgeois gigolos, such as Métayer, may have aroused Maurice's displeasure, but it was a displeasure that remained within limits. That the rigid class lines of rural society could be crossed in the bedroom was intolerable: hence the savagery of the beating—"a battered blood-stained face, with the nose nothing but a tumour and the upper lip split open" (132)—and the use of the landowner's power to expel summarily an employee from job and home. According to Vanoncini (1990):

> It is bad enough that the bourgeois Métayer penetrates the inner sanctum of the aristocracy. But that the bailiff's son, occupying exactly the same position in the social hierarchy as had the young Maigret, should sleep with the countess and swindle her is an act of usurpation liable to the harshest sanctions [95].

The novel symbolically ends with the funeral of the countess, where each social class finds its "proper place": Maurice de Saint-Fiacre looking down from the top of the chateau steps; the peasants "grouped at the foot of the steps"; the servants in the kitchen "their noses pressed against the window-panes"; the upstart Gautiers banished from the estate; and the bourgeois Métayer, "a little swine ... making his escape in the company of a lawyer with a hangover" (186–187). Effectively, with Maigret's tacit complicity, the practices of a bygone social order have prevailed over those of the capitalist Third Republic; the past has overcome the present.

Chez les Flamands: *Petite Bourgeoisie and Proletariat; Class Conflict in a Border Town*

Chez les Flamands was composed in Antibes in January 1932 as part of the burst of productive activity that also produced *L'Ombre chinoise* and *L'Affaire Saint-Fiacre*. It was published later in the same year as the fourteenth novel in the series. Uniquely in the Fayard Maigret stories, *Chez les*

Flamands includes characters from the working class, the Piedboeuf family, at the center of the narrative, thereby presenting an opportunity to consider Simenon's portrayal of the proletariat in relation to the petite bourgeoisie, represented by the other key family in the story, the Peeterses.

In *Chez les Flamands* Maigret goes to Givet, on the River Meuse, at the border between France and Belgium, at the request of Anna Peeters, who has come to Paris with a letter of recommendation from Madame Maigret's cousin in Nancy. The Peeters family, who are of Belgian origin, have a shop in Givet catering especially to the Flemish boatmen. In addition to Anna, there are two other children, Joseph, a law student, and Maria, a teacher in an Ursuline convent school in Namur across the Belgian border. Joseph is said to have fathered a son, Jojo, with Germaine Piedboeuf, although he had always been expected to marry his cousin, Marguerite Van de Weert. Last seen going to the Peeters's shop to get her monthly allowance for the child, Germaine has disappeared, and the Peeterses are suspected locally of having killed her. Although Germaine's corpse has not been found, Machère, the police inspector from Nancy, also believes the Peeterses to be guilty.

Germaine has a brother, Gérard Piedboeuf, who, Maigret learns, had a brief affair with Anna years before. There is also a bargeman, Gustave Cassin, who at first claims to have seen someone throwing a body into the Meuse and then denies it. Maigret visits his barge and finds Germaine's coat and a hammer. Then her body is found fifty miles downstream, killed by hammer blows to the head. Cassin disappears, leaving a bogus suicide note, and police suspicion turns to him. Maigret, who has his own theory but is present in only an unofficial capacity, confronts Anna privately. As he had worked out, she had killed Germaine in order to protect her brother's happiness, that is, so that he could marry Marguerite. Enlisting the aid of Joseph, she had hidden the body, finally throwing it in the river several days later, and asked Maigret to come to Givet as a ruse to try to deflect suspicion from her family. Gérard had paid Cassin to say he had evidence against the Peeterses; Cassin had then gone to Anna, who agreed to pay him more money if he would disappear. The official police conclusion is that Cassin is guilty, although he is never traced. Maigret stays silent about what he has discovered and returns to Paris.

Chez les Flamands has no explicit dating, but the context is clearly contemporary, that is, the very beginning of the 1930s. The French economy was beginning to slide into recession in the wake of the international depression signaled by the Wall Street crash of 1929, although according to Dard (1999, 11) and Montero (2001, 67) the effects of the recession showed themselves more gradually in France than in the other major capitalist economies. Thus, although the novel does not give the impression of a society in crisis, there are significant indications of the difficulties into which the French economy was drifting. Unemployment began to rise significantly from 1931 (Montero, 71) and when Maigret visits the factory where the Piedboeuf family all work he sees "a blackboard on which had been chalked: *No men wanted*" (*Chez les Flamands/Maigret and the Flemish Shop*, 72). One response of the French Administration to the economic situation was to institute tariffs on goods imported from countries other than their colonies (Braudel and Labrousse, 1979–1980, 757). This explains the importance of contraband in the economy of a border town such as Givet, an activity in which Machère, the police inspector from Nancy, perhaps based more on prejudice than any real evidence, believes the Peeterses are implicated.

While the 1930s were characterized by recession, the preceding decade had seen a significant expansion in economic activity based on postwar reconstruction and a substantial growth in world trade. As part of this general expansion, the French economy entered a period of technical advance and organizational restructuring, although this remained uneven according to the economic sector in question (Montero, 2001, 53–55). In industrial production, giant, semi-monopolistic corporations, using the latest systems devised by Bedaux and Ford, coexisted with small-scale businesses, whose methods had barely changed since the nineteenth century, and the same was also true in the realm of transport of raw materials and manufactured goods. In France, with its large surface area, sometimes difficult terrain and extensive network of rivers and canals, this coexistence was particularly evident in fluvial transport. This development is clearly seen in the Fayard Maigret novels, where there is a startling contrast between the owner-operators of the *Providence* in *Le Charretier de la Providence/Maigret Meets a Milord* (1931), whose barge is still horse-drawn, and the activity of Ducrau, in *L'Ecluse numéro 1/The Lock at Charenton* (1933), who by a process of horizontal and vertical integration has established a business empire of tugs and motorized barges, quarries and brickworks. In *Chez les Flamands* these different stages in the development of river transport are reflected in the shipping passing through Givet:

> Thanks to the stoppage of traffic on the river, Givet had quite the look of a big port. There were several Rhine lighters of a thousand tons—great black things of steel. Beside them the wooden barges from the north looked like varnished toys [*Chez les Flamands/Maigret and the Flemish Shop*, 23–24].

One of the fundamental features of capitalism is that in competition between large, forward-looking and small, backward-looking capitalists, the former will invariably prevail over the latter. This was true in general in interwar France, where it was less progressive businesses, usually those operating on a smaller scale, which bore the heaviest impact of the downturn (Dard,

1999, 22), and this was equally true in the specific conditions pertaining in river and canal transport:

> Maigret ... gathered that the Belgians were unpopular, not so much because they differed in character, as because they were competitors. Their boats were kept in perfect state of repair and were fitted with powerful motors, and they were generally in a position to undercut the French, often accepting cargoes at rates which the latter thought ridiculous [*Chez les Flamands/Maigret and the Flemish Shop*, 35–36].

By locating Simenon's narrative within the history of the period, it is clear how what may appear to be national or even "racial," antagonisms are frequently rooted in economic conditions and capitalist competition.

If it is true that within the capitalist class, in the broadest sense, the interwar period saw the advance of more modern, larger-scale capital at the expense of smaller capitalists, it should also be noted that, of all the groups in French society, the working class profited the least from the postwar expansion. According to Becker and Berstein (1990, 353), for the working class:

> This participation in prosperity ... remained relative.... Workers' wages were far from matching the growth in national income or employers' profits. The latter increased by 50% between 1913 and 1929, whereas blue-collar salaries only grew by 12% in Paris and 21% in the provinces.

For the commercial petite bourgeoisie, that is to say shopkeepers like the Peeters family, the 1920s were in general a period of prosperity. According to Zeldin (2003, 169), although the big chain stores like La Samaritaine, Les Galeries Lafayette and Bon Marché had been founded at the end of the Second Empire or the beginning of the Third Republic:

> In 1931, only around one hundred retail chains employed more than 500 staff, whereas there were more than half a million small shops: 91% of shops employed three workers or fewer.... These small shops played a particular role in French society. Gabriel Hanotaux praised them highly: their economic activity was the most democratic of all in that nowhere else was it so possible to start from nothing and earn a fortune.

Of course, there were also many small shopkeepers whose businesses failed, but the historical evidence suggests that the postwar expansion created conditions in which a hardworking petit bourgeois economic unit such as the Peeters family could prosper. And it is the relative prosperity, with its attendant lifestyle and ambitions, of the Peeterses, rather than any "racial" difference between Flemish and French speakers, which brings them into conflict with the proletarian Piedboeufs in *Chez les Flamands*.

Givet, the setting for *Chez les Flamands* was, in many ways, a typical French town of the interwar years. By 1931, a majority of the French population was urban, but the greater part of these urban dwellers lived in small towns of between 5,000 and 20,000 inhabitants, the size of Givet at that time (Abbad, 1993, 10). Although at the beginning of the narrative, Givet appears to be a busy river port (*Chez les Flamands/Maigret and the Flemish Shop*, 24), this is only as a result of the backlog of traffic caused by the flooding. As the river level falls, Anna explains to Maigret that in a couple of days there will be no more than three or four boats at a time (108). We are firmly in small-town provincial France, both materially—the telegram and telephone services do not operate after 11 o'clock on Sundays (128)—and mentally, as when Inspecteur Machère reports to Maigret that the *juge d'instruction* has insisted on a cautious approach to avoid disturbing small-town sensibilities (124). This is the kind of provincial setting in which small businesses, such as the Peeterses' shop, continued to exercise a significant social weight. As Dubois notes in Gothot-Mersche et al. (1980, 24):

> The association of the petite bourgeoisie with provincialism goes without saying. The petit bourgeois, and above all the traditional petit bourgeois, can best play out his role and assume a certain importance in the restricted setting of provincial life: he feels most at home in the small or medium-sized town.

Employment opportunities in Givet are limited. Despite the presence of the river traffic, employment in this sector seems confined to mariners from elsewhere, and the only local residents to benefit economically are owners of the bistros or shops, such as the Peeterses', that supply the river trade. The major employer of local workers appears to be the factory where Monsieur Piedboeuf and Gérard work and where Germaine had been employed before her disappearance. Although there is no mention of what the factory produces, it appears to be of a significant size, and Maigret notes that "through the gates dozens of workers, men and women, were pouring out" at lunchtime (*Chez les Flamands/Maigret and the Flemish Shop*, 51). In this, the economy of Givet reflects a general gradual change in French industry, with production shifting to larger factories: according to Braudel and Labrousse (1979–1980, 772), whereas in 1906, 40.2 percent of factory workers were in plants employing more than 100 workers, this figure had increased to 50.2 percent by 1931.

Yet it is the status of the river as the frontier between France and Belgium which gives Givet its distinctive character. The narrator, and perhaps Maigret, seems unsure how to understand this aspect of Givet:

> He was standing on French soil, but it was impossible to forget the nearness of the frontier. The houses were definitely Belgian houses, of ugly brown brick, with doorsteps of hewn stone, and copper flower-pots on the window-sills.
>
> The people, too, had in their lined faces something of the hardness of the

Walloon type. And then there was the khaki uniform of the Belgian customs officers.

Givet was unmistakably a frontier town, the meeting-ground of two nations. Even in the shops you could not forget it, as both French and Belgian money were accepted [*Chez les Flamands/Maigret and the Flemish Shop*, 34–35].

Thus, Givet seems an ideal setting for a consideration of the two key themes of *Chez les Flamands*: the relationship between the provincial petite bourgeoisie and the working class, and the impact of nationality and "race" on social relations. The main characters in *Chez les Flamands* can be divided into three groupings, namely the Peeters and Piedboeuf families and the communities they represent in Givet, that is, the Flemish and French populations of the Franco-Belgian border, and finally the "outsider," Maigret.

The Peeters family, in the person of Anna, is identified from the very beginning in terms of its social class through the phrase *des vêtements de petite bourgeoise* (*Chez les Flamands*, 9). The English translation has the less socially precise "Her clothes were sober and quite commonplace" (*Maigret and the Flemish Shop*, 3), and this explicit identification is repeated later in the narrative: "the atmosphere of this *petit bourgeois* house" (148). Monsieur Peeters, the father, is now a semi-senile semi-invalid, but in his earlier life he had been a classic example of what Fabre, following Poulantzas (1974), characterizes as the petite bourgeoisie traditionnelle (PBT):

> In general, it consists of small producers and small property owners. The first category includes artisans and small family businesses in which the proprietor while owning the means of production also directly expends his labor power. The employment of wage workers is only occasional and work by family members is not remunerated in the form of wages [Fabre, 1981, 137].

Indeed, we learn of Monsieur Peeters that "he was a basket-maker with four men under him, working in the workshop behind the house" (*Chez les Flamands/Maigret and the Flemish Shop*, 24). For reasons that are unstated but may well be connected to Monsieur Peeters's age (we learn on page 24 that he is twenty years older than his wife), the family has moved into the other sector of activity of the petite bourgeoisie traditionnelle, shopkeeping:

> The second category is composed of small property owners, principally shopkeepers, where, as with the artisan, the owner works, directly helped by family members and only occasionally employs wage labor [Fabre, 1981, 138].

This is a precise description of the Peeterses' family business. With Monsieur Peeters's worsening condition, the shop is run by his wife and their eldest daughter, Anna. Moreover, the business seems to have been very successful. While neither of them are impartial commentators, Anna and Inspecteur Machère both remark on the success of the Peeterses' shop:

> "Everybody's against us.... You see, we're foreigners ... and we've more money than most" [Anna, *Chez les Flamands/Maigret and the Flemish Shop*, 15].
>
> "They're supposed to be [rich]. The house is theirs and they've been known to advance money to bargees with no capital.... By all accounts, they're worth hundreds of thousands of francs" [Inspecteur Machère, 24].

Nevertheless, even a profitable family shop can support only so many family members, and in addition to Anna, there are two other children, Maria, 28, and Joseph, 25. The family's aspirations for these two lie in a movement into what Poulantzas and Fabre (1981, 139–144) call the nouvelle petite bourgeoisie (NPB), specifically the professions of education and the law. Although members of these professions do not directly own any means of production, it can be argued that their "knowledge" is the precondition for their economic activity, that they exercise a role which perpetuates the existing capitalist class system and that the hierarchical nature of these professions holds out the possibility of advance into the bourgeoisie proper:

> Hierarchical structures and career progression play the same role for the NPB as does the advancement of the best and brightest for the PBT, the artisan becoming a small businessman, then a capitalist. In both cases, this advancement is individual. Merit is recognized and new blood introduced into the elites.... For the NPB it depends above all on education [Fabre, 1981, 143].

The Peeters family holds strong ambitions for both Maria and Joseph. From Machère we learn that Maria is "a *régente* in a big convent in Namur.... That's more than an ordinary teacher" (*Chez les Flamands/Maigret and the Flemish Shop*, 25), and Anna tells Maigret that Joseph "is determined to pass [his exam] with distinction, as he has in all the others" (42).

The ambition for Joseph goes beyond his future profession and extends to his personal life: a marriage to Marguerite Van de Weert, a doctor's daughter, and therefore of a higher social status, would consolidate the family's respectability and provide another potential means of social advancement (13). The social implications of Joseph's possible future marriage to either of his two fiancées, Germaine, the mother of his child, or Marguerite, the doctor's daughter, are symbolized in the photos of the young women that Maigret finds in his room. On the chest of drawers is:

> A large framed portrait of Marguerite Van de Weert [the original French text continues *en robe claire, coiffée d'un chapeau de paille d'Italie*—"in a light-coloured dress, wearing an Italian straw hat"]. And on it the girl had written in a long pointed hand the opening lines of the *Song of Solveig* [*Maigret and the Flemish Shop*, 42–43, *Chez les Flamands*, 51].

In one of the drawers is a photo of Germaine which:

might have been a passport photograph, horrible as all such photos are with their harshly contrasting lights and shades. A girl who had obviously reached womanhood, yet was so small and frail that the word woman seemed quite inapplicable.... She was wearing an absurd hat and looked as if she was scared by the camera [*Chez les Flamands/Maigret and the Flemish Shop*, 44–45].

The reader sees more than a simple contrast in physiognomies; rather the difference is between young women of two distinct social classes, and Joseph's choice between them would have drastic consequences for the class position of his own family.

In contrast to the petit bourgeois Peeterses, the Piedboeuf family is prototypically proletarian in the Marxist sense that they own neither means of production nor property and they live entirely by the sale of their labor power. Monsieur Piedboeuf is a night watchman and Gérard a white-collar employee in the same factory, in which Germaine had been a typist before her disappearance (*Chez les Flamands/Maigret and the Flemish Shop*, 25). The fact that Gérard and Germaine are clerical rather than manual workers does not alter their proletarian status, which is ultimately determined by their relationship to the means of production rather than by the precise form of their labor. Indeed, they form part of a section of the working class which was growing gradually but consistently throughout the Third Republic, "a white-collar proletariat, with low wages and limited prospects of social mobility" (Braudel and Labrousse, 1979–1980, 63). Unlike Maria and Joseph Peeters, Gérard has no professional ambitions and his horizons are limited to having a good time during the hours when he is not working: "He doesn't seem to put in a great deal of work," says Machère, "judging by the time he spends playing billiards at the Café de la Mairie" (*Chez les Flamands Maigret and the Flemish Shop*, 26). Madame Piedboeuf has been dead for twelve years. According to her husband, "it was chest trouble that took her" (73), which seems to be a reference to tuberculosis, an illness closely linked to poverty and from which Maigret believes the whole family to suffer (54).

It is impossible to agree with Dubois (1992, 175) that: "What separates the small shopkeeping world of the Peeterses from the part blue-collar part white-collar world of the Piedboeufs is more a difference in aspirations rather than status." In fact, what *Chez les Flamands* presents us with is more than simply a portrait of two families with a different subjective view of life's possibilities; rather, the two families typify and represent two distinct social classes, whose daily life, and hence aspirations, are founded in an objectively different relationship to the means of production.

It is this objective class difference which underlies the contrasts between the material conditions of life and the behavior and attitudes of the two families. These contrasts recur throughout the narrative, sometimes explicitly and sometimes implicitly. The Peeterses' home is "a fair-sized building" (*Chez les Flamands/Maigret and the Flemish Shop*, 14); it has city-supplied electricity and a lounge/dining room "with a piano, a violin-case, a carefully polished parquet floor, comfortable furniture, reproductions of famous pictures on the walls" (9–10); on the table are "a check table-cloth, silver cups and saucers of fine china" (10); and when Maigret visits the upper floor, he notes, "The stairs were covered with linoleum so polished that you had to be careful not to slip" (21). By contrast, the Piedboeuf's home is "a poor two-storied cottage," with only a kerosene lamp for lighting (6). The interior is "in a fearful mess" (37): "everything was poor and ugly. The kitchen was the only sitting-room" (56). Joseph Peeters has a motorcycle (32), although as a student he has no independent source of income, while Gérard Piedboeuf, on his worker's wages, can only afford a pushbike (91).

The class difference is also realized in the social lives of each family. The Peeters family attend Mass, the Piedboeufs do not (138). The Peeters have family musical soirées (16, 156), Gérard Piedboeuf spends his leisure time playing billiards (33), getting drunk in bars (87) and taking factory girls to the cinema (155). Anna and Maria Peeters shun coquetterie and seem uninterested in sex (56), while Germaine Piedboeuf is "the sort you find kissing in any dark corner" (26). Finally, the class distinction can be seen in the two families' attitudes to the police. Although it later transpires that Anna has her own agenda, the Peeters family members are respectful to Maigret: they see in the police a defense of the existing social order, in which they feel they have a stake. For Gérard, "if you have got money, the police will eat out of your hand" (76), and in this opinion he is reflecting the common view of the Givet working class: "The police will always be on the same side as there's money" (39), says the woman who is looking after Germaine's child. In the eyes of the workers in the street, "Maigret was 'the detective from Paris,' an interloper who had been called in by the Belgians for the sole purpose of whitewashing them. And whenever he was recognized in the street, the glances that were turned on him were anything but friendly" (52).

However, this citation also raises the second major theme of *Chez les Flamands*: To what degree are the Piedboeufs and the general population of Givet motivated by a sense of injustice and working-class solidarity and to what extent are they driven by prejudice against the Peeterses because of their Flemish origins? In Anna's words, "Everybody's against us. The whole town. You see, we're foreigners" (15). How does the "national question" relate to the theme of class struggle in the novel's narrative?

Here it is necessary to make a number of distinctions. First, is the issue one of "nationality" or of "race"? In terms of nationality, the three Peeters children have all been born in France (66), although when Joseph enters the hotel where Maigret is staying, he "slunk in timidly" (30)—the original French is *en étranger*, "like an outsider or foreigner"—(*Chez les Flamands*, 37). Unlike their mother "[who] spoke with a decided accent" (*Chez les Flamands/Maigret and the Flemish Shop*, 11), the younger generation of Peeterses are completely bilingual and they see their future as being in France: although Maria works in Belgium, it is in the francophone town of Namur; Joseph's studies are in the French university of Nancy; and when, in the novel's coda, Maigret encounters Anna by chance, she has moved to Paris. Yet, Anna herself, on observing a young female factory worker in Givet, compares her to Germaine Piedboeuf with the words "It's one of the same sort" (7)—*C'est la même race* in the original French (*Chez les Flamands*, 13)—a remark which seems ambiguous as to whether it refers to social class or nationality.

The attitudes of the other characters are equally complex. The Piedboeufs seem to be motivated in the first instance by grief for the loss of Germaine, but their attitude to the Flemish origins of the Peeterses is mixed. For Monsieur Piedboeuf the key question seems to be one of class: "He'd never marry her. There's money in that family ... while we..." (*Chez les Flamands/Maigret and the Flemish Shop*, 72); but when Gérard is drunk, he refers to the national difference as an additional factor to class: "It seems to be a crime in France to be a Frenchman—particularly if you're poor" (76). Inspecteur Machère, who, as a middle-ranking police officer, shares the petit bourgeois class position of the Peeterses, seems to be full of prejudice against them, a prejudice that is expressed in the most virulent terms and which is directed against their Flemish origins, language and culture rather than the Belgian nationality of the older generation. The bargeman Cassin is Belgian too, from Tilleur, near Liège (28), but he is a francophone Walloon, so Machère's hostility to him is based on his character, not nationality. If the Peeterses were Jewish, rather than Flemish, Machère's attitude to the family could be the words of a virulent anti–Semite:

"They're not quite the same as us. A different outlook" [24].

"They've got queer ideas" [25].

"These people make me sick.... The smell of their coffee and their tarts is enough to turn me over" [140].

For some of the French boatmen, the dislike of their Flemish counterparts is based on economic competition rather than any particular national hostility:

The Belgians were unpopular, not so much because they differed in character, as because they were competitors. Their boats were kept in a perfect state of repair and were fitted with powerful motors, and they were generally in a position to undercut the French, often accepting cargoes at rates which the latter thought ridiculous [36].

For these French workers, the economic question is central: "Why don't they arrest the whole family.... Unless it's because they're well-to-do folk..." (36). Yet, when Maigret sums up local opinions on the Peeterses in his notebook, he notes another French boatman as saying: "In Belgium they're all like that!" (i.e., like the Peeterses) (29).

The narrator's voice on the national question is nuanced between objective observations of the distinctions between the French and Flemish communities in a border town and unsubstantiated remarks on "race." That there might be differences between the Peeterses' establishment and the French bistros of Givet (9, 29, 35) is a simple matter of observation, presumably rooted in Simenon's own experiences on his trips along the canals and rivers of northern France, Belgium and Holland on the *Ostrogoth* in 1929 (Assouline, 1997, Chapter 6). That many Flemish Belgians were more devoutly Catholic than their French counterparts in the border regions (*Chez les Flamands/Maigret and the Flemish Shop*, 126–127) may also be a historical point. But what can the reader make of the narrator's characterization of "two nations" (34)—*deux races* in the French original (*Chez les Flamands*, 43)—and his description of Docteur Van de Weert as "a real Flemish type. He could have stepped straight out of a picture or an advertisement for some brand of schnapps. Full, bright red lips, and clear blue eyes that revealed all the simplicity of his soul" (*Chez les Flamands/Maigret and the Flemish Shop*, 88)? What, too, of the narrator's description of the inhabitants of Givet with their "lined faces [with] something of the hardness of the Walloon type" (that is, francophone Belgians)? (34) Harder, more lined faces than whom? French people? *All* French people? Given that much of modern northern France was formerly part of the Spanish Netherlands, that the architecture of cities such as Lille and much of the culture of the Nord region of France is consciously "Flemish" and that the state of Belgium came into existence in its present form only in 1831, the logic of these remarks seems tenuous.

Maigret is disoriented by the situation he finds in Givet. The commissaire sees himself as a "typical" Frenchman, but he finds himself drawn towards the Peeters family, both the individual strength of character of Anna and the overall ambience of hard work, culture, piety and calm that reigns within the household. His first impressions of Anna are of sobriety and calm and that she is "really quite distinguished" (3). The atmosphere in the home is of "quiet" (9) and *harmonie* (118; in the original French; the English-language edition does not translate this word, 106). This contrasts with the "fearful mess" he finds in the Piedboeuf household (37) and the promiscuity of Gérard and Germaine. When he encounters the local *notables*, the assistant mayor and the local police chief, he feels disgusted by their hypocrisy and small-mindedness (127–129). Earlier in his inquiry, Maigret insisted "I'm not on anybody's side. I'm merely trying to find out what happened" (57). However, when he discovers the truth, that Anna has planned and carried out the brutal murder of Germaine, he stays silent. *Chez les Flamands* is not the only novel in which the commissaire chooses not to reveal what he has discovered, but it is perhaps the starkest example of Maigret setting himself up as a moral judge of a crime and a criminal, basing his decisions on his own evaluation of the characters and circumstances rather than acting as an impartial enforcer of the law. The accusation of the Piedboeufs that the commissaire has come to "cover up" for the Peeterses becomes a reality: although the identity of Germaine's killer is known to Maigret and although it is a member of the Peeters family, as the Piedboeufs and Machère have insisted from the beginning, no action is taken. For Maigret, the human qualities he has observed in Anna and, by implication, his class solidarity with the petit bourgeois Peeters family, are more important than the resolution of the case.

Le Port des brumes: *Social Class and Politics in the Final Years of the Third Republic*

Le Port des brumes was completed in Antibes in February 1932 and published in May of the same year as the sixteenth in the Fayard series (Eskin, 1987, 280). In Eskin's view, "The plot that Simenon contrives is highly uneven [but] *Le Port des brumes* is as successful as *Le Chien jaune* and *Au Rendez-vous des Terre-Neuvas* in building up a small town maritime atmosphere" (91). Unlike *Le Chien jaune*, where most of the principal characters are not directly involved in maritime affairs, and *Au Rendez-vous des Terre-Neuvas*, set in the deep-sea trawling industry of Fécamp, *Le Port des brumes* revolves around social relations within the small commercial port of Ouistreham in Normandy and in the regional capital Caen. All of the central characters in the story are, in one way or another, connected to the life of the port and its maritime commerce.

In *Le Port des brumes* a man found wandering around Paris unable to speak is identified as Yves Joris, the harbormaster of Ouistreham in Normandy. His housekeeper, Julie Legrand, comes to Paris to take him home, and Maigret accompanies them back to Ouistreham. Joris has been shot in the head and expertly operated on, but is suffering from complete amnesia. Among his letters there is a bank statement showing that someone has deposited 300,000 francs in his account. The following morning Maigret is called to Joris's house: Joris has been poisoned, and dies. Julie's brother, Grand Louis, is an ex-convict seaman who works on the *Saint-Michel*, which had been in port the night Joris disappeared. Maigret visits the *Saint-Michel*, which has docked again, and meets Louis and the ship's captain, Yves Lannec. Louis leaves to sleep on a dredger, and Maigret discovers that someone else has been on the boat as well.

Maigret visits the house of the mayor, Ernest Grandmaison, president of a shipping company, who is not helpful, and he then trails housekeeper Julie to a shrine in the dunes, where she wishes for success for her brother's project, although she won't reveal what this project is. Maigret sends for his colleague Inspector Lucas, who follows the unidentified man from the dredger to near the mayor's house, where he loses him. In the house they see Grand Louis and the mayor. Maigret sets the local police to work and has the missing man arrested and brought back to Grandmaison's: he confronts Louis and the mayor with the man, Jean Martineau, a naturalized Norwegian. All refuse to talk. Maigret learns that the mayor's wife, Hélène Grandmaison, knows Martineau as Raymond.

Maigret goes with Grandmaison to his offices in Caen, where the mayor shoots himself and the story is revealed. The "Norwegian" is his cousin, Raymond Grandmaison, who had been in love with Hélène. He had been caught stealing from the company funds, and Ernest had forced him to leave France forever, after which he himself married Hélène. But she had been pregnant with Raymond's child. Fifteen years later Raymond had been trying to steal back his son, and enlisted the help of Louis and Joris. A mistake resulted in Joris being shot. The plan aborted, Martineau managed to get Joris operated on, but when he returned, the mayor feared he would reveal the truth if he came to his senses, and poisoned him. Julie inherits Joris's legacy and Louis becomes owner of the *Saint-Michel*.

Although there are no precise dates given in the novel, other than "October" (*Le Port des brumes/Maigret and the Death of a Harbor-Master*, 3), we can assume that *Le Port des brumes*, like the other Fayard Maigret novels, is set in the same period as its publication, the early 1930s. Indeed, Simenon was in Ouistreham from the latter part of August to October 1931, aboard his boat the *Ostrogoth*, which he sold in Caen at the beginning of November (Assouline, 1997, Chapter 7). In May 1930 the index of industrial production in France reached its highest point since the end of the war (Dard, 1999, 13), and it seemed to many, including the administration, as if the national economy would be spared the depression into which the United States and Britain had been plunged in 1929 (12). However, by May 1931 the index of industrial production had fallen to 86 against a 1929 baseline of 100, and by 1932 this figure was down to 72. National revenue fell from 395 million francs in 1930 to 361 million in 1931, and fell again to 307 million in 1932. Bankruptcies and judicial liquidations of businesses rose from 755 a month in 1930 to 906 in 1931 and 1,169 in 1932 (22).

Maritime trade, in both its international and domestic forms, had generally prospered during the economic reconstruction of the 1920s. Certain raw materials had to be imported, as the replacement harbor master, Delcourt, explains when Maigret asks if Joris often went to Norway: "Yes.... Especially just after the war, when we were so short of wood" (*Le Port des brumes/Maigret and the Death of a Harbor Master*, 44). International trade was given a further stimulus when the Poincaré administration devalued the franc in June 1928, and by 1929 more than a quarter of industrial output was destined for export (Montero, 2001, 50). France's coastal geography, with its numerous wide river estuaries, also favored coastal rather than land transport. Delcourt explains the work of the coastal vessels: "These coasters almost always carry the same cargoes: vegetables, especially onions, for England, coal for the Breton ports, stone, cement, slates" (*Le Port des brumes/Maigret and the Death of a Harbor-Master*, 42); and he tells Maigret that he himself had always worked on the same route from Bordeaux to Nantes and back again (44).

The beginnings of the economic downturn had an inevitable impact on maritime commerce. The fall in economic activity affected internal trade and the international dimension of the crisis hit exports, a development which was reinforced as countries adopted increasingly protectionist trade policies (Braudel and Labrousse, 1979–1980, 753). As with other sectors of the economy, it was small businesses which felt the first impact of the downturn (877–888). Maigret overhears the following at a reception at the mayor's house:

> "I suppose the shipping crisis has hit people rather hard?"
> "Well, that depends. Here we hardly notice it; none of our vessels are laid up. Of course, small shipowners, especially those with only coasting-schooners, are beginning to feel the pinch. In fact, most of the people who own the schooners are trying to get rid of them; they don't cover expenses"
> [*Le Port des brumes/Maigret and the Death of a Harbor-Master*, 40].

We later learn that this is true of the *Saint-Michel*, when Julie tells Maigret that Lannec wanted to sell his schooner because of the slump in the economy (66).

Le Port des brumes is principally set in Ouistreham, a small port on the canal linking Caen to the sea, with a short episode in the home of Grandmaison and the company offices of the Société Anglo-Normande in Caen itself. In the 1930s, Normandy was a single province. The division into the two regions of Haute- and Basse-Normandie occurred with the administrative reorganization of 1955, but a clear difference between the two areas had been emerging from the beginning of the nineteenth century. Rouen (later to become the capital of Haute-Normandie), on the Seine, halfway between Paris and the sea, saw massive development of its textile industry, and the British traveler Arthur Young described it as "the Manchester of France" (Lewis and Picard, 1996, 51). Le Havre, at the mouth of the Seine, had essentially developed as a major deep-water port and was the main base for transatlantic passenger crossings. Although Rouen lost its predominance in textiles to the Nord-Pas-de-Calais at the beginning of the twentieth century, its status as the deep-water port closest to Paris placed it, along with Le Havre, at the center of the construction of petro-chemical plants and refineries during the expansion of the 1920s. Even as France nationally was sinking into recession, the Seine valley saw the construction of four major refineries by Shell, Esso, Mobil and Total from 1929 to 1935 (94).

In contrast, the period leading up to the Great War saw a deindustrialization of the *départements* of Manche, Orne and Calvados, which would later become Basse-Normandie. In ten years the number of textile workers fell from 20,000 to 5,000 due to lack of investment in new equipment and archaic practices and organization (92–93). The role of Caen, the only major city in these three *départements*, was essentially that of an administrative, commercial and cultural center for the surrounding region. Economic and social power lay with the traditional bourgeois families, such as the Grandmaisons: "A well-established, solid House: the typical provincial concern, handed down from father to son, generation after generation" (*Le Port des brumes/Maigret and the Death of a Harbor-Master*, 155). Unlike the capitalist owners of the rapidly expanding "new" industries (such as automobile manufacture, aeronautical production, petro-chemicals, electrical products and aluminum) which embraced new technologies and production methods and were often based in or around the very largest cities (Paris, Lyon, Toulouse), the bulk of the bourgeoisie in smaller provincial cities, such as Caen, remained resolutely "traditional" (Montero, 2001, 54–55; Braudel and Labrousse, 1979–1980, 649–650). Maigret sees something of this when at the offices of the Sociéte Anglo-Normande he meets the head bookkeeper, who has been with the firm for 42 years and who refers to the Grandmaisons, in the manner of a faithful family retainer, as "Monsieur Charles," "Monsieur Ernest" and "Monsieur Raymond" (*Le Port des brumes/Maigret and the Death of a Harbor-Master*, 156–157). Before becoming Ouistreham's harbormaster, Joris had been 28 years in the service of the company (32).

Through business association, marriage and friendship ("everybody knows everybody," 162) this numerically comparatively small group of haut bourgeois families dominated France's provincial cities and their hinterlands. According to Montero (2001, 61): "The *grande bourgeoisie* was a numerically small group of some two million, but it dominated social and economic life. It underwent little change between the wars ... when the majority of fortunes were ancient or dated back to the second industrial revolution." This seems a very accurate description of the group of Caennais bourgeois which attends the reception at Grandmaison's Ouistreham residence following the death of Joris.

As Maigret begins to orient himself, he discovers that, despite its relatively small population, Ouistreham is not a homogeneous village. Rather: "There were four distinct Ouistrehams: Port Ouistreham, the village of Ouistreham, residential Ouistreham (with a few private houses like the mayor's along the main road), and lastly Ouistreham-on-Sea, at present out of action" (49). The Ouistreham which interests Maigret is the port, which is small but busy as a result of its position at the head of the ship canal linking Caen to the coast and its capacity to take ships of five thousand tons and more (7). Material conditions in this Ouistreham seem fairly typical for small-town France in the period. Joris's house has municipal electricity (11), like 82 percent of French communes in 1932 (Becker and Berstein, 1990, 347; Abbad, 1993), but there is no running water, in common with four-fifths of rural dwellings at the time (Becker and Berstein, 1990, 347). Although there are occasional references to regional particularities in the speech of the protagonists (*Le Port des brumes/Maigret and the Death of a Harbor Master*, 52, 53, 55, 61) and regional drinks and foodstuffs (27, 82), the location in Normandy is not crucial to the development of the story. In short, Ouistreham is a fairly ordinary village, significant mainly for its typicality as a small port.

For Maigret:

> the only part of it that mattered was the harbor: a lock, a lighthouse, Joris's cottage, the *Sailor's Rest*. And what might be called the "rhythm" of the port—two tides every twenty-four hours, which timed the movements of the little group of men concerned with the canal-lock and of the fishermen [48–49].

For Maigret to solve the mystery of the disappearance and subsequent death of Joris, he must first try to understand the social relations within the port of Ouistreham. The development of the storyline in *Le Port des brumes* takes place against the backdrop of the port, and Simenon in the original French is quite explicit that we see the port as a "world," *le petit monde du port* (*Le Port des brumes*, 32) or *cet univers* (20). Even the hotel where Maigret stays is named L'Hôtel de l'Univers (*Le Port des brumes/Maigret and the Death of a Harbor-Master*, 16). But it is a little world fractured by class divisions, as Maigret discovers when in the Buvette de la Marine he inquires about Grand Louis:

> [MAIGRET:] "A tough customer, eh?"
> [DELCOURT:] "If you asked the mayor or any of the local bigwigs they'd say yes.... All I know is that he's never given us any trouble at Ouistreham" [43].

So within *le petit monde du port* there are separate "worlds" defined by the social class of their inhabitants. The *Saint-Michel* is described as "a universe" (128), the world of working people, and in contrast there is the bourgeois *petit monde de Caen* (*Le Port des brumes*, 50). What brings together the two worlds is the economic activity of the port. We are continually reminded of the importance of work in the lives of the characters:

> "Not till the ebb, thanks. I can't get away.... I come on duty here at ten for the morning tide" [*Le Port des brumes/Maigret and the Death of a Harbor-Master*, 16].
>
> "... even while he spoke, he didn't cease watching through the window the progress of the tide, and the steamer, which was now weighing anchor" [27].
>
> "You're stopping me from leaving Ouistreham. I've cargo to take on at La Rochelle, and there's a penalty for every day I'm overdue" [120].

Neither is Grandmaison, for all his wealth and status, a stranger to hard work. In his villa at Ouistreham the walls are decorated with structural plans of cargo ships and photographs of the company's steamers; the furniture is "strictly business-like"; the desk is covered with files, letters and telegrams (73–74). Similarly, in his Caen office the walls are hung with pictures of ships, statistical charts and graphs (155). What the characters have in common is the port; what separates them is their relationship to the means of production. Unlike the drinkers at the Buvette de la Marine, who own nothing but their labor power, "Monsieur Grandmaison had an assured position; he was the typical small-town magnate, member of a well-established upper middle-class family, not to mention the owner of a flourishing shipping concern" (77).

Grandmaison's economic position and lifestyle accord with all of the criteria outlined by Becker and Berstein (1990, 361) and Montero (2001, 61) for membership in the haute bourgeoisie: he is the director of a shipping company consisting of eleven ships (*Le Port des brumes/Maigret and the Death of a Harbor-Master*, 23); he owns two well-appointed homes—a country house in Ouistreham (39) and a palatial townhouse in Caen (153); he has servants (72); he owns an automobile (153); his family takes vacations on the Côte d'Azur (39); his son attends an exclusive private school in Paris (148). It is Grandmaison's economic position that underpins his political power. He is president of the Caen Chamber of Commerce (155) and has been mayor of Ouistreham for ten years (79). When Maigret accompanies Grandmaison to his Caen home:

> at least fifty hats were raised as the car passed by. Everyone seemed to know Monsieur Grandmaison's Renault. And the salutations were obsequious. The shipowner might have been a feudal lord visiting his domain [153].

Although the setting here is urban, the reader is reminded of the deference shown by the peasants to the *grand seigneur* Maurice de Saint-Fiacre when he enters the village inn in *L'Affaire Saint-Fiacre/Maigret Goes Home* (27).

Socially opposed to Grandmaison is Louis—le Grand Louis by nickname, Louis Legrand by patronymic. In a not particularly subtle piece of symbolism, Simenon contrasts Grandmaison, "grand" because of his property ownership, with Grand Louis, "grand" because of his physical presence. Where the physical descriptions of Grandmaison emphasize his elegant clothes, Louis, similarly to Léon Le Glérec in *Le Chien jaune*, is presented in terms of animality: he is described as "bestial" (*Le Port des brumes/Maigret and the Death of a Harbor-Master*, 79); his voice is like a "bearish growl" (79); his hands are described as "paws," *pattes* in the original French (*Le Port des brumes*, 148, 150). Grandmaison possesses wealth and power "handed down from father to son, generation after generation" (*Le Port des brumes/Maigret and the Death of a Harbor-Master*, 155), Louis and Julie come from "fisher-folk.... Her father never did a stroke of work if he could help it.... I expect her mother's still selling fish in the street" (44).

The opposing worlds of the bourgeoisie and the workers can be seen in the contrast between the reception at Grandmaison's home, where liqueurs, brandy, cigars, and petits fours are served (39–41), and Maigret's visit immediately afterwards to the Buvette de la Marine where beer is drunk, pipe tobacco is smoked and there is a game of dominoes (43–44), or when he goes below deck on the *Saint-Michel* to drink eau-de-vie served in dirty glasses surrounded by wet oilskins and boots (119–120).

There seems to be a clear contrast between the different social classes in the port. However, the relationships between social groupings in *Le Port des brumes* are actually more complex than the simple dichotomy between rich and poor or the relationship of individual characters to the means of production. Joris seems to occupy a position somewhere between the bourgeoisie and the popular classes. On the one hand, he is a former employee of the Société Anglo-Normande, yet he does not form part of the group centered on the Buvette de la Marine:

> [Maigret] had spent some hours in Joris's home, the tidy well-appointed home of a man of modest means and quiet tastes. The men here were of a

very different type—rougher, more free-and-easy in their ways. Here, short drinks went down, he guessed, at a high speed; voices rose, the atmosphere grew thick, the talk a trifle bawdy on occasion [29].

Grandmaison estimates Joris's savings at twenty thousand francs (32), which would be a considerable amount in the early 1930s. Although Grandmaison insists on the class difference between employer and employee (32), he nevertheless occasionally invited Joris on duck shoots (45). Moreover, Joris is himself an employer: Julie is his live-in servant, not simply a daily cleaner or cook. His lifestyle and aspirations are those of the petite bourgeoisie, an impression that is reinforced by Julie's account of why Joris had forbidden Louis to visit Julie in his (Joris's) home (115–116). In short, Joris occupies what Braudel and Labrousse (1979–80, 55) describe as the "fluid frontier" between the *"bourgeoisie populaire"* and the *"couches supérieures des classes populaires."*

Julie, despite her very modest origins and her objective class position as a servant, aspires, with her fake crocodile skin handbag (*Le Port des brumes/ Maigret and the Death of a Harbor-Master*, 3), to the petit bourgeois status of a Joris. Amusingly, this arouses resentment in both working-class and bourgeois circles. When Maigret asks about Julie in the Buvette de la Marine, he is told: "She fancies herself. At our local hops, for instance, she won't dance with anybody and everybody, not she! And if they treat her like a servant when she's shopping, she flies off the handle" (29). For Grandmaison, Julie is "a little fool. Joris treated her far too well and she's had her head turned. She ... fancies herself above her station" (43). In fact, Maigret's first impressions of Julie unconsciously, but very accurately, place her between two classes: "There were moments when she looked quite attractive, *chic* almost by Parisian standards; others when, though one couldn't say just why, her peasant origin showed definitely through" [10–11].

Neither does Maigret's own social position fall neatly into the rich bourgeois/*petites gens* dichotomy. His position as a senior police officer and his clothing set him apart from the crew of the *Saint-Michel*: "Maigret ... realized what a queer bird he must seem to them in his overcoat with a velvet collar and the bowler he was grasping firmly" (118–119). He is more easily accepted by the new harbormaster who speaks to him almost as a colleague, as one public servant to another (15). Nevertheless, solidarity between *fonctionnaires* seems to count for less than loyalty to other seamen: "Delcourt merely looked blank. And Maigret realized at that moment that he'd never get at the whole story; the sea-going folk hung together, weren't going to give one another away" [43].

With his open sympathy for Joris and Julie, not to mention his plebeian manners, Maigret is ill-received by the bourgeoisie at the reception at Grandmaison's house: "They made no effort to detain him; it was obvious that they no more desired his presence than he desired to stay" (41). The narrator describes a later visit by Maigret to the house in terms that are as much social as personal:

> There was an undercurrent of hostility on both sides. Due, perhaps, merely to the different social classes for which the two men stood. Maigret hobnobbed with fishermen and lock-keepers at the "local"; while the mayor entertained high officials with cups of tea, liqueurs and fancy cakes [77].

Nevertheless, as a police officer, Maigret tends to follow social convention and respect the status quo. The bourgeois are addressed with respectful suggestions: "May I assume, Monsieur Grandmaison, that you have no intention of leaving Ouistreham?" (108–109); "You, Monsieur Martineau, can take a room at the *Hôtel de l'Univers*" (109). When he speaks to Julie and Louis, his tone is much more direct: "You two, come along with me" (109), and in the original French text he addresses Louis with the familiar *tu* rather than the formal *vous* (*Le Port des brumes*, 150, 155).

At the climax of the story, when Grandmaison commits suicide, Maigret behaves sympathetically to the former's wife, despite their difference in social class: "He was conscious of an unexpected feeling of respect and understanding for this woman whom, the first time he had seen her, he had dismissed as a mere social butterfly" (*Le Port des brumes/Maigret and the Death of a Harbor-Master*, 163). With Grandmaison dead, Maigret is prepared not only to maintain silence on what he has discovered—"Grandmaison was dead. Was one bound to reveal the fact that he was a murderer?" (172)— but also to cover up the fact of his suicide, thereby preserving the respectability of the family name:

> "Monsieur Grandmaison has killed himself." Maigret's tone was heavily official. "It's for you to decide what form of illness led to his sudden death. That's your business. As for the police end—I'll see to it" [164].

At one level, the conclusion to *Le Port des brumes* can be seen as optimistic: Maigret has solved the murder of Joris, and the characters from all social classes, from Grand Louis and Julie to Raymond and Madame Grandmaison, will be able to resume their lives. But, at a broader social level, nothing has really changed: the *petit monde du port*, with its class distinctions, remains the same, and all that has happened is that a small number of individuals have altered their position within the system.

Conclusion to Chapters One and Two

In the seven novels discussed in Chapters 1 and 2, Maigret is obliged to operate across a wide spectrum of the social classes present in interwar

France and to work in a range of geographical settings. As can be seen by setting the texts alongside historical data, the portrayal of the different social milieus has a strong foundation in reality. The cases in which he is involved and the characters he encounters are framed and formed by issues of social class, in particular the conflicts between classes and between different factions of one of those classes, the bourgeoisie. Through Maigret's inquiries, Simenon introduces the reader to a number of social questions: the division between "old" and "new" money in the haute bourgeoisie; the tensions between ambitious and complacent elements within the petite bourgeoisie; the implicit class struggles between bourgeois *notables* and the plebeian popular classes and the petite bourgeoisie and proletariat in the small towns of provincial France; the uncertain future of the landed aristocracy; and the displacement of class contradictions into questions of nationality and "race."

Through Maigret's responses to the situations he encounters, the reader gains an insight into the commissaire's own class position and his attitudes to the capitalist society of France in the 1920s and 1930s. But what of his creator, Simenon? In the next chapter I will consider the extent to which Simenon's own perspective can be established from a close study of the plots and characters he creates, the content and omissions of the texts and the degree to which the narratives' outcomes reflect, either explicitly or implicitly, authorial values.

CHAPTER 3

The Fayard Maigret Novels: Simenon's Perspective

Introduction

We should not confuse the fictional works of an author with his or her own life and views: indeed, one biographer went so far as to title his study of Simenon *The Man Who Wasn't Maigret* (Marnham, 1992). Nevertheless, it is often instructive to explore the relations between the two, particularly when the writer's views are as extensively documented as those of Simenon. Clearly, it would be a mistake to identify Simenon's authorial intentions automatically with the points of view expressed by the stories' principal character, Maigret. Simenon stressed this point in an interview: "He isn't my spokesman. He is simply a character independent of me" (cited in Baronian et al., 2004–2007, "L'Univers de Maigret," 165); although he rather mischievously added: "People have said that I was Maigret. That is both true and false" (165). Moreover, an analysis of the texts suggests a certain similarity between the worldviews of the two.

Monsieur Gallet décédé

It would be too simple to identify the Maigret of *Monsieur Gallet décédé* with his creator. Neither can we assume the author's knowledge of Maigret's (fictional) boyhood spent on the Saint-Fiacre estate: *L'Affaire Saint-Fiacre*, which fleshes out the influence of Maigret's childhood on his social attitudes, was not written until January 1932 and published later the same year, more than a year after the publication of *Monsieur Gallet* and a good eighteen months after its composition.

Although the Maigret stories are written in the third person, the distinction between the narrator's voice and Maigret's perspective is often blurred. For example, in the "ordinary" passage (*Monsieur Gallet décédé/Maigret Stonewalled*, 24) it is the narrator who speaks but Maigret who "sees." As Maigret begins to understand what has happened, he gradually comes to a more sympathetic opinion of Gallet, that is, the "real" Saint-Hilaire. All Gallet wanted, Maigret surmises, was a quiet life: "Peace, of course! That's what he was waiting for!" (136). A peace that, paradoxically, he can only find in his death by suicide. The final judgments on Saint-Hilaire (the "real" Gallet), Madame Gallet, Henry and Eléonore (135) are much harsher, combining a general distaste for the values of petit bourgeois ambition which they represent with a specific dislike of their individual personalities.

Yet was not Simenon himself a highly ambitious man from petit bourgeois origins whose very decision to begin the Maigret series was part of a calculated project to advance in the literary world and so rise socially? If Maigret's perspective reflects that of Simenon, how can this apparent contradiction be reconciled? The answer lies in the means by which the "real" Gallet, the Préjeans, Henry and Eléonore seek to advance their social position. For Gallet, it is deception; for the Préjeans, marriage; for Henry and Eléonore, speculation and blackmail. In contrast, Simenon based his growing wealth and social status on hard work. In 1930, he had an income of 103,385 francs (Assouline, 1997, 111), which according to Abbad's statistics (1993, 16) would have placed him comfortably in the top 20 percent of incomes in the nation. When he came to Paris in December 1922, Simenon's intention had been to make his fortune by his pen. And this was what he did, writing 190 popular novels, under 17 pseudonyms, between 1924 and 1931 (Assouline, 1997, Chapter 5). It is hardly surprising, then, that Simenon held nothing but contempt for those who sought advancement by means other than their own personal merit and hard work and that this might be evident in his fiction.

The latent sympathy for the down-at-heel gentry is harder to understand. Simenon had worked as personal secretary to the marquis de Tracy from 1923 to 1924, simultaneously writing for reviews and magazines, but the position of the Tracys could not be identified in any way with that of the Saint-Hilaires, owning as they did several properties and employing around 25 servants (Assouline, 1997, Chapter 4). More probable is that the young Simenon had been impressed by all things aristocratic and he carried this over into sympathy for that layer of the aristocracy, such as the Saint-Hilaire family, which had lost its wealth and position with the onward march of capitalism.

Le Chien jaune

"We're taking a real plunge into small-town life," says Maigret to Inspector Leroy (*Le Chien jaune*/*The Yellow Dog*, *69*), and *Le Chien jaune* does indeed present a study of a typical provincial town and the relations between and within the various social classes which comprise its population. But what exactly is Simenon's attitude to provincial life and what are the intentions behind this portrait?

Assouline (1997, 167) asserts that "the myth of the 'noble provinces' is recurrent in [Simenon's] work." However, the Concarnois *notables* are presented in a highly unflattering light and the author, like Maigret, conveys his sympathy for the *petites gens* as they are represented by Léon and Emma. Simenon uses brilliantly his description of houses and rooms—the villas of the mayor (21, 87), Michoux (23) and Servières (29), Le Pommeret's apartment (46) and Emma's room (99–100)—to convey a sense of social difference. If Simenon has a notion of "the noble provinces," it is of a pre-capitalist society of aristocrats, craftsmen and peasants, in which there was an unstated and perhaps imaginary social stability unaffected by class conflict and social change. Yet, while Maigret and implicitly Simenon are sympathetic to the "little people," the ordinary inhabitants of Concarneau are presented as brutal when they throw stones at the wounded dog (38–39) and irrational in their panic as the plot develops (30–31). It is only when Maigret, who is, after all, an agent of the state which the *notables* support, and which supports them, enters into open conflict with the local ruling class with his arrest of Michoux (53) that the path is opened to a solution. It seems that Simenon's text demonstrates his lack of confidence that the *petites gens* might be able to resolve the problems they face without the intervention of an outside force.

While Simenon's text recognizes the existence of divisions based on social class and, furthermore, condemns the consequences of this division, it does so from a supra-class position. While Maigret may identify with Emma and Léon—"There was an instinctive rapport between the waitress and the superintendent" (32)—it is a form of humanism that motivates this identification rather than class solidarity. While putting social class at the center of the novel, Simenon simultaneously denies it by implying that class is somehow a "false" distinction and that all people are "equal." This reflects his idea that in one sense class society is something that is "unnatural," which, as he expressed it fifty years later, "the bourgeoisie, the rich, the well-to-dos invented all over the world and which made me angry. Aren't we all just men?" (Simenon, 1981, 11). Simenon's belief is that there is *un homme nu*, a fundamental human being, independent of his or her social class, "the quest for which constituted the alpha and omega of his work" (Assouline, 1997, 167).

This humanism is reflected in the difference between the methods of Leroy and Maigret. While the former bases his approach on "scientific" evidence, the latter relies on his intuitive understanding of "people" (*Le Chien jaune/The Yellow Dog*, Chapter 2). Yet here is Simenon's contradiction: "people" exist as members of social classes and it is their social class which determines their relations to each other; but, while recognizing this inescapable fact, Simenon wants simultaneously to deny it in his belief that we are "all just men."

La Tête d'un homme

In *La Tête d'un homme*, Simenon paints an overwhelmingly negative picture of Parisian life in the late 1920s in which the wealthy cosmopolitan set of Montparnasse is presented as being arrogant, morally decadent and lacking in taste. It is ironic that Simenon himself was a regular customer at La Coupole and similar venues from the mid–1920s onwards (Assouline, 1997, Chapter 5) and that the Maigret series would be launched in a Montparnasse nightclub at an event attended by what in *La Tête d'un homme* is described dismissively as "the somewhat tawdry crowd from Montparnasse" (*La Tête d'un homme/A Battle of Nerves*, 111). The very elements of the Crosbys' lifestyle that Maigret mistrusts — the expensive cocktails, the dinners in prestigious restaurants, the ostentatious limousine, the residency in exclusive hotels and the trips to select seaside resorts — would all become features of Simenon's lifestyle in the mid–1930s:

> It was not simply the author who had evolved but the man as well. He was becoming bourgeois in every sense: plump cheeks, early signs of stoutness, hints of a double-chin; Saville [*sic*] Row suits, custom-made silk shirts, designer ties and fedoras; a large green Delage sports car; a fat line in credit from the Banque Worms on boulevard Haussman; fine wines ordered directly from the great chateaux of Médoc; gourmet meals at the best restaurants...; a regular afternoon table at Fouquet's...; personalised invitations to ... premières of shows; supper at Maxim's; a bottle reserved in his name at Chez Florence.
> Far from making any attempt to disguise his taste for luxury ... he now cultivated it ostentatiously, as though it were incontrovertible proof of his success.... He had two official domiciles ... in Neuilly and Porquerolles.
> He would later claim that he did all this to make Tigy happy, but the truth is that he was leading exactly the kind of life he wanted.... His wife may have appreciated the lifestyle, but she was certainly not responsible for it [Assouline, 1997, 132–133].

How to explain this apparent contradiction? The simplest literary explanation would be that Simenon did not share the views of either Maigret or the narrator of *La Tête d'un homme*: the former being a fictional character, the latter a disembodied "voice" that was not necessarily that of the author. Alternatively, there could be a straightforward biographical explanation: Simenon had changed his views between the composition of the novel in 1930 and his own lifestyle from the mid–1930s onwards. There may be a third, more nuanced, explanation. Simenon's objection was not so much to the lifestyle of the Crosbys but to their character. Crosby had inherited his wealth, whereas Simenon had earned his fortune. This interpretation would enable us to reconcile the author's petit bourgeois origins, the narrative point of view, which broadly identifies with Maigret's perspective, and Simenon's subsequent behavior. His dislike was not for great wealth per se but for particular wealthy people whose wealth he felt was unearned or unmerited.

A similar contradiction appears to exist between *La Tête d'un homme*'s generally negative portrayal of foreigners in interwar Paris and the Belgian Simenon's own status as a foreigner in interwar Paris. It is hard not to conclude, as for the issue of great wealth, that Simenon's objection is not to non–French people in general but to particular national groups. In this, his opinion is in line with many of the preconceptions about foreigners that were common in France during the period. According to Abbad (1993, 42–44) the popular view was that Americans were all millionaires; the English were emotionally cold and overfond of whisky; Belgians were hardworking; Italians were happy but inclined to criminality; Asians were mysterious; North Africans were lazy, untrustworthy and debauched. To this must be added the notion that Jews constituted a "race," rather than a nationality, as they could be of any nationality, and that their "racial characteristics" were those of acquisitiveness, cunning and rootlessness.

It is fascinating to note how closely Simenon's non–French characters in the Maigret novels realize these stereotypes. In *Pietr-le-Letton*, the American, Mortimer, is a powerful but crooked millionaire businessman who installs himself at the Majestic when in Paris. Sir Walter Lampson (*Le Charretier de la Providence*), a former colonel in the British army in India, is rich, authoritarian, emotionally cold and alcoholic. James, the Englishman guilty of murder in *La Guingette à deux sous*, does not show his emotions and is an alcoholic. Even the unnamed English tourist who brushes past the commissaire in a nightclub in *Maigret* is characterized in a single phrase as "very drunk and stiffer than ever" (*Maigret/Maigret Returns*, 161). The Flemish Peeters family of *Chez les Flamands* are hardworking, aspirational and cultivated. The Martini women, mother and daughter, in *Liberty Bar*, French in nationality but presumably Italian in origin, judging by their family name, represent one facet of the Italian stereotype, while Pepito Palestrino, the assassinated nightclub owner in *Maigret* and Pepito Moretto, the contract killer in *Pietr-le-Letton*, embody the contrasting aspect of Italian participation in the criminal milieu. The Algerians of *La Tête d'un homme* are characterized as nameless violent elements (39) and the Algerian whom the commissaire encounters in the Paris streets in *Maigret* is "half-drunk" (106). East Europeans are either illegal immigrants (*La Tête d'un homme*, 40) or criminals—Pietr and Hans Johansson are not actually Latvians at all but "born at Pskov, Russia, of Estonian nationality" (*Pietr-le-Letton/Maigret and the Enigmatic Lett*, 136).

This leaves the presentation of the Jewish characters, whether of French or other nationalities, in the Fayard Maigret series. Anna Gorskine, the mistress of Hans Johansson in *Pietr-le-Letton* is often simply referred to as *la Juive* ("the Jewess") in the original French text, although English translators have not reproduced this; when Maigret searches her room in the Marais *quartier* (a predominantly Jewish area of Paris at the time), he finds:

> Hairs were scattered all over the place—coarse, greasy, black hairs.
> Hundreds of cigarette ends. Biscuits in tins and broken biscuits on the floor. A jar of preserved ginger. A big tin containing the remains of a preserved goose, a Polish brand. A pot of caviar, vodka, whisky. A little pot which proved, when Maigret sniffed it, to contain a remnant of unprocessed opium [*Pietr-le-Letton/Maigret and the Enigmatic Lett*, 103].

In *Le Fou de Bergerac*, the original murderer of women is "a man called Meyer, though known by the name of Samuel.... 'Samuel. Meyer. Sounds Jewish to me,'" remarks Maigret (74–75). The second killer is his son, who has assumed the name Rivaud: "One would hardly take you for a Jew," Maigret taunts him (80). Chapter 7 of this story (particularly pages 77–80) is an almost uninterrupted anti–Semitic diatribe, verbalized by the narrator but focalized through the eyes of Maigret. If Rivaud is a killer, Willy Marco in *Le Charretier de la Providence* is a victim. Nevertheless, he is treated to the same presentation of his "race": "Maigret looked hard at the young man's obviously Jewish features. 'Greek on my father's side ... Hungarian on my mother's...'" (*Le Charretier de la Providence/Maigret Meets a Milord*, 18). The theme is again one of the rootlessness of the Jew, a lack of national sentiment that is reflected in his or her multilingualism: Willy Marco, Anna Gorskine and Jean Radek all speak several languages, but rather than this being seen as a positive factor, it is viewed by Maigret and the narrator as a threat. Jews with less prominent roles in the stories are presented equally stereotypically: the intermediary in the blackmail of Monsieur Gallet, Monsieur Jacob, has "a long beard parted into two points, and above was a hooked nose" (*Monsieur Gallet décédé/Maigret Stonewalled*, 93); the initial victim in *Le Pendu de Saint-Pholien* is a rich and supercilious Jewish youth; in *L'Affaire Saint-Fiacre*, the moneylender to whom Maurice de Saint-Fiacre has recourse is "a certain Monsieur Wolf" (92); and in *La Guingette à deux sous* Maigret goes to the Marais in search of Ulrich, "second-hand dealer in the Rue des Blancs-Manteaux, suspected of usury" (81).

These overtly anti–Semitic characterizations may suggest that Simenon's own opinions were voiced in the texts through the medium of Maigret and the narrator. There can be no question that, as a young reporter for the *Gazette de Liège*, Simenon produced anti–Semitic articles between 1919 and 1922, including pieces on the *Protocols of the Elders of Zion* and *The Jewish Peril* (Assouline, 1997, Chapter 3). Eskin reminds us that these pieces were produced when Simenon was still a teenager and that he "probably both naïvely and calculatingly, adopted ... the paper's ideological line without a murmur" (1987, 37); and he concludes that: "Simenon (a) thoughtlessly wrote some anti–Semitic pieces in his youth; (b) retained unconsciously for some time some anti–Semitic vestiges from his culture; (c) was rid of all such vestiges at some indeterminate point in his maturity" (40). Had he reached this "maturity" by the time of the Fayard Maigret novels? The sheer insistence of the anti–Jewish sentiments expressed by Maigret and the narrator in the Fayard novels suggests that this was not the case, and this view is supported by comments in his journalistic output later in the 1930s, such as the following from the *Courier Royal* in January 1936: "I observed him carefully for he had a funny accent. He may have lived in a building in New York, but something about him seemed familiar. I soon discovered what it was: he had been born in Vilnius. He was a Polish Jew" (cited in Assouline, 1997, 170–171).

The issue here is not to stigmatize either Simenon in general or *La Tête d'un homme* in particular as consciously xenophobic or anti–Semitic; rather it is to recognize that texts are expressions of contemporary cultural perceptions and the society which forms these perceptions. The Fayard Maigret stories are no different in this respect from any other literature, either of the interwar period in France or of any other time or country. As the historian Eric Hobsbawm comments: "Dislike of Jews was indeed pervasive in the Western World," yet "the matter-of-course anti-semitism [*sic*] of Edwardian British intellectuals, such as the Bloomsbury Group [did not make] them into sympathizers of *political* anti–Semites of the radical right" (1995, 120). The casual anti–Semitic comments of Maigret and the narrator in the Fayard Maigret novels and Simenon in his 1930s nonfiction writings should likewise be seen as a symptom of intellectual and moral laziness rather than the deliberate expression of a social or political agenda.

L'Ombre chinoise

The narrative voice in *L'Ombre chinoise* often seems to merge with the voice of Maigret, since it is through his eyes that the action and characters are seen. The tone varies enormously according to which character is being described. The Dormoys and Saint-Marc, with their inherited wealth, are presented unfavorably, while Couchet, who is just as wealthy, is viewed in a favorable light: the approving "You old rascal/that rascal, Couchet!" is used three times by Maigret (*L'Ombre chinoise/Maigret Mystified*, 69, 88), and when he reads the will Maigret is delighted: "This will was the finishing touch that endeared Couchet to him" (86).

It seems incontrovertible that, through Maigret, Simenon is showing some of his own attitudes in his sympathy for Couchet and his young mistress. In contrast, the condescension of Colonel Dormoy and Saint-Marc and the narrow-minded mediocrity of the Martins, especially Madame Martin's obsession with becoming rich through someone else's efforts, were exactly the human characteristics that Simenon hated (Baronian et al. 2004–2007, "L'Univers de Maigret," 25). Simenon was a prolific user of prostitutes during this period of his life (Assouline, 1997) and Nine, although technically a mistress rather than a prostitute, is presented very sympathetically. Indeed, the "tart with a heart" is a recurring figure in the Maigret series, for example, Adèle in *La Danseuse du Gai-Moulin* and Fernande in *Maigret*.

In the autobiographical *Je me souviens* (1945) and *Pedigree* (1948), the latter a novel whose autobiographical elements Simenon freely acknowledged, the author recounts information about his early years which throws an interesting light on a reading of *L'Ombre chinoise*. Simenon presents his mother, Henriette, as a woman with many of the behavioral traits of Madame Martin: a domineering woman, constantly reproaching her husband (Simenon's father, Désiré) for his lack of ambition: "She didn't hold it against M. Mayeur [Désiré's employer] for being rich. Rather, she held it against my father for being incapable of rising further up the social ladder" (*Je me souviens*, 122). Significantly, Simenon gives Couchet some of the features of his own personality: great wealth achieved after years of struggle (*L'Ombre chinoise/Maigret Mystified* 67), a powerful physical desire for women (65, 67–68) and a tendency to spend money freely (20, 67). Yet he insists on his "popular" origins (85), just as he would later present himself as a poor boy made good who remained true to his roots: "I'm a poor boy, I've always been a poor boy, even when I played at being rich" (1975, 284).

The point here is not to interpret *L'Ombre chinoise* as an autobiographical text or a conscious statement of Simenon's attitudes to social class. Both his autobiographical writings and his biographies suggest that Simenon's deep-seated views on life were, often unconsciously, informed by his relationship to his mother, which was exceedingly complex. Fabre (1981, 156) proposes that while Simenon may have rejected his mother's personality he did not necessarily reject all of her attitudes to class, in particular her highly developed sense of ambition. Assouline (1997, Chapter 9) makes much of the contrast between Simenon's lavish spending and obvious pride in his fortune in the mid–1930s and his claim to be close to the salt of the earth. Inevitably, as authors necessarily draw, whether consciously or unconsciously, on the world they live in and their own experiences, so an acquaintance with Simenon's life helps to throw light on the presentation of social class and social change in his novels.

L'Affaire Saint-Fiacre

Simenon (*l'écrivain populaire*) shared with Maigret (*le policier populaire*) a reverence for the landed aristocracy which can be traced, in the writer's case, to his period in the employ of the marquis de Tracy and his residence in the chateau at Paray-le-Frésil (Assouline, 1997, Chapter 4), just as Maigret's attitudes are rooted in his (fictional) boyhood as the son of the steward on the Saint-Fiacre estate. However, both Maigret's feelings and Simenon's perspective are potentially ambiguous. While the commissaire's sympathies lie with the Saint-Fiacres, is this because he is an uncritical supporter of the class they represent or because their material and moral downfall threatens his childhood memories? The new steward has betrayed the values of service for which Maigret's father had stood as a servant of the aristocracy and, by her behavior, the countess has abandoned the standards which he believed her class represented:

> Admittedly he had no illusions about humanity. But he was furious that his childhood memories should have been sullied. The countess above all, whom he had always seen as a noble, beautiful person like a picture-book heroine.... And now she turned out to be a crazy old woman who kept a succession of gigolos [31].

The case solved, and "justice" summarily dispensed by Maurice, Maigret "felt the need to shake hands once more with Saint-Fiacre" (134). Why does he feel this need? Perhaps it is because Saint-Fiacre has solved a case that has proved beyond his abilities as a professional detective. Maybe he feels that the memory of the countess, and therefore his own childhood, has been redeemed. It could be that he believes that a "reformed" Maurice will restore the fortunes of the Saint-Fiacres.

> Was the inspector mistaken? It seemed to him that Maurice de Saint-Fiacre's lips were touched by the ghost of a smile. Not the smile of the sceptical Parisian, the penniless prodigal.... A serene, confident smile [139].

This interpretation is supported by Vanoncini (1990):

> Undoubtedly, the punishment takes on a ritualistic nature as a manner of restoring the momentarily wavering mythical and ideological values particular to Saint-Fiacre. In fact, the count re-establishes his authority by sealing an alliance between the throne and the altar—it is the priest who saves him from immediate bankruptcy—and by suppressing the power achieved by the social classes between the peasantry and the nobility. Not only does he physically thrash the usurper Gautier, but he makes clear his contempt for Métayer and his lawyer before dismissing them from his sight. Moreover, he reduces the police to the role of an awkward spectator [97–98].

It is never explicitly stated in the text whether Maigret believes that the decline of the house of Saint-Fiacre, and what it represents, is temporary or terminal. There is no definitive indication whether the character or the author sees the problems of the Saint-Fiacres as personal, caused by the death of the old count, the moral weakness of the countess and Maurice's tardiness in assuming his responsibilities to his family name and his class; or if the problem is structural, the working out in a single family and a single village of the historical forces of economic and social change. Maigret has lost his faith in the countess, but it is difficult to say whether he believes the "old values" can be reestablished, although his nostalgia for the past seems to suggest that this would be his wish.

In many ways, *L'Affaire Saint-Fiacre* sums up Simenon's complex and sometimes contradictory attitudes to social class. For Simenon and so for Maigret social class is a given, an inescapable and necessary feature of society. The division of society into social classes is often a negative factor, protecting the wealthy and excluding the *petites gens*, and, at a deeper philosophical level, dividing humanity along arbitrary and often unjust lines. This idea underpins Simenon's biological humanism, his search for *l'homme nu*, the essential human being, which underlies Maigret's role as a figure standing, somehow, outside the existing social classes of French society whose function is one of reconciliation of those divided by class barriers. According to Dubois (1992, 188):

> Simenon opposes the man imprisoned by class society and its barriers to the man who rises above them. The latter does not ignore social divisions but is able to stand aside from them, to understand them in a manner that is more anthropological then sociological. In doing this, he makes himself a Man, that is "l'homme nu," who is able to grasp the essence of the human condition.

At the same time, *L'Affaire Saint-Fiacre* reveals the reverse side of Simenon's notion of social class. If social class is seen as a given, then, logically, the existing social class structure should represent some kind of rational "natural order," corresponding to the existing development of social relations However, the global social order after which Simenon and his creation Maigret seem to hanker is not that of then-contemporary France (in which the *aristocratie nobiliaire* was in decline) but rather that of the pre-war and even pre-revolutionary period; in short, the political perspective of the marquis de Tracy: Catholic, quasi-feudal and implicitly anti–Semitic. Behind this perspective stands an ideological nostalgia for a past society in which the existence of social classes was recognized but class struggle was avoided by the willing acceptance of social hierarchy and a recognition that each group had its part to play within an organic social whole.

Chez les Flamands

Chez les Flamands addresses a number of themes which are central to Simenon's own personal background, most particularly the relationship between the petite bourgeoisie and the proletariat and the issue of nationality and "race." The author's own family background was similar in many ways to that of the Peeterses. His father was the son of a hatmaker, in other words a petit bourgeois artisan, who became an accountant with an insurance company, and hence a member of the nouvelle petite bourgeoisie. His mother was the daughter of a timber merchant, a member of the commercial petite bourgeoisie, and she herself worked as a salesperson in a department store before her marriage, during which she let out rooms to foreign students. In this latter capacity, although she may not have been an independent property owner, she used her control of a property, namely her own home, as a source of income (Marnham, 1992, 14–21, 34–35). When Simenon writes of *les petites gens*, which he frequently does in his nonfiction and autobiographical writings, he is generally referring to people of his own parents' background, not the proletariat. As Dubois (1980, 26) comments:

> It is well known that Simenon claims an interest in and sympathy for the "little people." All the evidence suggests that he understands by this expression not the proletariat, who are largely absent from his fictional universe, but a certain fraction of the middle classes.

Simenon's various memoirs describe vividly the ideological atmosphere of his childhood and the attitudes of his family to the industrial working class:

> A general strike, that must be worse still, a sort of awful spilling over, an invasion by tens of thousands of people whom one doesn't know, and whom

one wouldn't want to know, people from the mines, the copper and zinc foundries, whose children don't go to school, all these dirty uneducated people, who swear and drink genièvre, suddenly appearing from the darkness where they belong, hatred in their eyes and insults on their lips [*Je me souviens*, 1945, cited in Dubois, 1980, 23].

In *Chez les Flamands* both the petite bourgeoisie (the Peeterses) and the proletariat (the Piedboeufs) are present and it is hard not to see in the novel a certain realization of the sentiments by which Simenon had been surrounded as a child and youth in Liège. Of course, it cannot be assumed automatically that Maigret's attitudes are always and completely identifiable with those of Simenon, but it seems unlikely that the commissaire, who had been presented as a sympathetic character in the previous 13 novels, would suddenly be viewed in an unfavorable light. Significantly, in the coda to the novel, Maigret has no feelings of guilt or doubt over the decision he has made to let Anna literally "get away with murder." There is no implication that the author wishes the reader to question the conduct of the commissaire, so it seems probable that Simenon wants the reader to accept Maigret's silence as the best possible course of (in)action in a generally tragic situation.

Many of the prejudices expressed in *Chez les Flamands* against the Flemish inhabitants of Belgium were quite common among French-speaking Belgians at the time. In the early years of the twentieth century, the Flemish areas of Belgium were generally more backward than Walloon Liège, with its then "modern" industries of coal, steel and heavy engineering. Simenon's own family was mixed, a Walloon father and a Flemish mother, and the paternal Simenons were suspicious of the maternal Brülls (Marnham, 1992, 3). For many French people, Belgians were hardworking, like the Peeterses, but not necessarily to be trusted (Abbad, 1993, 44). Simenon seems to have a much more nuanced view: for the author what seems to ultimately define the Peeters family is not their language or culture but their class and their personal qualities. In a curious way, Simenon, through the narrative, seems to be arguing a message of tolerance of national differences, although this is inevitably brought into question by the insistent use of the word "race," with no justification for the idea that Flemish speakers form or formed a distinct "racial" rather than linguistic or cultural grouping within Belgium.

Le Port des brumes

References to social class are omnipresent in *Le Port des brumes*. Sometimes the references are explicit, as in the narrator's comments on the differences between Grandmaison and Maigret (*Le Port des brumes/Maigret and the Death of a Harbor-Master*, 77). At other times, Simenon uses descriptions of the various locations to situate characters within a specific social milieu: Joris's house (11, 22–23), Grandmaison's Ouistreham villa (39, 72–73) and his Caen house and offices (154–155), below decks on the *Saint-Michel* (54), La Buvette de la Marine (26–29). The characters' clothes and accessories reveal their social origins and ambitions: Joris's habitual uniform (7), Julie's blue suit and fake crocodile skin handbag (3, 44), Grandmaison's hunting costume (31), Madame Grandmaison's silk dress (39), Raymond's gold fountain pen (61). Often, the characters are referred to simply by their occupation or social position: "the Captain" (Joris), "the harbor master" (Delcourt), "the servant" (Julie), "the mayor" (Grandmaison), "the jailbird" (Louis).

However, although relations between the characters are generally determined by social class, Maigret's perspective seeks to transcend the restrictions of class. At the end of the story, Maigret sees Madame Grandmaison as a figure to be pitied, a prisoner of her class origins, whose explanation of the background to the case was "the summing up of a frustrated life" (161). Unable to marry Raymond because he led a dissipated life by small town standards and because he had no money, she is obliged to marry Ernest and effectively becomes part of the Grandmaison family property, "just part of his establishment" (162). Although by her birth, upbringing, marriage, lifestyle and behavior, Madame Grandmaison is inseparable from her social class, the haute-bourgeoisie of Caen, for which Maigret has little liking, he nevertheless feels deep sympathy for the individual woman:

> Maigret bowed himself out, tramped heavily down the stairs, trudged through the office, his shoulders sagging, a feeling of oppression on his chest. Once in the street, he breathed more freely.... A last look at the windows. Another at those of the house opposite, the scene of Madame Grandmaison's girlhood. The Inspector sighed [164].

By contrast, in what for them is a happy ending, Louis and Julie effectively succeed in changing their social class. With the *Saint-Michel* already transferred into his name by Raymond, Louis becomes a boat owner himself. Julie inherits Joris's estate, which, with the 300,000 francs deposited in the bank account by Raymond, makes her an extremely wealthy woman at a time when 75 percent of French people had an annual income of less than 50,000 francs (Abbad, 1993, 16).

The moral of *Le Port des brumes* appears to be that individual human qualities are more important than social class. Simenon seems to be arguing that while the division of society into social classes is an inevitable feature of modern life, the rigidity of class distinction and the forms of exclusion to which it leads can become a barrier to human happiness and elementary justice. Maigret's importance arises from the fact that as a result of his background ("popular," but not proletarian or peasant) and his values, he is able to stand aside from social class differences and work towards the resolution of problematic situations from a "humanistic" perspective. Whereas "Monsieur Grandmaison had an assured position; he was the typical small-town magnate," "Maigret was just a man" (*Le Port des brumes/Maigret and the Death of a Harbor-Master*, 77).

Dubois argues convincingly that Maigret's and Simenon's projects are one and the same:

> He [Simenon] recognizes his own petit bourgeois origins which he shares with his hero the commissaire. Through the latter, the petite bourgeoisie is assigned the semi-historical semi-utopian role of class conciliation or, better still, arbitration. The middle class is presented as the mediator of class conflicts: it promotes interaction and compromise but, knowing that in the final analysis there will be no significant changes, it favors above all class collaboration in place of exclusion and pretension (Maigret cannot abide condescension) [1992, 187–188].

For Simenon, the external intervention of a Maigret is required because the political institutions of civil society are fatally compromised by their relationship to the divisions of social class. Formal political democracy of the kind that existed in the Third Republic is seen as an obstacle to Simenon's particular brand of humanism. Hence the unflattering portrait of Grandmaison in his role as mayor of Ouistreham, which recalls the character of the mayor of Concarneau in *Le Chien jaune*. Grandmaison "pays tribute to democracy by shaking hands with all and sundry ... and, on occasion, patting their children on the head" (*Le Port des brumes/Maigret and the Death of a Harbor-Master*, 42); but, as the narrator explains: "True, he affected a democratic manner.... But his geniality was patronizing; put on to curry favor with the voters" (77).

The often superficial, opportunistic electoral democracy of the Third Republic is shown as a hypocritical and hollow façade in *Le Port des brumes*. Although he has no discernible popular mandate, Maigret is portrayed as the representative of a genuine, humanistic social order. While we cannot automatically identify all of the views expressed by Maigret, or the narrator, with Simenon's opinions, it would seem naïve not to recognize the parallels that can clearly be established. As Georges Sim, he had written in 1928, "There are crooks in politics and the worst they risk is to be named ministers" (Sim, 1928, cited in Lemoine, 1991, 156). In 1935 he briefly produced a regular column for the *Courrier royal*, produced by the de La Rocque brothers, defectors from the extreme right-wing *Action Française* (Assouline, 1997, 170–171), and in 1938, referring to the Third Republic, he told a journalist: "I love ordinary people, real ones, and am therefore horrified by democracy" (interview with Simenon by Doringe, *Toute l'Edition*, February 8, 1938, cited in Assouline, 172).

It is often argued (for example, in Eskin, 1987, Chapter 5) that the articles Simenon wrote for the *Gazette de Liège* from 1919 to 1922—"a reactionary, anti–Semitic, proto-fascistic paper" (Eskin, 1987, 37)—were the work of a naïve young man, desperate to be published. The same cannot be said of the mature Simenon's output in the 1930s when he was an established and successful writer. Assouline (1997, 167) characterizes Simenon's politics as "populist and conservative rather than reactionary" and argues, "His political sentiments (feelings more than ideas) were remarkably consistent—from his journalism of the twenties to his novels to the memoirs he wrote or dictated in the autumn of his life" (167).

Simenon was far from alone in his negative feelings about the institutions of the Third Republic. Becker and Berstein, describing a widespread public sentiment at the end of the decade, argue that:

> The disillusionment was complete. The Bloc National ... had failed to meet the expectations of the French people. The Cartel des Gauches came to an end with a spectacular fiasco which brought into question the capacity of the radicals to lead the nation. If Poincaré managed to return the country to stability, it was in a diminished form, a pale reflection ... of the pre-war golden age [1990, 392].

Shortly after the writing of *Le Port des brumes*, Simenon was to increase the time he spent reporting on politics, including a visit to Germany to write articles for *Voilà* magazine and a meeting with Trotsky in Prinkipo (Assouline, 1997, Chapter 8; Eskin, 1987, Chapter IX). The journalistic formulations are often ambiguous, as, for example, in the article of April 22, 1933, immediately following the Nazi accession to power:

> And there you have it! There are tens of millions of Germans who believe that it is all over, that they are back on their feet, that at last they have a goal in life. And it is Hitler's doing! The country was seething with disorder, people got by as best they could, each in his own way, without any real conviction, which ended up by creating a general lassitude. Hitler has put them back into step. He will polish them up, as good as new, from top to bottom.... No longer any need for individual worries.... All you have to do is march to the music shouting "Hoch! Hoch! Hoch!" to sense the frisson. And to feel once again the pride and joy of being born a citizen of Greater Germany [cited in Baronian et al., 2003–2007, "Le roman de Georges Simenon," 40].

Simenon's language is heavily ironic and his own political perspective is difficult to discern. Assouline (1997, 119) argues that in the tone of his reports on Germany: "Simenon sought to play down the horror of the situation, sometimes through irony. The more alarmist the news published by the Paris press became ... the more Simenon wrote about Germans bored with bloody exactions and lethal clashes between rival extremists." Soon after Simenon's return to France, the Stavisky affair erupted in December 1933 and the Daladier cabinet was forced to resign after the February 6, 1934, riots which left 15 dead and 2,000 injured.

For Simenon, events seemed to be confirming the political perspective underlying *Le Port des brumes*. In a system of morality which prioritized "human" values, "democratic" electoral politics of the kind practiced in the Third Republic had no place. As Assouline puts it (1997, 167–8):

> Politicians aroused his ire. The time he had spent with them during his days as a reporter left indelible images in his memory. One in particular often came to mind: the Café de Paris, across from the Opéra. Baron Edmond, patriarch of the Rothschilds, would mount his private stairway to the mezzanine, where he would receive visitors as though he owned the place, while ... Georges Mandel, minister of the interior, a post that put him in charge of "the garbage can of the republic" ... held court on the floor below, wielding the occult power of his portfolio to subjugate the citizenry [Simenon, 1978, 86–87].

As far as he [Simenon] was concerned, the people who exercised the arrogant profession of politician were swindlers and liars naturally inclined to despise others.

Conclusion

Judged by the formal criteria of plot and structure of many of the crime writers of the period, particularly those in the British and American "Golden Age," such as Christie and Van Dine, *Monsieur Gallet décédé* has numerous weaknesses. There are no clues available to the reader allowing him/her to solve the mystery by ratiocination and to deduce "whodunit" in competition with the detective. Furthermore, the plot, hinging on the exchange of identities, in the tradition of Gaboriau, is farfetched and Gallet's method of suicide is highly implausible at a practical level. However, these criticisms miss the point. There is no evidence that Simenon was trying to produce a novel either in the "Golden Age" tradition or a realistic "police procedural." Rather, the social themes of the story and the picture of the society that is portrayed represent the beginning of a new kind of crime story. The plot is driven and the characters formed by social forces which the contemporary reader can recognize. The puzzle, which was all in the Anglo-Saxon "Golden Age," is relegated to the background and replaced by a detailed and vivid view of social classes and social change as the motor force of human behavior. As Assouline puts it:

> Maigret is no intellectual: he is not wont to ponder. Intuitive and instinctive, he is intelligent but not cunning. He soaks up atmosphere like a sponge, penetrating a milieu so as to grasp its rules.... In the investigation, as in the writing that engenders it, atmosphere, milieu and characters are more important than plot, clue and suspense [1997, 93].

Even with its weaknesses, *Monsieur Gallet décédé* stands as the first step in the direction of a new form of crime writing that would be developed in the ensuing Maigret novels and subsequent detective fiction in both francophone and anglophone contexts.

Le Chien jaune is in many ways a fundamentally contradictory, or at least ambiguous, text. Despite some improbabilities in the plot, such as Léon being allowed to keep a dog in Sing Sing, the story is told with convincingly realistic description, believable characters and a strong sense of place and time. Social inequality and provincial backwardness are powerfully denounced and Simenon shows a deep sympathy for the oppressed in bourgeois society. But the oppressed are unable to resolve their oppression. This can only be achieved through the intervention of the bourgeois state, in the person of Maigret. Yet it is the same bourgeois state which the mayor of Concarneau and the criminal *notables* represent at a local level. At the end of the novel, justice is done: Léon and Emma are happy and Michoux is facing twenty years forced labor on Devil's Island. But is the author implying that capitalist society is ultimately and fundamentally just? Probably not, for without the intervention of Maigret it is almost certain that justice would not have been done, and the story could have ended very differently. Maigret's existence as simultaneously part of, yet somehow external to, class society realizes Simenon's own sharp description yet imprecise understanding of the society in which he lived.

Many of the features of the other Fayard Maigret novels are present in *La Tête d'un homme*: the conflicts between different social classes and fractions of classes, the contrasts between strong and weak characters, the origins of crime in the prevailing social conditions, and the essential role of the petit bourgeois commissaire in acting as a mediator between contending classes. However, *La Tête d'un homme* is unique in that it is the only case out of the nineteen Fayard Maigret stories where the criminal is caught, judged and executed. In two stories the guilty party is condemned to a prison sentence (*Le Chien jaune, La Nuit du carrefour*); two killers are imprisoned awaiting trial (*La Guingette à deux sous, L'Ecluse numéro 1*); two criminals go mad (*L'Ombre chinoise* and *La Danseuse du Gai Moulin*); four murderers commit suicide (*Pietr-le-Letton, Le Charretier de la Providence, Un Crime en Hollande, Le Fou de Bergerac*); and six cases are officially unsolved. In two cases (*Monsieur Gallet décédé* and *L'Affaire Saint-Fiacre*) there is no crime in the strict legal sense. *La Tête d'un homme* is also unique in that, alone among the Maigret stories taking place in France, a majority of the characters are foreigners, providing an insight into a very particular feature of social change and social class in interwar France, that is, the nature of immigration and its impact on society.

L'Ombre chinoise falls just over halfway through the Fayard series of Maigret novels and looks both back, in its reworking of themes from earlier stories, and forward, in its anticipation of the stories to follow. Certain character types in *L'Ombre chinoise* recur throughout the series: the self-made man (Ducrau in *L'Ecluse numéro 1*), the mediocre petit bourgeois (Michonnet in *La Nuit du carrefour* and Feinstein in *La Guinguette à deux sous*), the bullying and manipulative wife/mother figure (Madame Michoux in *Le Chien jaune*), the "bad girl" who is really a "good girl" (Fernande in *Maigret* and Adèle in *La Danseuse du Gai Moulin*), the condescending, "traditional" haut bourgeois (the mayor in *Le Chien Jaune* and Ernest Grandmaison in *Le Port des brumes*).

The overarching social framework of *L'Ombre chinoise* is also a familiar one in the series. The division of humanity into distinct social classes is an evil, insofar as it leads to inequality and exclusion. Nevertheless, for an individual to cross, or indeed attempt to cross, class boundaries, brings dangers of its own. As Dubois (1992, 186) puts it:

> "Crossing the line" is seen as the transgression which triggers off each crisis.... In this way, social mobility is often to blame. An individual rises in society (*Le Port des brumes*) or conversely suffers a social fall (*Le Charettier de la Providence*) when his past reappears to confront him once again. The reappearance of his social class origins, often by accident, is generally at the root of the drama.

Couchet has crossed the line separating the petite bourgeoisie from the haute bourgeoisie, but his past returns when his ex-wife moves into the building where he has his business. In *L'Ecluse numéro 1*, Emile Ducrau has become a wealthy entrepreneur, having started life as a humble barge worker, but his past, in the form of the daughter of his former comrade Gassin, who is actually Ducrau's natural daughter, triggers a chain of events leading to his committing murder. The *charretier* of *Le Charretier de la Providence*, Jean Darchambaux, had formerly been a doctor, but has become déclassé following a long prison sentence: it is his chance encounter with his ex-wife, now remarried to a wealthy Englishman and traveling the canals on a pleasure craft, that causes him to kill twice. The Compagnons de l'Apocalypse in *Le Pendu de Saint-Pholien* undergo a voluntary *déclassement* by their rejection of bourgeois society and its social order, which results in a murder and two suicides.

At a formal level of realism, *L'Affaire Saint-Fiacre* shares many of the weaknesses of the other novels. In particular, it is never explained why Emile Gautier would have sent his "A crime will be committed" note to the Moulins police, which by the most extraordinary coincidence comes to Maigret's attention at the Quai des Orfèvres (*L'Affaire Saint-Fiacre/Maigret Goes Home*, 6). Nevertheless, in terms of its portrait of French rural society between the wars, the story is a relatively accurate social document. Character and plot are formed and driven by the social environment, and social class and social change act as a trigger for the "crime" and its resolution. There is a certain ambiguity in Simenon's perspective on these questions and this is reflected in Maigret, the detective "hero" of the story who signally fails to detect. Another step had been taken in Simenon's development of the silhouette of the commissaire into a fully fleshed out, realistic character.

In *Un Banc au soleil*, published much later, in 1977, Simenon stated "I have never been preoccupied by social class." *Chez les Flamands* suggests quite the opposite: the whole narrative is underpinned and driven by social class, class consciousness and class conflict. The Peeters and Piedboeuf families are explicitly identified by their social class, and Simenon uses repeated contrasts between their occupations, their homes and their ways of life to emphasize their class difference. Although Anna tells Maigret that she has killed Germaine to save her brother's happiness, there is also a strong element of class consciousness in her act. If Joseph is able to marry Marguerite Van de Weert, the class position of the Peeters family will be maintained and it may even provide a means of advance into a higher stratum of the bourgeoisie. Monsieur Piedboeuf is aware that Joseph would not marry Germaine because of their difference in social class, while Gérard and the rest of the working-class francophone community resent Maigret's appearance in the town as a representative of a police force which defends the rich against the poor. If the conflict between the proletarian Piedboeufs and petit bourgeois Peeterses is resolved in favor of the latter, it is as a result of Maigret's intervention, the practical outcome of which is to conceal the planned violent killing of a daughter of the working class by a daughter of the petite bourgeoisie. For all of his "sympathetic" personal qualities and independently of, and almost certainly contrary to, the author's expectations, the class position of Maigret is revealed. The *policier populaire* is, in fact, the *policier petit bourgeois*.

Le Port des brumes is a highly significant text in the first series of Maigret novels. Eskin's evaluation that the "the plot that Simenon contrives is highly uneven [but] *Le Port des brumes* is ... successful ... in building up a small town maritime atmosphere" is undoubtedly correct. However, the importance of the text goes beyond "atmosphere": through a combination of largely accurate reporting of social conditions in the period and a highly effective literary technique, we are given a profound insight into, on the one hand, the deepening crisis of French society in the 1930s and, on the other hand, the development of Simenon's social and political thinking in interaction with the unfolding situation.

What gives the Fayard Maigret novels their interest and scope is that from one story to the next Simenon introduces a variety of social strata and geographical settings in which the question of social class and social change can be studied. The increased possibilities for social mobility in 1920s France, as a result of conjunctural factors, such as the postwar boom, and deeper underlying changes in the structure of capitalism, from the classical nineteenth-century model to the stage of monopoly capitalism, provide a marvelous framework for this project.

The settings of the Fayard Maigret novels follow closely periods from Simenon's own life. In some cases they hark back to earlier episodes, such as his period in Paray-le-Frésil from 1923 to 1924 or his subsequent residence in the place des Vosges. In other cases Simenon had briefly stayed in the location of a Maigret novel in the period immediately before composition. For example, he spent the winter of 1930-1931 in Concarneau, the setting of *Le Chien jaune*, written in March 1931 in La Michaudière; in August 1931 he was in Ouistreham, scene of *Le Port des brumes*, completed in Antibes in February 1932. Indeed, the only Fayard Maigret novel which cannot be linked with Simenon's own travels in France is *Le Fou de Bergerac*, in which Maigret is confined to his bed and is forced to construct his idea of the town from his wife's observations, guidebooks and postcards. The sense of on-the-spot reportage that results from the rooting of the narratives in the author's own personal experience contributes significantly to the highly realistic descriptions that form the backdrop to the stories discussed here. This is a France that is geographically and socially familiar to Simenon's public, which goes some way towards explaining the novels' outstanding sales. In Dulout's words (1997, 32): "He excels in his settings of daily life and in his art of depicting the everyday behavior of ordinary people."

A second reason for the popularity of the novels can be found in the character and underlying philosophy of Maigret himself. In comparison with Britain and the United States, France remained a society in which the petite bourgeoisie was still numerically and economically highly significant. Although there is no statistical data on the readership of the Maigret novels, it seems likely, given their greater length and significantly higher price than Simenon's 1920s output, that many readers came from the petite bourgeoisie rather than the workers, concierges and typists who were the targeted readership of the pulps (Baronian et al., 2004–2007, "Le Roman de Georges Simenon," 19–26). The continuing numerical mass and hence social influence in France of small business people and artisans provided a large readership which recognized and identified with Maigret's petit bourgeois perspective.

By his origins Maigret is "popular" but not proletarian. His clothes are those of a bourgeois (derby and velvet-collared overcoat), but, as Wenger ("Dans la garde-robe de Maigret: de l'élégance d'une charpente plébéienne") points out, the manner in which he wears them conveys his humble background: "His rather ordinary clothes emphasised his rather plebeian build" (*Le Pendu de Saint-Pholien/Maigret and the Hundred Gibbets*, 76). His tastes in food and drink are equally plebeian: sandwiches in *Monsieur Gallet*, *rognons à la Liégoise* in *La Danseuse du Gai Moulin*, sauerkraut in *La Guingette à deux sous*, beer rather than fine wines and coarse pipe tobacco rather than cigars throughout the series. His identification with the *petites gens* makes him a sympathetic character, yet he does not challenge the existing social order in any systematic way. In the character of Maigret, middle-class readers could recognize a (perhaps idealized) vision of themselves:

> Maigret is indeed an average Frenchman.... His lifestyle, his habits and his pleasures are remarkably consistent with his character, influenced simultaneously by his plebeian origins and his social position as a middle-class civil servant. Maigret appears, therefore, to be an ordinary man and not a mythical hero ... attractive to readers who can in a certain way identify themselves if not directly with him, then with a certain way of life, that of the middle classes [Alavoine, 1999, 32].

The commissaire's methods of work suggest a petit bourgeois humanist conception of professional activity rather than representing accurately how a highly placed *fonctionnaire* in the Police Judiciaire would really work. The humanism can be found in his identification with the oppressed in *Le Chien jaune* and *Le Port des brumes* and his willingness to suppress the truth about Grandmaison's role in the murder of Joris, out of sympathy for his wife, and Anna's murder of Germaine Piedboeuf in *Chez les Flamands*, out of a personal sense of right and wrong. Boileau and Narcejac (1964, 142) propose, "Deep down, Maigret is only attached to the Police Judiciaire as if by accident. He is a doctor, a lawyer, a confessor more than he is a police officer." In other words, his professional approach is that of the liberal professions or the church rather than the state bureaucracy. Fabre (1981, 222–225) compares the degree of independence Maigret exercises as akin to that of a self-employed businessman: sometimes, for instance in *Chez les Flamands* or *Maigret*, he initiates an unofficial inquiry in response to a personal request; on other occasions, such as in *Le Fou de Begerac* or *Le Pendu de Saint-Pholien*, he springs into unofficial action almost on impulse and acting entirely on his own initiative; and his relationship with specialists such as the pathologist Moers in *Monsieur Gallet décédé* resembles that between a small business and a specialist subcontractor.

This notion of Maigret as a small-scale employer is reinforced by the language of communication between the commissaire and his collaborators. Colleagues of a lower rank always address Maigret with the formal *vous*, which would be normal in contemporary standard French when speaking to a superior within a hierarchical organization, and brigadier Lucas habitually refers to him as *patron* ("boss") in *Le Port des brumes*. After *Le Charretier de la Providence*, the first inquiry in which Maigret and Lucas work together, Maigret increasingly addresses his subordinate with the familiar *tu*. Moers is addressed as *vous* when he first works with Maigret (*Monsieur Gallet, décédé*) but thereafter *tu* is often employed. At the same time as recognizing the hierarchical dimension of his working relationships, Maigret frequently demonstrates his humanistic side by the use of affectionate terms when speaking to lower-ranking colleagues: he calls Lucas *vieux* ("old chap") in *La Tête d'un homme* (138), while Moers is *mon petit* (*La Tête d'un homme*, 156) and Leroy is addressed as *vieux* (*Le Chien jaune*, 142).

With his combination of humanism and social conservatism Maigret speaks to the concerns of the petite bourgeoisie who were confused and disoriented by the rapid social changes taking place in the France of the 1920s. The decade had proved a turbulent one for French society as a whole as it lived through the aftermath of the Great War and the Russian Revolution, postwar reconstruction, a period of sustained economic expansion and the acceleration of the transformation from "classical" capitalism to its more "modern" monopoly form. For the petite bourgeoisie the strains were particularly pronounced. For this class, increasingly marginalized in economic life by the growing dominance of big capital and politically threatened by the emergence of a better organized and more politicized working class, the decade, despite the general economic prosperity, was one of social change and uncertainty.

Of the 19 Maigret novels published by Fayard between 1931 and 1934, the first to be written was *Pietr-le-Letton* in late 1929 or very early 1930, and a further 16 had been completed by the early months of 1932 (Marnham, 1992, 146–147). Baronian et al. (2004–2007, "Le Film dans le texte," 39) suggest that "Maigret's creator usually wrote his novels with a 'time delay,' setting the stories in places he had visited in the preceding months or years," and the author himself commented, "As I am completely lacking in imagination, I have to spend a lot of time in the settings and with the characters of my novels" (Letter dated December 2, 1931, cited in Baronian et al., 39). These comments help the reader of the first 17 Fayard novels to historically locate the narratives as belonging to the period between the late 1920s and the fall of 1931. It was not until the early months of 1931 that the French public began to become aware that the international capitalist recession signaled by the Wall Street crash of 1929 was beginning to have a major impact on the French economy (Dard, 1999, 21; Braudel and Labrousse, 1979–1980, 655), so it is unsurprising, given the time lapse for literary gestation and composition, that the developing economic crisis only begins to appear as a point of reference in the Maigret novels composed in January and February 1932 (for example *Chez les Flamands/Maigret and the Flemish Shop*, 72, and *Le Port des brumes/Maigret and the Death of a Harbor-Master*, 40). By the end of 1932, however, the recession was at full force and was affecting to one degree or another all of the classes of French society (Dard, 1999, 22). In the next chapter I will consider the extent to which the impact of the economic crisis, with its attendant social and political consequences, is realized in Simenon's Maigret writings of the mid– and late 1930s.

CHAPTER 4

Short Stories and Journalism: Maigret, Simenon and the Crises of the 1930s

From the Fayard Novels to Les Nouvelles Enquêtes

The final Maigret novel published by Fayard, entitled simply *Maigret*, which had the commissaire emerging from retirement to solve a case in an unofficial capacity, was completed in January 1934 and published in the spring of that year. There would be no further book-length publications of Maigret inquiries until *Maigret revient*, containing three novellas published in 1942 by Gallimard, with which Simenon had signed a contract after the publication of *Maigret*, followed by three more novellas, collected in *Signé Picpus*, and a collection of short stories, *Les Nouvelles Enquêtes de Maigret*, in 1944. After the war, Simenon would find a new publisher, Presses de la Cité.

It is tempting to divide the Maigret corpus into three clear periods: between the wars—Fayard; during the war—Gallimard; postwar—Presses de la Cité. However, this relies on the dates of book publications. The chronology of production of the materials is different. The stories in *Maigret revient* had been written shortly after the outbreak of war, in the winter of 1939-1940, whereas the inquiries which make up *Les Nouvelles Enquêtes* had been written and published in magazine format, in *Paris-Soir Dimanche* and *Police-Roman/Police-Film*, between October 1936 and December 1938. Thus, the gap between the Fayard series and the next group of Maigret texts is two and a half years rather than the eight or ten years often assigned to his absence and *Les Nouvelles Enquêtes* belong to Simenon's interwar Maigret writings.

Eskin (1987, 137) argues: "These stories of the 1930s do not constitute a substantive re-entry of Maigret, however. [They] are very light pieces of little import either to the Maigret saga or to Simenon's literary career, written probably for easy money." In what follows, I will not enter into an evaluative discussion of the "lightness" or otherwise of the stories in *Les Nouvelles Enquêtes*, their importance within the "saga" as a whole or Simenon's motivation for writing them. Rather, my focus will be on the perception and portrayal of social class and social change to be found in the stories. I have argued that in the Fayard novels Simenon shows great awareness of the social context of Maigret's inquiries, that the picture he paints of French society is generally accurate, and that social class and social change act as the engine in the development of many of the plots. In this chapter I consider whether the same is true of the stories making up *Les Nouvelles Enquêtes*.

The Context: French Society from 1934

Internationally, the period following the publication of *Maigret* witnessed a series of major developments. Following Hitler's election as chancellor in 1933, the National Socialist administration of Germany embarked on a policy of crushing its political opponents in the Communist and Socialist Parties and trade unions while simultaneously implementing a succession of anti–Semitic laws and encouraging "unofficial" violent actions against Jews by rightist street gangs. German rearmament was accelerated and in March 1936 the Rhineland was remilitarized. In September 1935, the Fascist administration of Italy invaded Abyssinia. In October 1936, General Franco, backed by the church, major landowners and sections of the bourgeoisie, led a military revolt against the reformist Republican administration in Spain, starting a civil war that would last until 1939. The Francoist forces received financial and military aid from the German and Italian administrations while the administrations of France, Britain and the United States pursued a policy of neutrality.

The international recession triggered by the Wall Street crash of 1929 seemed slow to affect the French economy: according to Braudel and Labrousse (1979–1980, 655), "Until the first months of 1931, many French people might have felt that their country would be spared the crisis." Dard, however, suggests that "there is an ambiguity in the dating of the French economic crisis. The chronology of its actual unfolding is not in fact the same as that of its perception" (Dard, 1999, 21). Industrial production and national revenue had in fact started to fall very soon after the other countries'. The index of industrial production based on a figure of 100 for 1929 dropped to 86 in 1931, before falling again to 72 in 1932. National revenue, which stood at 395 million francs in 1930, fell to 361 million in 1931 and 307 million in 1932. Bankruptcies rose from 755 a month in 1930 to 906 in 1931 and 1,169 in 1932, particularly hitting "the independent middle classes" (22).

Whether or not the recession came later to France, it is indisputable that its duration there exceeded that of the United States and Britain. Montero (2001, 67) points out that "there was no recovery from the crisis after 1935, but rather a further fall until 1938–39"; and the volume of production did not return to the level of 1930 until 1940 (Braudel and Labrousse, 1979–1980, 83). Stock market values fell by 64.5 percent between 1929 and 1936 and did not return to their pre-crisis level until 1939. Hourly wages for manual workers fell by 6.6 percent, while the monthly salaries of civil servants declined by 12–14 percent (Agulhon et al., 1993, 168). Unemployment rose to 500,000 by 1935 and showed little sign of falling until 1938. Although this figure was lower than in the United States or Britain, Montero (2001, 71) points out that the real number was over a million as between 300,000 and 400,000 women and 175,000 foreign workers lost their jobs but did not appear in the official statistics.

The crisis of the 1930s brought to the fore structural weaknesses evident in the French economy compared to those of its rivals. Dard (1999, 21) describes the recession as "the brutal awakening." Although concentration of capital in industry and finance continued, this was at a slower rate than in the United States, Britain and Germany (Zeldin, 2003, Volume 1, Chapters V and VI). According to Montero (2001):

> The crisis revealed the weaknesses in the French economy. In agriculture it brought to the fore the structural gaps.... In industry it deepened the disparities: above all, it struck at the small independent businessman and accelerated the concentration of capital [70].
>
> The middle classes were most affected by the crisis. Managers and engineers experienced unemployment, lawyers and doctors saw a reduction in their clientele. Small shopkeepers and small manufacturers were particularly undermined [72].

Braudel and Labrousse (1979–1980, 877–888) make a similar point:

> The economic crisis led to a certain social restructuring. The problems facing big capital were evident ... but few of the well-known family names or long-standing fortunes collapsed entirely. Whilst the capitalist class faced great difficulties, certain sectors were better protected than others.... These were the businesses catering to the immediate needs of the population, in retail as well as manufacture, which were the least susceptible to economic fluctuations. The crisis brought down a large number of artificial business empires built on speculation and easy money. But this restructuring intensified confusions and conflicts between different fractions of the bourgeoisie.

Given the manner in which the Fayard Maigret novels had tended to focus on precisely those social groups mentioned above, the relations between and the impact of social change on them, we might expect to find the effects of the crisis at the center of Simenon's authorial concerns in the stories collected in *Les Nouvelles Enquêtes de Maigret*.

In *Le Chien jaune* (1931) and *Le Port des brumes* (1932) Maigret comes into close contact with the local political institutions of the Third Republic, and I have considered in a previous section Simenon's views on French political life in the late 1920s and early 1930s. The economic recession of the 1930s provoked major changes in the political sphere, and it is worth considering these in order to see whether and how these developments are realized in the Maigret short stories of the mid- and late 1930s.

Most historians of the period are agreed that a significant change in attitudes to the political institutions of the republic occurred with the onset of the recession. According to Montero (2001, 7):

> The 1920s were marked by a search for consensus, which prolonged the social unity of the war years.... The French people sought to lessen national tensions (anticlericalism in particular), attempted to enjoy the return of peace and began to adopt consumerist habits. The contrast with the 1930s is marked, a decade of crisis and pessimism, when ideologies of hatred and practices of social exclusion intensified.

As the recession continued, so the political crisis deepened:

> The duration of the crisis accelerated disillusionment with national political institutions.... Liberal parliamentary democracy came under repeated fire.... The political establishment was deemed incapable of renewing itself or providing the solutions that public opinion expected [Agulhon et al., 1993, 100–101].

Dard (1999, 8–9) argues that while the economic crisis had begun in 1931, the political turning point was in February 1934 (just as the final Fayard Maigret novel was being prepared for publication): "The point of rupture then was the February 1934 crisis of which the Stavisky affair was more a trigger mechanism than a deep-lying cause.... The turning point of 1934 marked the beginning of a deepening ideological polarisation."

The Stavisky affair was a financial scandal which broke in December 1933. Its main importance was as a pretext for anti–Republican demonstrations by forces of the extreme right. L'Action Française and Les Croix de Feu, the two main groupings, which shared an ideology not dissimilar to that of the marquis de Tracy, for whom Simenon had worked in the early 1920s, both underwent significant growth under the impact of the recession. According to Agulhon et al. (1993), the former organization:

numbered about 60,000 members in the 1930s. Its militants included country squires, army officers, members of the liberal professions, representatives of the petite bourgeoisie, shopkeepers, insurance agents, small manufacturers and students [76].

The Croix de Feu had 150,000 members in 1934: "corporatist in outlook, the Croix de Feu addressed itself to and defended very specifically the middle classes and the peasantry" (79).

On February 6, 1934, tens of thousands of rightists launched a coordinated attack on the Chambre des Députés. Six hours of fighting with the police ensued, at the end of which the insurgents had lost 14 dead and 200 hospitalized, while police casualties were one dead and 100 injured (Cobban, 1965, 145). The attempted coup d'état failed, but the legitimacy of the republic was further compromised among those sections that looked towards the extreme right for inspiration in the face of continuing economic recession and deepening political crisis. At the same time, from 1934 onwards, the political strength of the organized workers' movement was also growing. Between 1934 and 1936 labor union membership increased from one million to five million workers (Zeldin, 2003, Volume 1, Chapter X) and on February 12, 1934, more than one million workers participated in strikes to protest the attack on the Chambre des Députés (Trotsky, 1979, 24), an event which was followed by the signing of a pact between the Socialist and Communist Parties in July. In the local elections of May-June, 1935, the two workers' parties increased their vote significantly, and in July of the same year the Popular Front was formed with the adherence of the Radicals. In the parliamentary elections of April-May 1936 the Popular Front won a large majority (378 seats out of 598) and Léon Blum formed the first ever Socialist Party–led administration. The Communist Party grew from 40,000 members and 11 deputies in 1934 to 235,000 members and 72 deputies in 1936 (Agulhon et al., 1993, 61).

On June 4, 1936, before Blum could take office, workers in Toulouse, Le Havre and Lyon began to occupy their factories, quickly followed by the major plants in the Paris region. Soon, two million workers (about one-quarter of all wage earners) were on strike (Trotsky, 1979, 152). In response, the employers were forced to concede wage increases of between 7 and 12 percent, a 40-hour working week (down from 48 hours) with no loss of pay, two weeks paid vacation and collective bargaining (Cobban, 1965, 152). The Blum administration proved no more able to "manage" the recession using traditional capitalist economic measures than had its predecessors. A financial crisis developed and in September the franc was devalued by 25 percent. When, in June 1937, Blum asked Parliament for special powers to deal with the crisis, and was refused, the administration resigned, Blum being suc-

Popular Front demonstration in 1936. Although the Popular Front had been unable to meet the expectations of the industrially and politically organized workers in the big urban centers, the workers had now incontrovertibly entered into French political life in a way that had never been seen before. The complacent domination of the *notables*, depicted by Simenon in *Le Chien jaune* and *Le Port des brumes* had been shaken to its foundations. (Courtesy Bibliothèque nationale de France.)

ceeded by the Radical Chautemps. The level of labor union militancy fell, although in January 1938 there was a further strike wave which succeeded in shutting down virtually all transport and public services in Paris (Trotsky, 1979, 188). Although the Popular Front had been unable to meet the expectations of the industrially and politically organized workers in the big urban centers, the latter had now incontrovertibly entered into French political life in a way that had never been seen before. Political life could no more return to the 1920s model than could the economy and society return to their pre-recession forms. The complacent domination of the *notables*, portrayed by Simenon in *Le Chien jaune* and *Le Port des brumes*, had been shaken to its foundations.

Dard (1999, 239) argues that the crisis of the 1930s was qualitatively different from anything the Third Republic had previously experienced and distinct from the effects of the recession in the United States and Britain:

In the first place, it must be emphasised that unlike many other states, and in particular its British ally, France underwent a multi-faceted crisis. That is to say, in addition to a generalized economic and social crisis, France also went through an unprecedented political crisis. Of course, the Third Republic had already experienced far-reaching crises such as Boulangism and the Dreyfus affair. However, they were relatively short-lived and their resolution was to the benefit of the republican model which emerged strengthened. This was not at all the case for the crisis of the 1930s.

Simenon would offer an analysis of the early effects of the crisis in a series of 28 articles published in *Le Jour* from October 31 to November 27, 1934 (Simenon, 1976), and I will return later to the implications of these texts for an analysis of his Maigret writings. In the following paragraphs I will consider how the effects of the crisis are realized directly or indirectly in the stories which make up *Les Nouvelles Enquêtes de Maigret*.

Les Nouvelles Enquêtes de Maigret: *Analysis*

Les Nouvelles Enquêtes de Maigret consists of 17 stories. The nine texts published in *Paris Soir-Dimanche*, written in October 1936, range from 14 to 18 pages; the remaining eight, which originally appeared in *Police-Roman* and *Police-Film*, written in the winter of 1937-38, are between 37 and 44 pages long. In this section I will consider in some detail two texts from the first group ("La Fenêtre ouverte" and "Les Larmes de bougie") and one from the second ("La Vieille Dame de Bayeux") as offering the best points of comparison with the Fayard Maigret novels. Other stories from the collection will be referred to as necessary.

The most obvious point of comparison and contrast between *Les Nouvelles Enquêtes* and the Fayard texts is that the former are short stories while the latter are full-length novels, albeit not particularly long ones, of around one hundred and eighty pages in paperback format. This change in form has important implications for Simenon's treatment of social class in Maigret's inquiries. A short story necessarily tends to concentrate on a smaller group of characters and deals with a shorter period of time than a novel. Inevitably, this allows less possibility for the development of protagonists with real depth of character or for the creation of a particular social ambience by the steady accumulation of descriptive detail. It might, therefore, be thought that the short story form is particularly appropriate for the ratiocinative subgenre of crime fiction, pioneered in Poe's Dupin stories (1841–1845), focusing on an enigma to be solved rather than the social causes of particular crimes or the social origins of criminality in a particular historical context. Many of the most successful early ratiocinative crime fiction texts in English, from

Poe to Chesterton, were short stories, a feature that Kayman (2003, 43) ascribes to "the fact that the detective story is a product of the emergent magazine culture and the economy it promoted."

Vanoncini asserts that in the eyes of many critics the Sherlock Holmes short stories are superior to the novellas precisely because they center on the rational solution of a problem rather than the development of character, "action" or social description:

> Many critics point to the clumsiness of these texts [the novellas]. They prefer the structure of the short stories, entirely based around the investigation and often driven by a permanent conflict between Holmes and his antagonist [2002, 29].

This appears to be the view of Julian Symons (1992, 78), who proposes that: "The two novels, and indeed the two other long Holmes stories [Conan] Doyle wrote, cannot be counted as successes." In the first two Sherlock Holmes novellas, *A Study in Scarlet* (1887) and *The Sign of Four* (1890), the investigation, in which Holmes solves the mystery, occupies the first half of the narrative, indeed, even less in *A Study in Scarlet*, as the first two chapters are Watson's account of his first meeting with Holmes, while the second half of each book consists of an extended flashback, in the tradition of Gaboriau's *Le Crime d'Orcival* (1867) or *Monsieur Lecoq* (1868) and Stevenson's "Story of the Avenging Angel" in *The Dynamiter* (1885), explaining the origins of the crime.

The development of French crime fiction in the years preceding the Great War was somewhat different than the Anglo-Saxon model, with the ratiocinative short story format occupying a less prominent place than in Britain. Maurice Leblanc's Arsène Lupin series, starting in 1905, owes more to the tradition of the *roman d'aventures*, exemplified in Eugène Sue's *Les Mystères de Paris* (1842–1843), than to the Poe model of a detective solving a mystery by rational deduction or Holmes's use of "science" to solve an apparently intractable problem. Gaston Leroux's detective Rouletabille claims to work exclusively *par le bon bout de la raison* ("the correct application of logic"); however, his best known case, *Le Mystère de la chambre jaune* (1907), although it is a "locked room" story in the tradition of Poe's "Murders in the Rue Morgue" (1841) and Conan Doyle's "The Speckled Band' (1892), is also influenced by the *feuilleton* tradition in mid- and late nineteenth century French fiction. This influence is even more strongly felt in Marcel Allain and Pierre Souvestre's crime *roman-feuilleton Fantômas* (1910–1914).

Simenon had already written a significant number of detective short stories in the period immediately preceding the publication of the first Maigret novels by Fayard. These originally appeared in 1929 in *Détective* magazine under a pseudonym but were collected and republished under Simenon's own name in 1932 as *Les 13 Coupables*, *Les 13 Enigmes* and *Les 13 Mystères* (Marnham, 1992, 129). The stories are short, usually about 14 pages, and have little by way of complex characterization or social context. The methods of inquiry used in the "13" series are in fact much closer to the ratiocinative anglophone short story model than to what would become the "Maigret method." The "detectives" Froget, G-7 and Leborgne, act by reasoning and deduction, unlike Maigret, one of whose catchphrases is "I don't think anything" (*Un Crime en Hollande/Maigret in Holland*, 1994, 75), and their cases are usually narrated in the first person by an admiring "straight man" in the style of Doctor Watson or Archie Goodwin. Indeed, Eskin goes so far as to describe the "13" short stories as "anti–Maigrets," "as if he [Simenon] were zigzagging toward Maigret and this was a last zag in the opposite direction" (1987, 76).

The impact of Simenon's change in format from novel to short story in the mid– and late 1930s Maigret narratives is immediately obvious in three areas: first, the duration of the inquiries; second, the limitation of Maigret's physical movements in the course of the inquiries; third, the implications for Maigret's method in solving cases. Typically the Fayard novels span a period of five days to a week, with the passage of time often being explicitly recorded. Most of the stories in *Les Nouvelles Enquêtes* are restricted to a period of 24 hours or less. The action of "La Fenêtre ouverte" occupies an afternoon and an evening; "Rue Pigalle" and "Les Larmes de bougie" a morning and an afternoon; "Jeumont 51 minutes d'arrêt" and "L'Etoile du Nord" a single day from early morning to evening; "La Péniche aux deux pendus" a single evening and night. The Fayard novels often involve Maigret in travels from one location to another: in *Le Pendu de Saint-Pholien* he moves from Brussels to Bremen to Paris to Liège; in *Monsieur Gallet décédé* the action is divided between Sancerre, Paris and Saint-Fargeau; in *Pietr-le-Letton* the commissaire moves back and forth between Paris and Fécamp. Even where the inquiry is confined to a single area, as, for example, in *La Tête d'un homme* (Paris) or *Le Chien jaune* (Concarneau), Maigret moves rapidly from one scene to another. In contrast, many of the stories in *Les Nouvelles Enquêtes* unfold in a single setting: the lock at Coudray in "La Péniche aux deux pendus"; an office building in the rue Montmartre in "La Fenêtre ouverte"; a nightclub in "Rue Pigalle"; a railroad car in "Jeumont, 51 minutes d'arrêt!"

The short time span and the confinement of the commissaire to a single location have important consequences for his method of working. In the Fayard novels, Maigret works by what might be termed "progressive penetration." Sometimes this involves him in gradually immersing himself in the social context in which the crime has been committed. Thus in *Le Charretier de la Providence*, he gradually enters into the world of the canal and the people who live and work on it before penetrating the more enclosed worlds of two vessels, *The Southern Cross* and *La Providence*. In *Le Port des brumes*, Maigret first attempts to understand the port of Ouistreham in general and, in order to do so, is obliged to immerse himself in the various environments that compose it—the mayor's house, la Buvette de la Marine, where the harbor workers drink, and below decks on the *Saint-Michel*.

In other inquiries, Maigret attempts to identify with the victim of a murder by entering into the different social settings in which he has lived. This is the method of *Liberty Bar*, where Maigret attempts to recreate the life of William Brown with his mistress and her mother in his villa at Antibes and then in the bar of the title where Brown regularly disappeared for long drinking sprees in the company of the *patronne*, Jaja, and Sylvie, a young prostitute. Although Maigret does not spurn conventional clues or the use of techniques such as forensics and handwriting analysis, his approach is based on atmosphere and instinct and his sensitivity to people and places. In short, it is a social rather than a logical or technical approach to police investigation. The approach is summarized by the narrator of *La Guingette à deux sous*:

> He had handled hundreds of cases in his time, and he knew that they nearly always fell into two distinct phases. Firstly, coming into contact with a new environment, with people he had never even heard of the day before, with a little world which some event had shaken up. He would enter this world as a stranger, an enemy; the people he encountered would be hostile, cunning, or give nothing away. This, for Maigret, was the most exciting part. He would sniff around for clues, feel his way in the dark with nothing to go on. He would observe people's reactions—any one of them could be guilty, or complicit in the crime.
> Suddenly he would get a lead, and then the second period would begin. The inquiry would be underway. The gears would start to turn. Each step in the inquiry would bring a fresh revelation, and nearly always the pace would quicken, so the final revelation, when it came, would feel sudden [*La Guingette à deux sous/The Bar on the Seine*, 85].

In the short stories of *Les Nouvelles Enquêtes* there is insufficient space or time for the full deployment of such a method. Maigret relies much more on conventional clues, such as a close analysis of the different times given by witnesses for the events surrounding the death of Madame Croizier in "La Vieille Dame de Bayeux" or the seating plan of the victim's railroad car compartment and the details of which passengers got off and back on the train at different stations in "Jeumont, 51 minutes d'arrêt!" Logic and deduction play a much greater part in the resolution of many of the cases in *Les Nouvelles Enquêtes* than they do in the Fayard novels, as both Maigret and the narrator explicitly note:

"It's like this! I've been looking for the only logical explanation of the facts. It's up to you to prove it or get somebody to confess" ["Jeumont, 51 minutes d'arrêt!"/"Jeumont, 51 Minutes' Stop!," *Maigret's Pipe*, 244].

This was one of those rare cases which might have been solved from diagrams and documents, by deduction and by scientific police methods. Indeed, when Maigret left the Quai des Orfèvres he was already acquainted with every detail ["Les Larmes de bougie"/"Death of a Woodlander," *Maigret's Pipe*, 110].

"What made you think of Caroline?" the prosecutor asked after a pause.

"Logic!" ["La Vieille Dame de Bayeux"/"The Old Lady of Bayeux," *Maigret's Pipe*, 159].

Does this mean, therefore, that the social dimension of the Fayard Maigret texts is absent from *Les Nouvelles Enquêtes*, and that a sensitivity to social class and environment plays no part in Maigret's approach? In the analysis that follows, I will contend that, despite the restrictions of the short story format, social class continues to be an important feature of many of the inquiries in the sense that it often provides the background to the crime as well as determining the behavior of the protagonists. I will also consider the extent to which the changes in French society ushered in by the depression and the rise of the organized workers' movement, embodied in the coming to government of the Popular Front, are realized in the narratives of *Les Nouvelles Enquêtes*.

In "La Fenêtre ouverte," Maigret arrives at 4 o'clock in the afternoon at an office building in the rue Montmartre to arrest Oscar Laget, a crooked financier. When Inspector Lucas had visited at 3 o'clock, the clerk, Ernest Descharneau, had said Laget was out and would be back at 4. But, as Maigret is being met by Descharneau in the reception area, there is a detonation and Laget is discovered dead in his office, an apparent suicide. But Maigret is suspicious: Why is a window open in the corridor, when it is cold enough for the heating to be on, and why is the smell of gunpowder in Laget's office stale? Maigret questions Madame Laget and Descharneau, discovering that the latter had been Laget's superior officer during the war but had subsequently been employed by him as a clerk after his gun shop failed, although he disapproved of his employer's shady business practices. When he learns from Madame Laget that her husband usually returned at 3 o'clock for a sleep in his office, Maigret deduces that Descharneau had shot him in his sleep with a silenced pistol at 3:45; then when Maigret arrived he pressed a button under his desk setting off a firecracker in the open window in the hall. This explained the detonation and appeared to clear Descharneau of any involvement. Descharneau denies all, but hangs himself in his cell that night while under arrest.

Superficially, this seems to be a classic story in the Poe/Conan Doyle mold, with Maigret putting together his knowledge of Laget's routine, Descharneau's background with guns and munitions and the stale smell of the gunpowder to solve the mystery. However, in the space of sixteen pages, Simenon gives the narrative a significant social dimension and the killer an important social motive. Laget's business activities had started during the feverish economic expansion of the early 1920s when "the post-war period consolidated the position of the *nouveaux riches* and multiplied new openings" (Braudel and Labrousse, 1979–1980, 874). Although his first business venture lasted only a short time—"the chemical products firm lasted three years.... One fine day Laget shut up shop" ("La Fenêtre ouverte"/"The Open Window," *Maigret's Pipe*, 54)—the prolonged period of expansion created an economic space in which even inefficient companies could survive, providing they were not too scrupulous in their operations. As Descharneau explains to Maigret:

> At that point there was some talk of prosecution, which did not prevent Laget, a year later, from launching a new concern, *Le Commerce Français....* You can't imagine what it was like.... Even when there was a staff of sixty, we were sometimes hard put to it to lay our hands on two thousand francs.... Laget had his own car and Madame Laget had hers. They had built themselves a country house for eight hundred thousand francs, but the servants were left without wages for three months at a time. We had to rob Peter to pay Paul. Laget would disappear for two or three days, then come back in a state of great excitement by a side door and make me sign some papers: "Hurry! ... This time we're going to make our fortunes!" [54–55].

Just as the postwar boom provided opportunities for the likes of Laget, the turbulence of the economic situation saw other small businesses, such as Descharneau's, disappear as part of the *reclassements brutaux* (Abbad, 1993, 18) of the period. Laget's rise and Descharneau's fall show the two sides of the coin of a decade in which "social mobility was high as a result of the enrichment of some and the impoverishment of others" (Montero, 2001, 62). As Descharneau recounts to Maigret:

> When we were demobbed I found my shop closed down and my wife ill. I had a little money left and I was unlucky enough to invest it in a concern that collapsed soon after.... Then my wife died. ["La Fenêtre ouverte"/"The Open Window," *Maigret's Pipe*, 54].

In this financial and social turbulence it is, paradoxically, the honest man, Descharneau, who finds himself economically dependent on the unscrupulous Laget: "I didn't even know what I was signing. Whenever I hesitated, he'd accuse me of ingratitude, reminding me that he'd rescued me out of the gutter" (55).

It is not difficult for Maigret, or the reader, to feel sympathy for Descharneau:

One of those failures who are perhaps the most pitiful legacy of the last war or at any rate its most lamentable victims. A man who had been Lieutenant Descharneau and whose character must then have been above reproach. At the armistice he found nothing left of his former life. His business was ruined, his wife died. And it was Laget, whose vulgarity and unscrupulousness had worked wonders in that uneasy period, who took him on [58–59].

It may be debatable whether Descharneau is a more pitiful and lamentable victim of the war than the hundreds of thousands of men mutilated in the fighting: "3,153,000 wounded, including 20,000 brain-damaged, 14,000 with severe facial injuries, 42,000 blinded, 19,700 having lost an arm and 24,900 a leg and 61,200 'severely disabled,'" according to Abbad (1993, 6). Indeed, it might be more accurate to describe him as a victim of the peace, a victim of the unbridled expansion of capitalism during the postwar boom.

In "Les Larmes de bougie"/"Death of a Woodlander," Maigret is called to a tiny village near Vitry-aux-Loges in the forest of Orléans. An elderly woman, Marguerite Potru, has been stabbed to death and her sister, Amélie, who has not spoken since the attack, has numerous knife wounds. Share certificates and money are missing. The principal suspect is Marguerite's son, Marcel. Basing his deduction on a close reading of the report by the Orléans police and a thorough examination of the scene of the crime, including the discovery of drops of candle wax near a barrel in the outhouse, Maigret decides that Amélie has killed her sister, hidden the valuables in order to implicate Marcel and that her wounds are self-inflicted to divert suspicion from herself. In this way, she hopes to get rid of the two people she hates the most, her sister and her nephew.

Again, it seems like an ingenious story of ratiocination, in which the solution can be attributed to Maigret's impeccable logic and analysis of the evidence. In fact, as in "La Fenêtre ouverte," the story has a strong underlying social theme and Maigret's solution of the enigma owes much to his understanding of French rural society—its material backwardness and the limited horizons of its poorest inhabitants—as well as to his reasoning. Maigret's fictional childhood in the Allier had been documented in *L'Affaire Saint-Fiacre* (1932) and the narrator reminds the reader that "Maigret had been born forty kilometres away, on the banks of the Loire" ("Les Larmes de bougie"/"Death of a Woodlander," *Maigret's Pipe*, 110). Nevertheless, the commissaire is unprepared for what he finds in the forest hamlet:

He expected to make a brief journey through space, and it proved to be an exhausting journey through time. Barely a hundred kilometres from Paris, at Vitry-aux-Loges, he alighted from a preposterous little train such as one only sees in old-fashioned picture books, and his request for a taxi was taken as a joke and met with disapproval. He nearly had to complete his journey in the baker's cart, but at the last minute he persuaded the butcher to drive him in his van [110].

Becker and Berstein, describing French society in the interwar years insist:

> One can therefore say that in the 1920s France had a truly dualist economy. Alongside a limited number of dynamic businesses ... there was still a France living to the rhythms of the nineteenth century on its farmsteads and in its shops and small workshops [1990, 339].

Maigret goes even further: "And yet he came from a peasant family! He *knew* that certain hamlets still live today as they did in the thirteenth and fourteenth century" ("Les Larmes de bougie"/"Death of a Woodlander," *Maigret's Pipe*, 114) An exaggeration, perhaps, but it was nevertheless true that:

> In 1939 productivity in agriculture and livestock rearing across all sectors was behind European averages as a result of several factors—the small size of farms, ineffective use of fertilizer, less mechanization, poor nutrition of livestock [Zeldin, 2003, 281].

Moreover, it should be remembered that Zeldin's analysis refers to *average* productivity; the most backward regions of rural France, usually in the mountains and forests, were even further behind in terms of productivity and social development. This is reflected in the fact that much of the area around the hamlet in "Les Larmes de bougie" is given up to hunting by the local aristocrat rather than agricultural production ("Les Larmes de bougie"/"Death of a Woodlander," *Maigret's Pipe*, 110) and to the economic activities of the local population: Marcel is a woodcutter (112), Yarko hauls timber from the forest with horses (113), the husband of Madame Lacore is a blacksmith (111), implying that horses are more common than machinery, and even the mayor is only a tenant farmer (117). These were precisely the rural areas which saw the biggest exodus of inhabitants to the towns, 12.6 percent of the active population between 1929 and 1942, according to Agulhon et al. (1993, 166), leaving the remaining residents even more isolated. Social conditions are primitive. The hamlet consists of:

> Some thirty low, poky little houses ... huddled round a church with a pointed steeple. Every one of these houses must have been at least a hundred years old, and their black slate roofs added to their grimness ["Les Larmes de bougie"/"Death of a Woodlander," *Maigret's Pipe*, 110].

Apart from the few items sold by the Potru sisters, there are no shops, the butcher visits only twice a week (110), the baker comes from Vitry in a horse-drawn cart (110) and there is no telephone service (117). Brutality and alcoholism are rife among the male population: Yarko is a drunkard (113) and Marcel

> ... was a brute in every sense of the word. He had repeatedly stayed away from home for weeks on end without giving any sign of life to his wife and

five children, who got from him more kicks than sous. A drunkard into the bargain, a real bad one [112–113].

Significantly, there is no electricity in the hamlet (111), even though the electrification of the countryside had been a major governmental campaign of the postwar period (Becker and Berstein, 1990, 347), and it is the drips of wax from Amélie's candle which provide Maigret with a critical clue for his solution of the case ("Les Larmes de bougie"/"Death of a Woodlander," *Maigret's Pipe*, 115).

Amélie's motives in killing her sister and trying to implicate her nephew are personal—greed and hatred—but these sentiments have been nurtured in the claustrophobic, backward world of an isolated hamlet:

> The basis of his theory was hatred, a hatred exacerbated by long years spent tête à tête, by life together in this constricted house, nights spent in the same bed, identical interests.... Marguerite had had a child, she had known love, whereas her elder sister had not even had that joy [116].

In a less isolated setting, the two sisters would not have been obliged to pass their whole lives in such close proximity. Opportunities for them to find husbands and to live lives apart from each other would have been greater. Despite the hard situation facing working-class women before the First World War, when the Potru sisters would have been in their early twenties, at least the conditions of urban life offered the perspective of social interaction with work colleagues and the wider world at a time when 38.9 percent of women were in paid employment (Zeldin, 2003, 509). With their own homes, husbands and jobs, and with the greater access to the modern patterns of consumption that were available to urban workers in the 1920s, it is unlikely that the avarice which fed the hatred of Amélie for her sister would have developed to such a degree:

> Money which belonged as much to Amélie as to Marguerite! Even more, indeed, *since she was the elder and had worked longer to earn it!*
> A hatred fomented by the countless incidents of daily life, such as Marcel's killing of the rabbit, his eating of the cheese which was there to be sold and which he had quite shamelessly spoiled without protest from his mother ["Les Larmes de bougie"/"Death of a Woodlander," *Maigret's Pipe*, 116].

The causes of the crime are, then, as much social as personal. Where in *L'Affaire Saint-Fiacre* Maigret had shown a nostalgic longing for the rural life of his childhood, here his response to life in the very depths of *La France profonde* is a negative one from beginning to end. On the first page of the story, we learn that "he had not expected to find tragedy lurking in the forest of Orléans" (110); as he spends more time in the home of the sisters, he feels that it is like "a visit to those homes or hospitals where some of the worst deformities of the human race are concealed" (114); and having solved the case, he feels so sickened by "the scene [that] seemed to belong to a different era, to a different world," that "he would have liked to leave immediately, or else ... treat himself to a hefty draught of rum straight from the bottle" (117). At a time when, according to Zeldin, nearly one-third of French people still lived in rural areas, compared to only 5.7 percent in Britain (2003, 259), Maigret's sentimental boyhood memories in *L'Affaire Saint-Fiacre* are stripped away and replaced by a brutal vision of the harsh realities of life in the most isolated regions of the French countryside for the most economically and socially backward sections of the nation's population.

"La Vieille Dame de Bayeux," as one of the stories originally published in *Police-Roman*, is one of the longer texts in *Les Nouvelles Enquêtes* at 37 pages, which allows greater space and time to develop the social portrait of characters from different classes. While in Caen, reorganizing the Brigade Mobile, Maigret is visited by Cécile Ledru, a lady's companion, who claims that her employer and benefactor (whom she calls her "aunt") has been murdered at the house of her nephew, Philippe Deligeard, although the death has been attributed to a heart attack. After close questioning of Cécile, Deligeard, the doctors who examined the body and Deligeard's servants, Maigret is able to solve the case: Deligeard had brought the body of his childhood nurse, who *had* just died of a heart attack, to the house to be examined by the doctor, and then killed his aunt in the next room so that he could inherit her fortune.

In parallel with Maigret's solution of the "problem," which is essentially based on small discrepancies in the accounts of the timing of Deligeard's movements on the day of the murder, Simenon paints a highly critical portrait of the provincial bourgeoisie of Caen. *Le Port des brumes* had already exposed the pretentious condescension of one Caennais haut bourgeois, Ernest Grandmaison, the mayor of Ouistreham, and the snobbish narrowness of provincial bourgeois life. In his personality and behavior, Deligeard has many similarities to Grandmaison. The key difference is that, while Grandmaison's fortune is based on a family business, the Anglo-Normand shipping company, which remains prosperous, Deligeard, originally an ambitious petit bourgeois, has married into wealth but has squandered his wife's money, hence his preparedness to kill his aunt in order to inherit her fortune:

> Philippe Deligeard ... had on the contrary made a showy start when he married the daughter of a rich horse-dealer. He had bought a splendid mansion which was said to be one of the most handsomely furnished in all Caen. Unlike his aunt, he had made some unfortunate investments, and according to public rumour, for the past three or four years he had been living on credit, borrowing from money-lenders against a future inheritance from his aunt ["La Vieille Dame de Bayeux"/"The Old Lady of Bayeux," *Maigret's Pipe*, 137].

Although the events of the story take place at the height of the recession of the mid–1930s, it is not the depression that has caused Deligeard's financial difficulties but his own extravagance and speculation during the 1920s economic expansion. Nevertheless, he continues to live the life of luxury to which he believes himself entitled and to behave with an air of superiority common to his class. He characterizes Cécile as "that low-class adventuress" (140), her lover Jacques Mercier is from a family that "was, to say the least of it, scarcely respectable" (141) and even his own son is criticized for frequenting the public cafés of Caen: "Young men nowadays do not realize that a gentleman's place is in his club and not in some establishment frequented by all and sundry" (143).

The narrator makes it clear that Deligeard is not simply an individual to whom Maigret feels a strong antipathy, but is rather a representative of his class:

> He was every inch the rich bourgeois whom one meets in all provincial towns, fashionably correct, living in style, a stickler above all for decorum, for certain details of dress, certain forms of speech and bearing which distinguish him from the common herd [140].

Deligeard is cut from the same cloth as the Caen *procureur*, whose note warns the commissaire, "A family affair ... act only with the utmost circumspection" (135), and "the ladies in black, gentlemen in formal dress—all the top people of Caen" (139) whom he sees arriving at Deligeard's home. Maigret's hostility is to the provincial haute bourgeoisie as a whole. He has misapprehensions at the beginning of the inquiry following the *procureur*'s note:

> Did this mean that once again he was going to be involved with the family problems of some high-up official or local bigwig? It was incredible how many people of standing in this part of the world had cousins, brothers- or sisters-in-law who had taken a wrong turning! [135].

As the case proceeds, and as he is obstructed at each development by the *procureur*'s class solidarity with Deligeard, Maigret realizes that his initial feeling was correct: he is not just confronted by a murderer but by a social milieu where snobbery and hypocrisy mask criminality:

> A respectable façade, solemn prudish people, all the outward signs of virtue carried to the point where it exudes boredom.
> And he, Maigret, was to probe all this, to search in every corner, to sniff on every side, until at last, behind the freestone and the panelling, the sombre clothes and the haughty or sullen faces, he discovered the human beast, the nastiest and most unforgivable sort of beast, the kind that kills out of sordid self-interest, for motives of gain! [150].

At the end of the narrative, with Deligeard charged, but still admitting nothing, Maigret's only wish is to go back to Paris and he is apprehensive as to whether, in the closed provincial society of Caen, the killer will be convicted. He tells the *procureur*:

> I feel somewhat ill at ease myself in this part of the world. My wife is expecting me back in Paris. I can only hope that the jurors of this town will not let themselves be overawed by the grand mansion of that utter scoundrel Philippe, and that he'll get the death penalty [160].

Deligeard's financial difficulties are self-induced, rather than a result of the economic crisis of the 1930s; however, Jacques Mercier, Cécile's lover, has been affected by the slump, which Dard says "struck particularly hard at the independent middle classes" more than the big business interests (1999, 22):

> "I joined up with a friend to buy three lorries to collect and transport fish from in the small seaports of the Cotentin region. Unfortunately the lorries, which were not new, have cost us a lot to repair."
> "How long will it be?"
> "What d'you mean?"
> "Before you go broke?"
> "The lorries have been out of action for three days, because the rent of the garage hasn't been paid" ["La Vieille Dame de Bayeux"/"The Old Lady of Bayeux," *Maigret's Pipe*, 145].

Further, there is a fleeting reference to the political dimension of the mid-1930s crisis and the sharpening of class antagonisms when the *procureur* makes a scarcely veiled threat to Maigret in his attempts to warn him off from his pursuit of Deligeard:

> Do what's necessary but be prudent! ... You would pay dearly for one false step, and so should I ... Philippe Deligeard is a prominent man who may owe money but who is received everywhere. As for the girl, Cécile, as you call her, if you lay a finger on her you'll have all the left-wing press defending her as a victim of the rich.... Watch out, Superintendent! [150].

Cécile herself, however, has no real sense of class consciousness and no political agenda. Despite her own humble origins as an orphan and then as maid to Madame Croizier, her identification is with her wealthy employer and benefactor. In becoming a lady's companion she is still objectively a paid employee, no different from a cook, chauffeur or gardener, but at the level of her own consciousness she feels an affinity with the millionaire Madame Croizier rather than seeing herself as part of the working class.

There is an interesting contrast between Madame Croizier and Caroline, Deligeard's childhood wet nurse, whose body is substituted for that of the murdered woman in order to fool the doctor into delivering a death certificate showing the cause of Madame Croizier's death as a heart attack, and this provides Maigret with a crucial clue. The bourgeois Madame Croizier was, according to Deligeard's valet, "very well-preserved" (151), while the doctor who examined Caroline's body, believing it to be that of Madame Croizier, tells Maigret, "She had been in very poor health. It must have been her tenth attack at least" (148). Maigret recognizes that not only is there a discrepancy in the descriptions, but that the woman described by the doctor was probably working class, which helps him towards his solution of the mystery.

Once again, as in "La Fenêtre ouverte" and "Les Larmes de bougie," Maigret's ability to resolve a mystery is as much a function of his awareness of social class as of his deductive logic. If Chesterton's Father Brown is able to unravel problems using an understanding of the human soul and the nature of sin gained in the confessional, then Maigret's success is based on an awareness of capitalist society, the relations based on social class that it creates and perpetuates between its members and how these relations influence the behavior of individuals.

Les Nouvelles Enquêtes de Maigret: *Conclusions*

As in the novels published by Fayard between 1931 and 1934, the *Nouvelles Enquêtes* of 1936 to 1938 show Maigret operating in a wide range of geographical and social settings: Paris, provincial towns and the countryside; the haute and petite bourgeoisie, the peasantry, the world of the canals, the criminal milieu. Moreover, many of the themes of the Fayard texts are revisited in *Les Nouvelles Enquêtes*: the consequences of the social mobility opened up by the economic expansion of the 1920s, which had been at the center of *L'Ombre chinoise*, is the backdrop to "La Fenêtre ouverte"; the condescension and snobbishness of the provincial haute bourgeoisie, typified by Ernest Grandmaison in *Le Port des brumes*, reappears in another Caennais haut bourgeois, Philippe Deligeard, in "La Vieille Dame de Bayeux"; the opposition between Maigret and the legal establishment of the Third Republic, more concerned by potential scandal than by the pursuit of truth and justice, which in the latter story brings the commissaire into conflict with the Caen *procureur*, is an echo of the former's uneasy relations with juge Coméliau in *La Tête d'un homme*; the restricted horizons of the peasantry, which are evident among some of the villagers in *L'Affaire Saint-Fiacre*, are given a sinister twist in "Les Larmes de bougie."

While the short story format may often be less amenable than the novel to the development of social analysis, I have demonstrated that in the selected stories from *Les Nouvelles Enquêtes* Maigret's approach is rooted in his awareness of social class and how this informs the behavior of individuals. For Maigret, and it seems for Simenon, criminal acts are not simply a function of individual personality but rather they result from defined class positions and relations within a given society.

The question must therefore be asked whether the France of 1936–1938, when the *Nouvelles Enquêtes* were written and published, is recognizable in the society depicted in the texts. Significantly, the context for each of the three stories I have considered in detail is one that looks backwards. The relationship between Laget and Descharneau in "La Fenêtre ouverte," which leads to the murder of the former by the latter, is essentially based on Laget's rise and Descharneau's fall during the economic expansion and turbulence of the immediate postwar period. "Les Larmes de bougie" is not informed by the changes taking place in rural life but rather by the absence of change and development in a particularly isolated region of the French countryside. In "La Vieille Dame de Bayeux," the provincial city in which the inquiry takes place is not one such as Toulouse, Lyon or Le Havre, with their rapidly expanding aeronautical, vehicle production and petrochemical industries, but Caen, where the narrator is at pains to point out the old-fashionedness of social life: only the streets in the city center are paved (151), the Palais de Justice is literally "dusty" (153) and the society metaphorically so (150).

There are in the three stories some oblique references to the economic and political crises of the mid–1930s, with Jacques Mercier's pending bankruptcy and the *procureur*'s comments about the left-wing press, but these are the exception rather than the rule in *Les Nouvelles Enquêtes*. There is little to indicate that changes were taking place in French society that were just as fundamental as those which had occurred in the immediate postwar period. The industrial, and increasingly organized, working class is as largely absent from the *Nouvelles Enquêtes* as it had been in the Fayard series. The non-bourgeois classes are once again represented by servants, such as Cécile in "La Vieille Dame de Bayeux," aspirants to the petite bourgeoisie and the distinctive, but highly untypical, world of the canals inhabited by the characters of "La Péniche aux deux pendus." Neither is there any sense of the developing international situation, specifically the consolidation of the National Socialist dictatorship in Germany and the Spanish civil war. Although Otto Braun, the victim in "Jeumont, 51 minutes d'arrêt!," may be a German Jew seeking to expatriate part of his fortune from Stuttgart to Paris, this is essentially a pretext to set up a *huis clos* robbery and murder on a train, rather than the persecution of German Jews forming a defining social context for the crime.

Les Nouvelles Enquêtes de Maigret contains elements of both continuity and difference in relation to the Fayard Maigret novels. The continuity is evident in the importance of social class to the narratives; the difference can be found in the fact that the author appears to be less and less describing the tendencies towards social change in the society in which he is writing: the perspective is increasingly retrospective rather than contemporary. One possible explanation for this could be that, with his own rapidly increasing wealth and ostentatious consumption following the huge success of the Fayard novels, Simenon was no longer in such close contact with the petit bourgeois and popular social layers about whom he was writing. While the texts in the 1931–1934 Maigret series were based on close, direct personal observation, often gathered from the author's travels around France at the time, the *Nouvelles Enquêtes* were composed from the luxury of Simenon's Paris home in Neuilly and his vacation residence in isolated Porquerolles. His social contacts were no longer with the *petites gens*, but rather with the clientele of Fouquet's and Maxim's. As Assouline observes: "These were the days of the Popular Front. The fight for collective bargaining, paid vacations, and the 40 hour week was at its height, but Simenon played the great bourgeois as never before" (1997, 132). It would hardly be surprising if this increasing immersion in the society of the rich made Simenon less aware of social developments outside his new circle of friends and acquaintances, and that this should be realized in his fiction.

An alternative, but not exclusive, explanation could be that Simenon was reacting like an ostrich, hiding his head in the sand, in the hope that if he ignored developments with which he was not in sympathy then they might disappear. Just as his newspaper reports on Germany in 1933 had tended to downplay the significance of the coming to power of the National Socialists by mocking them (Assouline, 1997, 119), so he remained virtually silent on the rise of the organized workers' movement and the Popular Front, of which he equally disapproved (167). Simenon's own origins, although they were modest, were petit bourgeois rather than proletarian and from his childhood his mother instilled in him a distaste for and fear of the organized miners and steelworkers of Liège, their labor unions, their strikes and their mass demonstrations (Fabre, 1981, 252). Throughout his entire life, he always distinguished between *les petites gens*, essentially the petite bourgeoisie or those with petit bourgeois aspirations, and *la foule* or *les masses*. This petit bourgeois ideology, which sees the way forward for the *petites gens* as being individual and based on hard work and merit, was fundamentally opposed to the working-class socialist conception of social change through organized collective action which the Popular Front represented. The *petites gens* who appear in a most positive light in both the Fayard novels and the *Nouvelles Enquêtes*, such as Léon and Emma in *Le Chien jaune*, Julie and Louis in *Le Port des brumes* and Cécile in "La Vieille Dame de Bayeux," escape their modest origins through their personal qualities as individuals, often, perhaps significantly, with the help of Maigret (Léon and Emma) or a benefactor from a higher social stratum such as Captain Joris, in the case of Julie, and Madame Croizier, in the case of Cécile. Simenon would later succinctly state his position as "I see the individual; I don't recognize 'the masses'" (Interview in *Le Nouvel Observateur*, July 13, 1970, cited in Fabre, 1981, 294).

Although Simenon's personal circumstances were changing rapidly in the 1930s, his ideology remained remarkably consistent. France and the world were changing radically too, but it remained to be seen if and how the inquiries of Maigret, whether in short story or novel form, would respond to these changes.

Reportage *and Fiction: Simenon's 1930s Journalism and Its Relation to the Maigret Series*

Simenon's prodigious literary production in the 1930s was not limited to the Maigret novels published by Fayard between 1931 and 1934 and the short stories of 1936 to 1938 featuring Maigret published in *Paris-Soir Dimanche* and *Police-Roman/Police-Film*. In addition, there were 34 non–Maigret novels (*romans durs*) and around thirty collections of articles for various newspapers and magazines. These can be basically divided into articles in which Simenon wrote about his foreign travels and those in which he analyzed developments in France. The former are not relevant to my theme, but the latter, edited by Lacassin and Sigaux (Simenon, 1976), may help to inform a reading of the Maigret stories of the same period.

From the early 1930s onwards, France, in common with the rest of the advanced capitalist economies, had been sliding into recession. Simenon personally, in contrast, was passing through a period of hitherto unknown financial prosperity. Whereas it is sometimes suggested (Marnham, 1992, 69) that his early journalism in Liège reflected not his personal views but rather what he felt was desired by the editor of the *Gazette de Liège*, by the mid–1930s Simenon was a wealthy and successful author—"a celebrity whose signature was coveted by editors in chief" (Bocquet, 1998, 83)—whose nonfiction writing, it can be supposed, fairly reflected his own personal perspectives. It might therefore be expected that Simenon's analysis of social developments in France in the 1930s might throw an interesting light on his fiction writing, that the explicit vision of French society contained in his journalism might illuminate perspectives that are both veiled and refracted through the characters and plots of the Maigret texts.

While the earliest articles are essentially travelogues and many of the reports from the mid–1930s focus fairly narrowly on the Stavisky scandal, two collections are of particular interest in relation to Simenon's contemporary crime fiction. These are the 20 articles published in *Le Jour* from October 31 to November 27, 1934, collected under the title *Inventaire de la France. Quand la crise sera finie*, and the 10 articles from *Paris-Soir* entitled *Police-Secours*, published between February 6 and 16, 1937. The former collection is an analysis of France's society and economy in the early years of the economic downturn and the origins of the situation in the postwar boom of the 1920s. These articles, therefore, consider the period that acts as a backdrop to the Fayard Maigret novels. The latter collection is a snapshot of Parisian society in early 1937, based on a two-week period Simenon spent observing the Paris police's emergency response service, and is, therefore, contemporaneous with the short stories of 1936 to 1938. A third piece, "Police Judiciaire," written in 1933 (Simenon, 1976, 77–101), although it provides background into Simenon's growing awareness of real police practices, and is obliquely referred to in the later *Mémoires de Maigret* (1951), is fundamentally procedural rather than analytical.

What follows will focus on three main themes. First, there will be an exposition of the contents of the two series of articles, including a consideration of the similarities and differences between them. Second, I will examine to what degree the vision of French society explicitly propounded by Simenon in his journalism corresponds to the settings, stories and characters of the contemporary Maigret texts. Finally, I will synthesize these two themes in a consideration of how Simenon's journalism can give an insight into possible authorial perspectives that can be inferred from a study of the Maigret stories of the period.

Inventaire de la France *and* Police-Secours

In the first article of the *Inventaire* series (Simenon, 1976, 311–316) Simenon states his motivation, his methods and his aim:

> Because ever since people have been talking about the crisis and bankruptcy, I have wanted to know what was left for us ... what will be left of France tomorrow [314].
>
> I have been traveling for weeks, from North to South ... stopping at farms and workshops, at the greengrocer's shop and the solicitor's office [313–314].
>
> Would you like to have in simple terms, without statistics or theories, an inventory of France from the cellar to the attic? [315].

At first sight, a review of the articles suggests that the reader can take Simenon at his word. There are articles on the situation in the countryside, agricultural production and trade policy, the peasantry, the fishing industry, manufacturing, the situation in Alsace and Lorraine, the impact of the crisis on shopkeepers and professionals and unemployment. In articles XVI and XVII, Simenon reflects on how the crisis can be overcome, and in the final two articles he gives his conclusion in response to the questions he has posed in the first article. However, a closer reading of the articles reveals both significant omissions in the scope of the inventory and a strong suggestion that the author's conclusions draw heavily on preconceptions and prejudices rather than research.

Although Simenon's tour of the horizon takes him to all four corners of France, he speaks not at all about the main industrial centers, such as the Parisian suburbs, Marseille, Lyon, Toulouse and Le Havre, which had undergone substantial expansion and transformation in the postwar years (Montero, 2001, 53–55; Braudel and Labrousse, 1979–1980, 650). Instead, his focus is on the smaller provincial towns, which, although they still constituted a majority of the urban population (Abbad, 1993, 10), represented France's past rather than reflecting the actual tendency of demographic change in the interwar period. Likewise, the two social groups which had become increasingly important in the 1920s—"modern" monopoly capitalists, such as André Citroën, and the industrial working class concentrated in developing industries such as vehicle production, aerospace and petrochemicals—have no voice in the *Inventaire*. The areas of manufacturing which concern the *Inventaire* are porcelain, footwear and clothing, which had been classic examples of artisan or small workshop craft production. The discussion of unemployment in article XVIII does not concern industrial workers but the middle class (Simenon, 1976, 393–397).

For Simenon, the profound changes which occurred in France's economy and society in the 1920s, and which themselves reflected the changing nature of capitalism internationally, were an aberration rather than signs of the natural development of a mode of production with its own inbuilt tendencies to evolve in a particular direction. Thus, in seeking to explain the causes of the crisis, Simenon focuses on the innovations which had taken place within French and international capitalism in the postwar period. So the crisis in the countryside can be laid at the door of the increasing weight of speculative finance capital:

> Now, land is no longer land, wheat is no longer wheat, copper is no longer copper. There is *long-dated* wheat, *long-dated* copper, *three-month* wheat, *carried-forward* wheat.... In other words, there is speculation.... As the banks have the most power, Maloin [a farm owner whom Simenon has been discussing] will, sooner or later, lose his farm and all the profits from his activity, at the same time, no doubt, as he will lose his confidence in modern methods [324–325].

The crisis facing wine producers is due to the fact that "the majority of them were families who, during the years of plenty, forgot their former principles and threw themselves into speculation" (334). The crisis in the fishing industry is ascribed to speculators who during the easy credit years of the 1920s had boats built which were then repossessed when the price of fish fell and they could no longer repay their creditors (345–350).

The decline of the porcelain and footwear industries in Limoges is explained by three other features of "modern" capitalism, namely increasing mechanization of production to raise output and benefit from economies of scale, mass consumption as a means of capital realizing surplus value and reproducing itself, and the internationalization of trade as part of the struggle between national capitalist powers.

> A Czech, a Pole, who yesterday still knew nothing about machinery, is capable, for eight hours a day, of pushing the same lever with a regular rhythm. Their life is basic, their needs are almost non-existent.... Are they not, with the Japanese and some other nations, the ideal fodder for this new machine-slavery? Bata has understood this clearly and he has built factories in the middle of a poor country, a whole town of factories capable of providing the entire world with shoes [352].

> A major shoe manufacturer told me a few days ago: "a pair of shoes doesn't have to last more than three months. That's why we keep changing the fashions...." And it seems that is what the public wants, that people prefer three pairs of one hundred franc shoes to a solid pair at two hundred francs [356].

Simenon's final target in his assault on "modern" capitalism is the increasing intervention of national and local administrations into production and trade:

> The peasant has confidence.... Not in you! Not in the economists or the politicians, but in himself, in his tools, in his land, which he knows better than anyone.... What he wants no more of are laws which he doesn't understand and which, from one hour to the next, can ruin all of his work faster than a hailstorm [337].

> Everyone has understood, with a few exceptions. Everyone has reduced his expectations, brought his budget into harmony with the new situation. Everyone except the State! ... One thing hasn't gone down, one thing has only gone up and continues to rise: taxes [382].

In summary, Simenon's verdict is that France's crisis is the result of being deceived by the mirage of modernism, of failing to respect its national traditions. In this analysis he was not alone: according to Borne and Dubief (1989, 24) this resistance to modernization constituted "the most distinctive social feature" of the interwar period. Simenon proposes that to overcome the crisis, it is necessary to look backwards. In agriculture, he longs for the prewar days when "a good farmer worked for twenty years, thirty years before having the idea—and even then it was rare!—of owning the land he worked on" (Simenon, 1976, 324). The problems of manufacturing are to be dealt with by persuading consumers to limit their purchases to the higher priced but better quality products made by French artisans (359). In contrast to "modern" methods and attitudes, Simenon waxes lyrical about the wisdom of the small manufacturers of Lorraine and Alsace:

> Here, people set up a business when they have the ready cash to do so. They order goods when they have the money to pay for them.... Outside certain specific industries, I have found the same attitude in all the towns of Lorraine and Alsace. People there don't like speculation. They mistrust money that has been too easily gained. They know that the only solid things are those which have been built brick by brick. They talk reprovingly, almost crossing themselves, about certain "big shots" who let themselves get carried away and have now bitten the dust.... Isn't a workshop good enough, and why, from one day to the next, would anyone want to turn it into a factory? [366–368].

According to Simenon, the same principles can be applied to large-scale industry. He cites the case of a third-generation industrialist, whom he calls Moret III:

> So in 1922, 1923, 1924, what happened after 1870 started again. By speculating on raw materials, you can from one week to the next earn much more than a factory brings in in a year. Moret III gets carried away, builds up a fortune, buys chateaux and even thinks about racehorses. Until the day when.... The boom cannot last forever. The bust is just as spectacular, and so our man panics, tries to recoup his losses by new speculations, flounders, endangers the factory, his family heritage [385].

Moret III is forced to retire and is succeeded by his son who, in total contrast, follows a regime of hard work, responsibility and not spending what he does not have:

> The son has lived quietly and has put money on one side.... He has reserves. He uses them up little-by-little. Other factories have closed around him, but it is a matter of pride that he should be the last man standing [387].

For Simenon, only a return to France's prewar traditions, which he identifies with petit-bourgeois values and practices, can overcome the crisis. His conclusion is an optimistic one, exemplified by the title of the final article, "And We Are Sure We Will Overcome Thanks to Our Traditions and the Courage of All Those Who Produce in This Country," in which he calls on the French population not to follow those who have been influenced by foreign ideas of modernity:

> What has been constructed elsewhere in these last ten years is starting to appear to us in an extremely dim light. Bankruptcy follows bankruptcy, from one side of the world to the other. Are you telling me that we won't escape,

that it won't happen to us too? If you wish! In any case, it will be less serious, less generalized, precisely thanks to our tumbledown town halls, to our manure-soaked farms, to our Balzacien shops and to our millions of savings bank deposit books. And look! I bet that the biggest disasters will be those of the foreigners who have brought their methods here without understanding that the Frenchman is a crafty old devil who, even if he doesn't get angry often, knows what is going on. And who, above all, takes precautions! [404].

In one sense alone, Simenon was correct. The French economic crisis of the 1930s did not have the same depth as the crises in the United States, Great Britain and Germany, although it did, however, last longer (Montero, 2001, 67; Braudel and Labrousse, 1979–1980, 83). The October to November 1934 articles are subtitled *Quand la crise sera finie*, but by the time of the *Police-Secours* reports in 1937 the crisis was anything but finished. When the crisis did end it was not as a result of a return to an earlier socio-economic model: the concentration of capital continued, small businesses of the kind exalted by Simenon were the worst hit (Montero, 2001, 70–72) and the organized movement of industrial workers gained in strength (Zeldin, 2003, Volume 1, Chapter X) as did the Communist Party (Agulhon et al., 1993, 61).

Therefore, when the ten articles composing *Police-Secours* were published in February 1937, the French economy remained deep in recession. Furthermore, the political impact of events had taken a turn not envisaged by Simenon in the fall of 1934 with the election of the Popular Front administration in May 1936, a wave of factory occupations in June and the winning by the labor unions of significant improvements in wages and conditions. Whereas the canvas on which the *Inventaire de la France* is sketched is national and intended to cover a range of social milieus, the focus of the *Police-Secours* articles is much more narrow, drawing as they do on ten nights that Simenon spent in the control room of the emergency response service of the Paris police. He would draw on this experience in the 1938 short story "L'Etoile du nord" (in *Les Nouvelles Enquêtes*, 1944), *Signé Picpus* (1944) and *Maigret et l'inspecteur malchanceux* (1947) as well as his observations forming the basis for a non–Maigret police short story, "Sept Petites Croix dans un carnet" (1951). By their very nature, the articles tend to be snapshots rather than in-depth studies, but in the final two articles of the series Simenon engages in a slightly deeper consideration of the social origins of the events to which the unit responds. What interests Simenon, and he will later put almost identical words into the mouth of Maigret in *Les Mémoires de Maigret* (1951, 148), are not the crimes committed by professional criminals, "people who live more or less on the fringes of society" (Simenon, 1976, 196) but rather:

> The dramas that matter, those which reveal the soul of a period, of a given moment in time, are the others: dramas of love and jealousy, the suicides, the child murders, the three-line news-in-brief articles which affect rich areas as much as poor [198].
>
> There have always been thieves and there have always been certain of them who killed in the hope of getting away. You will discover the real temperature of Paris by studying the other crimes, those committed by amateurs, and the long succession of suicides [202].

Indeed, the suicides in the different arrondissements of Paris are explicitly linked by Simenon to the economic development of postwar France and its impact on different social classes:

> Look! The simple fact that there are most suicides in the XVI arrondissement [one of the wealthiest bourgeois areas of Paris].... Do you understand? People who have lived through a brilliant time of false prosperity, the extremes of pleasure, and cannot resign themselves to a severe setback.... And these little old men and women in Montmartre who decide to put an end to it all? Haven't their savings been destroyed and their incomes from interest become derisory? Doesn't our industrial development prevent thousands of fifty year old men from finding work? And these young families who end their lives, taking their child with them? Is it as if there remained the slightest hope for them? [202].

Interestingly, given its almost complete absence in the Maigret novels, the impact of the 1914–1918 war is also presented as a contributor to crime and suicide: "Oh yes! The war! Nerves stripped bare.... Irritability pushed to the point of illness because you feel your life is a failure. And this lump of wood that you've been dragging round for years where your leg should be" [202].

At the level of professional crime, Simenon concludes on an optimistic note:

> The total figure for Paris in 1935? Sixty-nine murders for more than four million inhabitants. A lower proportion than for apparently the most peaceful country in the world: I mean Switzerland [196].
>
> I'm telling you that I have the statistics at my finger tips. And they reveal that there were more petty crimes in 1900 or 1913 than today [201–202].

However, for crimes committed by non-professionals, with the recession continuing and no signs of a turn to the recommendations of the "*Inventaire*," Simenon is more pessimistic: "Nowadays, disappointment in love counts for less than jealousy.... And jealousy even less than anger at the idea of a life that has failed, a balance that you feel incapable of regaining" (202). If Simenon is right that "you will discover the real temperature of Paris by studying the other crimes, those committed by amateurs" (202), then it must be assumed from the foregoing lines that his disillusionment with developments in French society conveyed in the *Inventaire*, which had nevertheless been tempered by a rousing call to action in the final article of the series, had deepened and hardened with the progression of the 1930s.

Reportage *and Fiction: Conclusions*

When we study the articles of the *Inventaire* and *Police-Secours* alongside the 1930s Maigret texts, it is immediately evident that many of the same themes, settings and attitudes occur in both the *reportages* and the fiction. Maigret's respect for the aristocracy in *L'Affaire Saint-Fiacre*; his hostility to the complacent haut bourgeois Grandmaison (*Le Port des brumes*) and the in-laws of both Couchet (*L'Ombre chinoise*) and Ducrau (*L'Ecluse numéro 1*); the dislike of property speculation and the louche business practices of the 1920s (*Monsieur Gallet décédé*, *Le Chien jaune*, "La Fenêtre ouverte") combined, paradoxically, with sympathy for characters such as Couchet and Ducrau who have benefited from the postwar expansion to become immensely wealthy; the almost casual racism and anti–Semitism of *Pietr-le-Letton*, *La Tête d'un homme* and *Le Fou de Bergerac*; the sympathy for *les petites gens* (*Le Chien jaune*, *Le Port des brumes*, "La Vieille Dame de Bayeux") but the almost complete absence from the texts of the industrial proletariat (the Piedboeufs of *Chez les Flamands* being the notable exception); the identification of the Parisian banlieue with "les classes dangereuses" (Issy in *La Tête d'un homme*); the loathing of politicians (the mayor of Concarneau in *Le Chien jaune*, Grandmaison in *Le Port des brumes*); even a small detail such as the increasing importance of motor transport and its connection to changing patterns of professional criminal activity (*La Nuit du carrefour*).

There are some differences in emphasis between the two sets of articles and between Simenon's journalism and the fictional output in the Maigret texts, but these tend to be at the level of nuance or less important details. For example, river and canal transport, which is central to three Maigret novels (*Le Charretier de la Providence*, *Chez les Flamands* and *L'Ecluse numéro 1*) and one of the *Les Nouvelles Enquêtes* stories ("La Péniche aux deux pendus") is barely mentioned in the *Inventaire*. In contrast, the war, which is almost completely absent from the Maigret narratives, appears as an important element in the social consciousness at the end of *Police-Secours*. Finally, the conclusion of the *Inventaire* seems to be more optimistic than that of *Police-Secours*, perhaps because the predictions of the earlier articles had not been borne out by subsequent developments nor their proposals for action taken up by any significant social forces.

The overlap between the social concerns and attitudes of Simenon as author/reporter, the narrator of the fictional stories (if indeed the narrator can be considered as a separate entity to the author) and the central character of Maigret is striking. All three share a perspective that can best be described as *passéiste* (Gouttefangeas, 1991, 86). This is evidenced at a number of levels. Whether writing as a reporter or as an author of crime fiction, Simenon's social vision of France is a partial one. Certain social classes, essentially the declining traditional petit bourgeoisie and landed gentry, are given a prominence that exceeds their actual weight in society, while the rising classes, the "modern" bourgeoisie, along with their associated subgroups of technicians, engineers and administrators, and the industrial proletariat, are notable by their absence.

The geographical settings of both the journalism and the Maigret stories are usually those that typify prewar French society: small provincial towns and Paris *intra muros* provide the backdrop rather than the expanding industrial centers or the rapidly growing Parisian suburbs. The targets of the Maigret narrator's disapproval are the same as those of Simenon the journalist, namely the speculator, the snobbish haut bourgeois, the narrow-minded provincial *notable*, the scheming, social-climbing petit bourgeois and the rootless cosmopolitan foreigner. Journalist and narrator alike evince sympathy for the landed aristocracy, self-made men owing their fortune to hard work and personal dynamism and *les petites gens*.

Georges Simenon, author of 75 Maigret novels and 28 short stories published between 1931 and 1972. While Maigret may not be reducible to a mouthpiece for Simenon, the latter's nonfiction writings reveal important correspondences between them in agenda, analysis and attitudes. (Courtesy DR Collection John Simenon.)

Maigret's own social views parallel those of the narrator and Simenon and the commissaire's *passéisme* is confirmed by his lifestyle: a deep respect for tradition, living within his financial means, his conservative dress sense, the liking for traditional French peasant cooking, a taste for homemade country liqueurs and his lack of any desire to learn to drive an automobile. It is at the level of personal behavior that the most important difference between author and character can be found, despite the similarity of their social vision. While the commissaire leads the kind of lifestyle that his creator is keen to propound in the *Inventaire*, the author himself was, according to all of his biographers, an extravagant, ostentatious, social-climbing womanizer. Yet, despite this difference, and despite Simenon's protestations that he and Maigret could not be identified with each other, at the level of their social vision and their response to the social changes of the interwar period as realized in the former's journalism and the latter's fictional character, the similarities are remarkable. While Maigret may not be reducible to a mouthpiece for Simenon, the latter's nonfiction writings reveal important correspondences between them in agenda, analysis and attitudes.

CHAPTER 5

What Maigret Did Next

Introduction

If Simenon's output of novels and short stories featuring Maigret had been prolific between 1931 and 1945, he showed no signs of slowing down in the postwar years. Now with a new publisher, Presses de la Cité, he was to produce a further 48 Maigret novels and eight short stories and novellas of varying lengths between 1947 and 1972 (Eskin, 1987, 283–286). I have proposed in the preceding chapters that the 1930s Maigret texts are significant in the history of crime fiction in terms of their approach to social class and social change, not only in the way in which contemporary society provides the backdrop to the stories, but also in the manner in which the evolving class formation of contemporary French society acts as a driving force in the development of the narratives. In this chapter I will consider whether, in addition to being historically significant in their own context, the 1930s Maigret texts are also distinctive within the corpus as a whole; that is to say, whether there is a continuity or a rupture between the pre- and postwar texts in terms of the function of social class and historical change in the realization of plots, characters and themes.

Numerous commentators have, indeed, seen a clear break between the pre- and postwar novels. Carter suggests that:

Many fans prefer the earlier Maigrets [the Fayard series from 1931 to 1934], and feel that the later ones are more philosophical and expansive. In the later ones, however, Simenon often attained greater subtlety of character and insight into motivation [2003, 15].

Alavoine expands the point:

Unlike the output of the 1930s, the Presses de la Cité Maigrets contain on the whole the same themes as the contemporary *romans durs*: solitude, guilt, the weight of destiny, criticism of the judicial system.... We have seen that above all in the early inquiries, Maigret sets himself up as judge and jury, preventing the legal system from proceeding in the normal way: this is almost always to the benefit of the criminal, except when the latter is almost driven towards suicide. In the post-war inquiries ... the theme of culpability is much more present, and now it is the judicial system which is called into question by Maigret. The examining magistrate, the public prosecutor's office, legal procedures or the criminal law are the objects of the commissaire's criticism [1999, 15, 29].

Vinen argues that:

Significant parts of most [later] Maigret stories take place in Maigret's head. One only has to list a few titles (*La Colère de Maigret*, *Maigret se fâche*, *Maigret a peur*, *Maigret s'amuse*) to realize how much they revolve around Maigret's personality, as well as how formulaic they become [2003, a, 2].

Bresler clearly distinguishes between "earlier" and "later" Maigret novels, but he places the dividing line in 1966:

Most informed French critics would agree with the view expressed by Maurice Dubourt that [Simenon's] last good novel was *Le Chat*.... Of the eighteen more novels, equally divided between Maigrets and non–Maigrets, that Simenon was to write after *Le Chat*, none has anything like its stature ... for the most part they are no better or worse than any other competent storywriter could have produced.... Even his beloved Maigret had lost his sparkle for him; the last Maigret novels are clockwork, automatic things with sloppiness in the plotting and a palpable disenchantment on Simenon's part for all the new gadgetry of forensic science with which a modern policeman would have to work [1983, 221, 222, 228].

In order to see whether the function of social class and social change changes in the postwar Maigret stories, it is necessary to consider whether the texts are susceptible to any clear periodization. Murielle Wenger proposes four essential periods: first, the Fayard series, in which Maigret is "rocklike" (*Pietr-le-Letton*/*Maigret and the Enigmatic Lett*, 12), essentially sure of himself and his role; next, a "lighter" Maigret of the Gallimard period (for example, *Félicie est là* and *Signé Picpus*); then a period of transition, represented by the texts written in North America, in which the author balanced new experiences of a different society with his memories of France; finally, the Presses de la Cité novels from 1956 in which Maigret becomes "more and more questioning of his profession and his role, taking up in his doubts Simenon's own concerns ... about the real responsibility of men and criminals" ("Maigret of the Month: *Maigret tend un piège*").

Any attempt to periodize the Maigret novels is complicated by the fact that the chronology of the narratives is in radical contrast to their dates of publication. In the penultimate text of the Fayard series, *L'Ecluse numéro 1*

(1933), Maigret is only days away from retirement, and in the final Fayard novel, *Maigret* (1934), he has retired; this despite the fact that in the remainder of the series, published in 1931 and 1932, he is described as being in his mid-forties. Yet all of the stories have a contemporary, that is, late 1920s/early 1930s setting; in fact *Monsieur Gallet décédé* (1931) even begins with the precise date "27 juin 1930" (7). Of the postwar Maigret novels, *La Première Enquête de Maigret* (1949) is openly retrospective—"It was the 15th of April, 1913" (*La Première Enquête de Maigret/Maigret's First Case*, 6)—and Maigret's age (early twenties) is consistent with the chronology of the 1931 and 1932 Fayard stories; *Maigret chez le ministre* (1955, 63) refers explicitly to the occupation and resistance and the postwar political climate, thereby suggesting a contemporary setting for the narrative. But the only other exact date in the remainder of the corpus is in Chapter 1 of *Maigret et l'homme tout seul/Maigret and the Loner* (3)—"This was 1965"—and the commissaire is still in post, aged about 75, if the dates are accurate, but giving no evidence of this in the text. Maigret had been recently retired (again) in *Maigret à New York* (1947) but in *Maigret aux assises* (1960) he is once more days away from retirement.

In short, it is pointless to seek a coherent chronology for the postwar Maigret novels in terms of the age of the central character. However, if the age of the commissaire is inconsistent, even as a matter of imagination, it may be that the settings of the narratives can help to establish their historical context in relation to developments in French society in the postwar years. In the following sections of this chapter I will look at how France evolved in the period after 1945; I will consider the extent to which this evolution is realized in the Presses de la Cité novels; and I will evaluate the implications of this for an understanding of whether there is a continuity or a rupture between Simenon's approach and perspective, in terms of the role of social class and social change, in the earlier and later Maigret stories.

Postwar France

Asselain (1984, 105) essentially divides the period in which the Presses de la Cité Maigret stories were composed, that is, 1945–1972, into three phases. First, postwar reconstruction, which was effectively completed by the end of the 1940s; secondly, a period of sustained, if uneven and sometimes unstable, economic expansion from 1950 to 1958; finally, a phase of unprecedented, continually accelerating growth from 1958 to 1973. Other historians agree that the period represented a new stage in the development of French capitalism: "For the growth which started at the beginning of the 1950s was a new phenomenon as much in its duration as in its continuity and which, until 1972, even showed a clear tendency to acceleration" (Braudel and Labrousse, 1982, 1011). The postwar expansion was common to all of the advanced capitalist countries, but France's economy grew more quickly than most. In the 1950s, French growth was faster than that of Great Britain and the United States (albeit from a lower starting point) and by 1968 the economy was growing at an even more rapid rate than the much-hailed West German "miracle" (Asselain, 1984, 105).

Growth was evident across all sectors of the economy, and the shift in the nature of the economy can be seen in the change in the structural activities of the working population.

	Primary (agriculture, extraction)	*Secondary* (manufacturing)	*Tertiary* (services)
1946	36.5%	29.5%	34.0%
1962	21.0%	39.5%	39.5%
1972	12.0%	39.0%	49.0%

SOURCE: Asselain, 1984, 140.

In agriculture, productivity increased by an average of 6.8 percent per year between 1949 and 1962 (against 5.5 percent for the economy as a whole), and by the end of this period, output per capita was approaching the levels of the most advanced European economies. This was primarily due to mechanization, with five times as many tractors in use in 1950 as in 1938 and the number tripling again between 1950 and 1957 (Asselain, 1984, 118). Industrial output and productivity also soared. Between 1951 and 1973 industrial production more than tripled, and by 1967 French industrial output had overtaken that of Britain (Ardagh, 1988, 28). This was partly due to a dramatic concentration of production in each industrial sector. The chemical and steel industries were dominated by three groups, vehicle manufacturing by four companies, the seven largest aerospace firms accounted for 80 percent of sales, and even in the stagnating textile industry the market share of the twenty largest manufacturers doubled between 1962 and 1970 (Asselain, 1984, 139; Braudel and Labrousse, 1982, 1286, 1290). The average annual number of industrial mergers and fusions grew from 32 between 1950 and 1958 to 136 from 1966 to 1972 (Asselain, 1984, 138).

The second key factor in French capitalism's dramatic growth was the role of the state. There was massive governmental investment in new machinery, technology and infrastructure in areas such as coal, steel, shipbuilding, petrochemicals, power generation and the railroads (Cobban, 1965, 218–219). Moreover, the state itself assumed an increasingly directive role in the planning of the economy. In the winter of 1945-1946, the credit and insurance, gas and electricity and coal industries were nationalized; in 1948, sea and air transport was reorganized into mixed public-private companies (Asselain, 1984, 111). Coordination and planning was assured through the creation of the Commissariat Général du Plan in 1946 and the adoption of a series of growth plans from January 1947 onwards (Asselain, 1984, 112). Links between big business, the state and the "technocracy" of the elite Grandes Ecoles were established to a hitherto unknown degree (Ardagh, 1988, 33). The administration's international trade policy, from the creation of the European Coal and Steel Community in 1951 to the signature of the Treaty of Rome in 1957, creating the "Common Market," was determined by the need to advance the modernization and expansion of French capitalism (Ardagh, 1988, 36; Asselain, 1984, 126).

Improvements in family allowances and health care led to an increasing birthrate and longer life expectancy, resulting in an average annual excess of births over deaths of between 250,000 and 300,000 from 1945 to 1974 (Ardagh, 1988, 15). However, the rapidly growing economy could not draw on children and the elderly for labor power, so the expanding sectors were obliged to look elsewhere. On the one hand, the increasing mechanization of agriculture and the concentration of farm ownership liberated millions of small farmers and agricultural workers to work in the boom industries. Over one quarter of the working population in rural occupations left the land between 1949 and 1954 (Cobban, 1965, 220) and by 1968, 66.2 percent of the population was in towns and cities (Braudel and Labrousse, 1982, 997). On the other hand, as in the postwar expansion following 1918, the labor force was boosted by the arrival of immigrant workers. Initially, displaced Poles and Yugoslavs were employed, but from the mid–1950s increasing numbers of Algerian, Moroccan, Portuguese and Spanish workers were recruited. The growth in the working population was further augmented by the return of almost 800,000 white Algerians following the independence of that country in 1962. According to Braudel and Labrousse, (1982, 994): "Around one-third of the total increase in France's population between 1945 and 1968 was the result of net immigration.... From 1962 to 1968, out of every three industrial jobs created, one was performed by a foreigner." By 1974 there were over three million immigrants in France, including workers, their families and the unemployed (Braudel and Labrousse, 1982, 1539):

Algerians	871,223
Portuguese	840,460
Italians	564,660
Spanish	548,600

Moroccans	302,225
Tunisians	162,479
Poles	90,896
Yugoslavs	79,445

Not only was the population as a whole changing, but its distribution within the country was also evolving rapidly. In addition to the exodus from the countryside, there were also significant changes in the urban areas themselves. The Paris region was still the main beneficiary of internal and external immigration, but its proportion of the national population remained stable between 1936 and 1968 at around 16 percent (Braudel and Labrousse, 1982, 1000). What was significant was the movement within the region from the Ville de Paris to the suburbs. The former numbered 2.9 million residents in 1911 but only 2.1 million in 1980; the latter had 2.1 million inhabitants in 1911 and 5.9 million in 1980; so, by 1980 three-quarters of Parisians were *banlieusards* (Ardagh, 1988, 252). This shift was driven by three main factors. First, the chronic housing shortage caused by the growing population; secondly, the fact that there had been little building between 1900 and 1950, and little updating of apartment blocks by private landlords, meant that the housing stock was often in very poor condition and beyond renovation; thirdly, the removal of rent controls in 1958, which had been imposed in 1914 to protect soldiers' families from profiteering landlords, resulted in soaring rents in the city and the gentrification of formerly popular quarters (280). The large-scale development of public housing (*habitations à loyer modéré*, or HLMs) in the suburbs began in the early 1950s, and the construction of the massive Sarcelles project, to the north of Paris, which would house 40,000 people by 1971, was started in 1956 (281–282, 290).

A similar process occurred in the major provincial cities between 1946 and 1968. The population of Marseille increased from 636,000 to 964,000 (including suburbs), Lyon from 461,000 to one million (including suburbs), Toulouse from 264,000 to 444,000 (including suburbs), Nice from 211,000 to 322,000, Grenoble from 102,000 to 162,000, Dijon from 101,000 to 145,000, Montpellier from 93,000 to 162,000 (Braudel and Labrousse, 1982, 999). France was increasingly becoming not just an urban nation but a country of major city dwellers. By 1968, small towns of between 5,000 and 20,000 inhabitants accounted for only 9.4 percent of the population (1000), whereas in the 1930s they had contained a majority of the urban population (Abbad, 1993, 10).

There were also significant changes in economic activity and demographic spread between and within the different French regions. In 1939, France was, with a few exceptions, essentially divided between an urban, industrialized east and a rural, agricultural west, with 85 percent of industry lying to the east of a line from Caen, in the northwest, to Marseille, in the southeast (Ardagh, 1988, 121). Although much of the postwar economic expansion took place in the traditional industrial areas of the north, the east and the Paris region, and although the regions of Poitou-Charentes, Limousin and the Centre continued to decline, a governmental policy of financial incentives, and the availability of labor released by an increasingly mechanized agriculture, led to significant economic development in the major cities of the west and center-west, such as Caen, Le Mans, Tours, Orléans and Rennes. Whereas in 1954 for the west, southwest and center regions taken together, the distribution of the workforce was 45.5 percent in agriculture, 25.1 percent in industry and 29.4 percent in the tertiary sector, by 1975 these figures had changed to 18.4 percent, 33.4 percent and 48.2 percent respectively.

While the need for factory labor had been primarily met by the exodus of farm workers and small farmers and by foreign immigration, the evolution of the French economy also had serious consequences for the petite bourgeoisie, both in manufacturing and commerce, which found itself increasingly threatened by modern manufacturing and retail organization and techniques. Braudel and Labrousse (1982, 1533–1534) summarize the decline of this layer which had been one of the economic, social and political bulwarks of the Third Republic:

> Craft industries continued to decline, with the artisan often obliged to give up his economic independence and the creative nature of his work. After 1950 and above all from the beginning of the 1960s, small-scale retail businesses felt the heat of an increasingly ruinous competition: in addition to the traditional department stores and various Prisunics, the years from 1958 saw the growth of an increasingly dense network of supermarkets.... Little by little, the independent shop sector retreated to the benefit of the big retail chains. At the beginning of the 1950s, about 10% of retail activity was controlled by the capitalist sector, rising to 20% ten years later and 35% in 1972. The elimination or satellisation of large layers of craft production and retail business was accompanied by a growth in the number of salaried employees who represented 71.6% of the economically active population in 1962.

The last significant attempt by the petite bourgeoisie to defend itself against modern monopoly capitalism was the Poujadist movement of the mid-fifties. However, despite winning three million votes and 50 seats in the 1956 legislative elections, it was unable to reverse the tide of economic and social change (Cobban, 1965, 221).

Certain aspects of social life failed to keep pace with the economic boom of the postwar period. For example, as late as 1968, 30 percent of French homes did not possess running water (10 percent for Paris and the main urban centers) and 60 percent had neither plumbed-in baths/showers nor flushing toilets (around 40 percent in Paris and major towns) (Braudel and Labrousse, 1982, 1545). Telephone services remained poor: in 1970 France had fewer lines per capita than "underdeveloped" Greece (Ardagh, 1988, 179). On the other hand, automobile ownership was on the rise. In 1953, 20 percent of households owned an automobile, a figure which rose to 50 percent in 1967 and 62 percent in 1973, of which 9 percent possessed two vehicles (Braudel and Labrousse, 1982, 1289). Domestic electrical appliances also became common, one consequence being the decline in the number of domestic service workers as bourgeois housewives required less help in the maintenance of their homes.

Social attitudes changed in a number of areas, reflecting the changes in material economic life. Women won the vote in 1945 and were increasingly represented in the universities and professions, although they were still virtually absent from the Grandes Ecoles and the higher echelons of industry and big business (Ardagh, 1988, 333). The extended family, which had been rooted in land ownership in the countryside and inherited wealth in the urban bourgeoisie, gave way increasingly to the nuclear family as revenue became more important than property (350). The influence of the church continued to decline (430), although abortion was not legalized until 1974 and in the 1960s clandestine abortions were estimated at between 700,000 and 800,000 per year (347–348). The French remained the second heaviest drinkers in Europe (after the inhabitants of Luxembourg) but alcohol consumption per head declined by 20 percent from 1951 to 1980, partly as a result of a series of governmental campaigns (427).

Ardagh (1988, 13) summarizes the period as follows:

> During that time France went through a spectacular renewal. A stagnant economy turned into one of the world's most dynamic and successful, as material production moved along at a hectic pace and an agriculture-based society became an increasingly urban and industrial one. Prosperity soared, bringing with it changes in lifestyles, and throwing up some strange conflicts between rooted French habits and new modes. The French themselves were changing.... Many of them grew fired with a new energy, a zealous new faith in the cure-all of economic growth and technical progress. Long accused of living with their eyes fixed on the past, they now suddenly opened them to the fact of living in the modern world.

In previous chapters, I have argued that the Maigret texts of the 1930s represent a generally successful realization in crime fiction of the social class structures of interwar French society. In the next section, I will consider whether the changes summarized by Ardagh above are equally realized by Simenon in the postwar Maigret novels.

Maigret in the Postwar World

The first thing that would strike a casual reader comparing the Maigret narratives of 1931 to 1944 with those of the postwar period would be the titles. Of the 19 Fayard novels, only the final one contains the central character's name, the eponymous *Maigret* (1934). Of the Gallimard novellas and short stories, although two of the collections include the commissaire's name (*Maigret revient*, 1942, and *Les Nouvelles Enquêtes de Maigret*, 1944), only one story ("L'Erreur de Maigret" in *Les Nouvelles Enquêtes*) has Maigret's name in the title. By contrast, in the Presses de la Cité series, only four narratives, all short stories, do *not* have "Maigret" in their title — "Le Témoignage de l'enfant de choeur," "Le Client le plus obstiné du monde," "On ne tue pas les pauvres types" and "Vente à la bougie" — and these appear in the collections *Maigret et l'inspecteur malchanceux* (1947) and *Maigret et les petits cochons sans queue* (1950). One could conclude, with Vinen (2003, a, 2), that this is because the stories have become more introspective, "revolve around Maigret's personality" and "take place in Maigret's head." However, a simpler explanation is that as astute businessmen Simenon and his new publisher, Sven Nilson, realized that they had a highly marketable product and that a key part of marketing is brand recognition. A "new Maigret" would leap off the shelves in bookshops and railroad stations all the more easily if the faithful readership could recognize it immediately by the title. For all that Simenon liked to portray himself as a kind of literary artisan, he had in his armory both a promotional organization and a business know-how far beyond that at the disposal of any artisan in the real world of manufacturing or retail distribution.

A second general feature of the Presses de la Cité novels is the importance of the past. In this there is a certain structural continuity with the Fayard series. Of the 19 Fayard novels, over half have at their heart a past crime or event leading to the inquiry of the narrative: *Monsieur Gallet décédé* (an exchange of identities), *Le Pendu de Saint-Pholien* (a murder in the past), *Le Charretier de la Providence* (the desertion of the imprisoned Jean by his wife), *Le Chien jaune* (the betrayal of Léon Le Glérec by the Concarneau notables), *La Guingette à deux sous* (the murder committed by James six years before), *L'Ombre chinoise* (Couchet's humble beginnings and first marriage), *L'Affaire Saint-Fiacre* (Maigret's childhood), *Le Fou de Bergerac* (the crimes and escape of Samuel in Algiers), *Le Port des Brumes* (the dispute between the Grandmaison cousins and the "banishment" of Raymond) and *L'Ecluse numéro 1* (Ducrau's fathering of a child by Gassin's wife).

This retrospective theme is restated, perhaps even deepened, in the Presses de la Cité series. In several of the postwar Maigret novels, it is a crime that has been committed years before that is the key to Maigret's inquiry (*Maigret à New York*, 1947, *Maigret en meublé*, 1951, *Maigret et le clochard*, 1963, *Maigret et l'homme tout seul*, 1971). In other cases, Maigret encounters figures from far back in his professional career (*Mon ami Maigret*, 1949, *Maigret et la grande perche*, 1951, *Maigret et le voleur paresseux*, 1961) or his personal life (*Maigret a peur*, 1953, *Un Échec de Maigret*, 1956, *L'Ami d'enfance de Maigret*, 1968). Often Maigret's pursuit of a case is overlain by personal memories (*Maigret à l'école*, 1954, *Maigret et les vieillards*, 1960), and in *Une Confidence de Maigret* (1959), the commissaire recounts a past case in flashback. *La Première Enquête de Maigret* (1949) takes the reader back to before the Great War and *Les Mémoires de Maigret* (1951) offers a retrospective of his professional and personal lives from childhood onwards.

There are differences and similarities in the settings of the Fayard and Presses de la Cité novels. After 1945, Maigret's inquiries are much more concentrated in Paris than they had been in the 1930s, which is arguably more realistic from the point of view of his professional jurisdiction. Yet it is invariably the city of Paris itself, whose population was declining, and not the rapidly expanding *banlieue* which is the commissaire's theater of operations. When Maigret leaves Paris, it is to conduct inquiries in locations which are symbolic of France's past (and his own) rather than the actual demographic developments of the postwar years: Les Sables d'Olonne (*Les Vacances de Maigret*, 1948), Etretat (*Maigret et la vieille dame*, 1950), Fontenay-le-Comte (*Maigret a peur*, 1953), Saint-André-sur-Mer (*Maigret à l'école*, 1954) are all small towns or villages in the west or northwest of France, largely bypassed by the immediate postwar economic expansion and social change. Vichy (*Maigret à Vichy*, 1968) as well as being identified with the Belle Epoque is also in the Allier *département* in central France, which includes Maigret's fictional birthplace of Saint-Fiacre. All, in some way, represent the past rather than contemporary developments. Writing in *Le Populaire* in 1950, a reviewer of *Maigret et la vieille dame* noted, "the extent to which this novel freezes the image of a lost France testified to in Simenon's novels, a point of reference in the sentimental geography of France" (cited in Baronian et al., "Le film dans le texte," 36). The settings of the Presses de la Cité novels are usually places with which Simenon was familiar, but it was a familiarity which dated back to the 1930s. After his departure from France in 1945, he lived first in North America and then in Switzerland; he had left Paris in 1938, returning thereafter only for short visits, and the city he described in the Maigret novels was in reality changing rapidly.

The social classes from which the protagonists of the postwar stories are drawn are similar to those of the Fayard series. Equally, those social classes which are largely ignored in the 1930s Maigret stories are also absent from the later narratives. The reader of the 48 Presses de la Cité novels will search in vain for the urban workers, industrial capitalists and "technocrats," the central social groups in the postwar economic life of France. Likewise, Maigret encounters hardly any of the millions of immigrant workers whose labor was essential to the expansion of industry and the major construction projects of the period. Foreigners fall into a number of defined categories drawn either from the earlier narratives and/or popular stereotype: professional criminals, such as the Czech killers of *Maigret et son mort* (1948), recalling the Polish gang of "Stan le tueur" (1938); stereotypical characters such as the alcoholic Englishwoman Mrs. Wilcox of *Mon ami Maigret* (1949), who has much in common with Sir Walter Lampson in the 1931 *Le Charretier de la Providence*, and the wealthy foreigners of *Maigret voyage* (1957), resembling the clients of the Hotels Majestic and George V in 1931's *Pietr-le-Letton* and *La Tête d'un homme*; the Flemish bargemen of *Maigret et le clochard* (1963), harking back to *Chez les Flamands* (1932); and a range of figures (criminal or otherwise) of Italian origin from Montmartre's nightlife, such as Maurice Marcia in *Maigret et l'indicateur* (1971), who are not dissimilar to Pepe Palestrino from the 1934 *Maigret*.

Montmartre in 1925. The settings of the Presses de la Cité novels are usually places with which Simenon was familiar. (Courtesy Bibliothèque nationale de France.)

The Paris suburb of Sarcelles in 1970. After his departure from France in 1945, Simenon lived first in North America and then in Switzerland; he had left Paris in 1938, returning thereafter only for short visits, and the city he described in the Maigret novels was in reality changing rapidly. (Courtesy Agence Roger-Viollet.)

Such capitalists as Maigret meets tend to be from economic sectors which represent France's past: the wholesale butcher, Fumal, in *Un Échec de Maigret* (1956) or the wine merchant, Chabut, in *Maigret et le marchand de vin* (1970). Significantly, both of these activities are connected to distribution of agricultural products rather than industrial manufacturing. The distance between the economic world inhabited by Maigret and contemporary developments, particularly from the late 1950s onwards, is illustrated by the difficulty (even impossibility) of imagining novels entitled *Maigret and the aerospace engineer* or *Maigret and the public relations consultant*.

Other bourgeois figures are notable for their criminal attempts to preserve inherited fortunes, for example Madame Besson and Madame Serre, in *Maigret et la vieille dame* (1950) and *Maigret et la grande perche* (1951) respectively, or for their cupidity and corruption, for example, the society lawyer Gaillard in *La Colère de Maigret* (1963) or Mélan, the wealthy dentist with a profitable sideline as an illegal abortionist, in *Maigret se défend* (1964). In summary, two features characterize the bourgeois figures of the postwar novels: first, they represent sectors which were unconnected to France's contemporary economic expansion; secondly, they are portrayed in a highly unflattering light. By contrast, despite his initial difficulty in understanding their social milieu, behavior and attitudes, Maigret feels a certain respect, even affection, for the aristocrats of *Maigret et les vieillards* (1960), who are even more distant from the socioeconomic realities of France in the third quarter of the twentieth century than the wholesale butchers and wine merchants.

Petit bourgeois criminals, such as the bar owner's wife Madame Calas in *Maigret et le corps sans tête* (1955) or the picture-framer Meurant in *Maigret aux assises* (1960), receive a much more favorable treatment from the commissaire and from the author, as does Planchin, proprietor of a small painting and decorating business, who is the victim in *Maigret et le client du samedi* (1962). As in the Fayard novels, Maigret is generally sympathetic to the *petites gens*, but, postwar as interwar, they are never proletarians. Ginette in *Mon ami Maigret* (1949), Ernestine in *Maigret et la grande perche* (1951) and Louise in *Maigret se trompe* (1953) are (ex-) "tarts with a heart," like Adèle in *La Danseuese du Gai Moulin* (1931) and Fernande in *Maigret* (1934). Victor in *Un Échec de Maigret* (1956) has his origins in the rural poor; Keller in *Maigret et le clochard* (1963) is a voluntarily déclassé doctor; the victim of *Maigret et l'homme du banc* (1953) and the killer of *Maigret et le marchand de vin* (1970) are both former white-collar employees.

In his personal life, Maigret is faced with changes attendant on the evolution of French society. In *Maigret et son mort* (56), colleagues and friends suggest that the Maigrets move to another apartment more in keeping with the commissaire's professional status, but Maigret refuses: "What he dreaded was not so much the actual house moving, as the change of scene. The thought of no longer ... making the same journey every morning" (*Maigret et son mort/Maigret's Special Murder*, 1972, 327). The respect for tradition and social conservatism, in the broadest sense, that Maigret reveals in his dealings with the different social classes is reflected at a personal level in his attitude to his apartment in the postwar stories. Whereas in the Fayard novels he had spent little time at home, partly because so many of the cases take place in the provinces, the great majority of the later inquiries unfold in Paris, and Maigret's reasons for liking his apartment reflect his desire for social stability and tradition. The same words and expressions recur like a litany—*retrouver, à leur place, familier*:

> It was good to find Madame Maigret's voice again, the smell of the flat, the furniture and objects in their place [*Maigret a peur/Maigret Afraid*, 154].
>
> The door of the apartment opened as usual and Maigret rediscovered the light, the familiar smells, the furniture and other objects which had been in the same place for so many years [*Les Scrupules de Maigret/Maigret Has Scruples*, 128].
>
> He ensconced himself in his familiar world, got back into his habits, his slippers [*Maigret aux assises/Maigret in Court*, 62].

In some aspects of his domestic life the commissaire eventually makes concessions to "modernity," but only after a long resistance and then only partially. For years, Maigret resists buying an automobile, despite their affordability for a man with his salary and though they were by now commonplace in French society, before eventually purchasing a *quatre chevaux* for weekend trips to the countryside or the house at Meung-sur-Loire that the Maigrets are renovating as a retirement home, but it is Madame Maigret who is obliged to learn to drive (*Maigret et monsieur Charles*, 1972, 123). For years he also resists installing a television, the other great symbol of postwar capitalist consumerism, in the apartment, only giving way in *Le client du samedi* (1962, 498); but the novelty does not last long and the Maigrets rapidly become highly selective in their viewing. At a time when French eating habits were beginning to change (Ardagh, 1988, 389), Maigret continues to enjoy the traditional slowly simmered *plats mijotés*, cooked by Madame Maigret who, unlike most Frenchwomen of the period, having neither children nor employment, has time to prepare such dishes.

If Maigret's lifestyle changes are few during the postwar economic expansion, then his attitudes change equally little. He remains uncomfortable and unsure of himself in the presence of the aristocracy, although he respects them in an almost reverential fashion: "All their attitudes, their remarks, their reactions were unfamiliar to him, and he tried in vain to classify them.

He wanted to like them.... He discovered, in their way of life, a grace, a harmony, a certain innocence too which appealed to him" (*Maigret et les vieillards/Maigret in Society*, 779).

Maigret feels equally ill at ease with the very highest echelons of the bourgeoisie (*Maigret et la grande perche*, 1951, *Maigret hésite*, 1968) but he feels no such respect for them; rather he detests their arrogance and condescension, a dislike that goes back to his pre–Great War dealings with the Gendreau-Balthazar family in *La Première Enquête de Maigret* (1949). He distrusts politicians: although Auguste Point, the government minister of *Maigret chez le ministre* (1954), is himself an honest man (and, perhaps significantly, from the conservative heartland of the Vendée), the bourgeois democracy of the Fourth Republic is seen as a dirty business, symbolized by the ambitious and corrupt *député* Mascoulin. In this, Maigret's view seems to reflect that of his creator:

> In *Maigret chez le ministre* ... we discover the moral that can be drawn throughout the whole of Simenon's writings concerning political activity.... An honest man cannot engage in a political career without risking the worst. The lesson is a hard one and it is probably for this reason that the minister and the commissaire "had the same heavy sad look, the same hunching of their shoulders" [Gallot, 1999, 211, cited in Baronian et al., 2004–2007, "Le film dans le texte," 49].

Maigret's traditionalism is partly realized through his nationalism, which generally takes the form of an intense pride in his Frenchness. He is glad to return from the United States in *Maigret à New York* (1947) and his observation of the coroner's court in Tucson in *Maigret chez le coroner* (1949) suggests that he believes France has little to learn from the American legal system. His final sustained dealings with the New World, in the form of American organized crime, come in *Maigret, Lognon et les gangsters* (1952). These criminals are better organized and more ruthless than in the milieu of Pigalle with which he had dealt in *Maigret*, but Maigret is on his own territory and a good part of his irritation stems from the fact that the American gangsters behave "as if the fact that the police knew their identity, as well as their activities, was a matter of complete indifference to them" (*Maigret, Lognon et les gangsters/Maigret and the Gangsters*, 127). In the end, it is the Frenchman, Maigret, who triumphs and, national pride satisfied, he reflects with satisfaction in the final lines of the book: "Well, anyway, he'd shown them.... Precisely!" [168].

This pride in his roots in the French provincial heartland often leads Maigret to nostalgic reflection, to the extent of still dreaming of the Comtesse de Saint-Fiacre (*Maigret et les vieillards*, 110) as she was during his childhood over forty years before. His visit to a country primary school (*Maigret à l'école*, 1954) brings back memories of his own school days in Saint-Fiacre. However, as the years go by, many of Maigret's memories are tarnished. Chabot, a friend from university days, is revealed as a weak, vacillating mediocrity (*Maigret a peur*, 1953); he discovers that the Saint-Fiacre chateau has been sold to the son of the village butcher, Fumal, whom he had known and disliked at primary school, now a vulgar businessman (*Un Échec de Maigret*, 1956); and his lycée friend, Valentin, whom he had admired and envied, reappears in *L'Ami d'enfance de Maigret* (1968) as a shallow confidence-trickster and blackmailer.

Above all, throughout the Presses de la Cité novels, Maigret reveals the same essentially ambiguous combination of social conservatism (everyone has their right and proper place in life and society, which they should not attempt to change) and humanism (all people are equal and those at the bottom of the class ladder should not be abused by those at the top). As a result of his job, Maigret comes into contact with all social classes, and in *Maigret voyage* (1958) his professional philosophy is outlined in a manner that reveals his underlying view of humanity:

> "A policeman—the ideal policeman—ought to feel at home in any surroundings." Maigret had said this one day, and all his life he had striven to forget the surface differences between men, to scrape away the varnish and discover the naked human being under the various appearances [*Maigret voyage*/*Maigret and the Millionaires*, 142].

In *Maigret et la grande perche* (1951) he seems to take pleasure in his alliance with the ex-prostitute burglar's wife, Ernestine, in scraping away the varnish of the haut bourgeois Serre family to reveal their greed. In *Maigret se trompe* (1953) his instinctive sympathies are with Louise Filon and her boyfriend, a penniless musician, rather than the renowned surgeon Gouin and his wife. At times, his humanism combined with his own humble origins causes him to question his professional role:

> It was curious that this drama should have begun at Saint-Fiacre, the tiny village in the Allier where Ferdinand Fumal and he had both been born. Maigret had come into the world at the château, or rather in a house on the estate, of which his father was bailiff. Fumal had been born in a butcher's shop.... As for Victor, he had been born in a wooden hut and his father used to eat crows and carrion. Was that what gave the Superintendent the impression that he understood them. Did he really want the man-hunt to succeed and the ex-poacher to go to the scaffold? [*Un Échec de Maigret*/*Maigret's Failure*, 148].

The same humanism, and the same wish to understand, is equally extended to those at the very top of the class system, the aristocracy:

> He felt that the solution was within reach, and tried to guess what it was, not so much in his capacity as a chief-inspector of the Judicial Police whose duty

it was to identify a criminal and get a confession out of him, as in his capacity as a human being. For it was as a human being that he had conducted this case, as if it had been a personal matter, so much so that in spite of himself he had brought childhood memories into it.... If he hadn't a very high opinion of men and their capabilities, he went on believing in man himself [*Maigret et les vieillards/Maigret in Society*, 778–779].

Perspectives

Wenger ("Maigret of the month: *La Première Enquête de Maigret*") suggests that "more and more, as the years go by, Maigret has the same responses to and feelings about life as Simenon." In this section I will evaluate this comment in relation to the role of social class and social change in the postwar Maigret texts and consider whether the author's and character's views realize or diverge from the reality of postwar France. In order to do this, I will make use of Asselain's division (1984, 105) of the period in which the Presses de la Cité Maigret stories were published into three phases, namely postwar reconstruction from 1945 to 1950, the beginnings of sustained but uneven development and expansion from 1950 to 1958, and the continually accelerating economic growth and attendant social change from 1958 to 1973.

Simenon's vision of provincial and Parisian society in the immediate postwar period is summarized by the social settings of *Les Vacances de Maigret* (1948) and *Maigret en meublé* (1951). In the former, the *notables* of Les Sables-d'Olonne who gather in the Brasserie du Remblai represent a provincial bourgeois social milieu that has not changed significantly from that of the Hôtel de l'Amiral clique in *Le Chien jaune* (1931). There is a doctor, a shipowner, a police inspector, a real estate agent, a builder, a retired magistrate, a shipbuilder and the deputy mayor (*Les Vacances de Maigret/No vacation for Maigret*, 30). Economically and socially, this group is as representative of the Third Republic as of the Fourth. The microcosm of Parisian *petites gens* that Maigret encounters in Mademoiselle Clément's *pension* in *Maigret en meublé* also shows little change from the petit bourgeois milieus portrayed in the 1930s stories: Monsieur Valentin, a former "light opera singer" who "gives singing lessons" (32); Mademoiselle Blanche, "a dramatic artiste," who receives male "visitors" (34); Mademoiselle Isabelle, "a typist in an office in the Rue Montmartre" (36); Oscar Fachin, "a student" (35). Nevertheless, the other residents realize, in different ways, the realities of postwar Paris: the Yugoslav Monsieur Kridelka, a displaced former lawyer, now working as a nursing assistant in a mental hospital (38); Monsieur Saft, a Polish chemist, working as a druggist's assistant, unable with his pregnant wife to find accommodation (38–39); the Lotards, with their baby, arrived in Paris from the provinces and unable to find an apartment (34). Mademoiselle Clément is herself very aware of the postwar housing crisis in Paris:

> When a couple come to see me, I know in advance what they're going to say, that it's only temporary, that they will soon be finding a flat. The Lotards have been waiting for one for three years. The Safts hope to move before the baby comes [39].

The housing shortage, caused in large part by the lack of any major new building projects in Paris in the first half of the twentieth century, resulted in a certain "freezing" of the social geography of the capital in the immediate postwar years. The association of particular areas of the city with particular social classes, which underlies many of the settings of the Fayard novels and the Gallimard short stories, continued to hold good, in general, in the late 1940s and early 1950s. Blanc (1991, 176) suggests that:

> For Simenon, the city is socially divided into zones, and this division imposes itself on the characters. The series of Parisian Maigrets is quite well-known and rich enough to show the whole range of correspondences between the social position of the characters and their urban space.

For Modenesi (1996): "In the commssaire's view, there is a necessary correspondence between the area, and therefore the street, where a particular character lives and his social status."

The use of the geography of Paris as a symbol of the opposition between social classes is a frequent theme in the early Presses de la Cité novels. In *Maigret et la grande perche* (1951), the haut bourgeois dentist Serre lives in Neuilly, while the burglar Jussiaume and his wife, *la grande perche*, have two rooms by the canal Saint-Martin on the Quai de Jemmapes, and the Serres' cleaner lives in the then working-class place de Puteaux. In *Maigret se trompe* (1953), the luxurious apartment building of Docteur Gouin on avenue Carnot is contrasted with the poverty of the La Chapelle and Barbès-Rochechouart districts from which his murdered mistress, Louise Filon, and her boyfriend, Pierrot, hail and where the latter still lives.

If the Maigret novels of the immediate postwar period can be subjected to the same charges as those of the 1930s—that is, having a focus on a France that was disappearing and an inadequate realization of the dynamic forces that were driving social change—they nevertheless continue to be rooted in a version of contemporary reality, albeit a very particular and partial vision of French society. As economic expansion accelerated and forced a speeding up of social change, this connection between the fiction of the Maigret stories and the reality of their social context would come under increasing strain.

The key text in which Maigret and Simenon are forced to engage with the economic and social changes in 1950s France is *Maigret a peur*, written

5. What Maigret Did Next

The central Paris wholesale market in 1933 (Les Halles). If the Maigret novels of the immediate postwar period focus on a France that was disappearing and are an inadequate realization of the dynamic forces that were driving social change, they nevertheless continue to be rooted in a version of contemporary reality. (Courtesy Bibliothèque nationale de France.)

in Lakeville, Connecticut, in March 1953. Maigret is returning from an international police conference in Bordeaux and decides to visit a friend from university days, Julien Chabot, the *juge d'instruction* in Fontenay-le-Comte in the Vendée. Chabot is mystified by a series of murders that have been committed using the same weapon but with victims from completely different backgrounds. One is an old aristocrat, Robert de Courçon, the second a retired midwife, the third a local drunkard. The suspicion of the local population is directed at members of de Courçon's own extended family. Although he has no official brief, Maigret helps Chabot and the local police to solve the case, discovering in the process the impact of contemporary economic developments on the *notables* in a small rural town and the deepening conflict between the ruling class on the one side and an increasingly organized and politicized working class and their allies on the other.

Maigret learns from Chabot that the traditional aristocratic landowners have been progressively ruined and displaced:

The central Paris wholesale market in 1969 (Rungis). As economic expansion accelerated and as this forced a speeding up of social change, this connection between the Maigret stories and the reality of their social context would come under increasing strain. (Courtesy Agence Roger-Viollet.)

> For a long time the only people who counted were the owners of châteaux, counts, viscounts, anyone who had a "de" to his name, who lived amongst themselves and formed a closed society. They still exist, almost all impoverished, and they hardly matter any longer.... Now, others have taken their place [*Maigret a peur/Maigret Afraid*, 32].

The "others" are exemplified by Hubert Vernoux, the murdered de Courçon's brother-in-law, son of a livestock trader. In conversation with Maigret, Chabot continues:

> "In the last years of his life, the father started buying farms and land as well as cattle and it was that business that Hubert continued.... He has his offices near the station."
> "He married a nobleman's daughter?"
> "In one way, yes.... She was a Courçon...."
> "I suppose that, at the time of the marriage, the Courçon's had descended the scale again and found themselves without money?"
> "Pretty well" [32–33].

Just as economic and social change had ruined the aristocracy, so the rural parvenus who have supplanted them also find themselves increasingly marginalized in a French economy increasingly based on modern capitalist industry. As Chabot explains:

> Hubert Vernoux, for example, is in fact, I would swear, a man overwhelmed with worries. He has been very rich. He is less so now, and I even wonder if he still is at all, because, since the majority of farmers have bought their own properties, the trade in land is no longer what it used to be [34].

Chabot's impression is confirmed by Louise Sabati, the mistress of Vernoux's son Alain:

> I too, at one time, used to have notions about people who are supposed to be rich. It's all on the outside! A large house with nothing indoors. They're always squabbling to squeeze a bit of money out of the old man and the tradesmen sometimes wait months to get paid [78].

Despite their financial difficulties, the gentry, represented in one form or another by Vernoux and de Courçon, maintain their hold on political power in a small provincial town like Fontenay, "a town of eight thousand inhabitants" (20). Their waning economic strength is still sufficient for them to form a bloc with the other local *notables* to exercise social power on a day-to-day basis:

> The smaller of the two groups, the one standing near the corpse, appeared to be composed only of men who knew each other, who belonged to a particular set: the judge, the two doctors, the men who, doubtless, had just been playing bridge with Doctor Jussieux, all of whom were probably local worthies [25].
>
> Chabot and Doctor Vernoux, who had heard, looked at each other, still with that air of belonging to the same set, of knowing each other so well that words are no longer necessary.... Rarely had Maigret had such a strong sense of a clique. In a little town like this there are, of course, the local worthies, few in number, who, through force of circumstances, meet each other, if only in the street, several times a day [27].

However, this group finds itself under threat from two quite distinct angles. On the one hand, "modern" capitalism threatens the rural-based economy from which the provincial ruling class drew its strength. As has been demonstrated, from the 1920s onwards, surplus value and income were supplanting property and inheritance as the source of economic and social power within the ruling class. The same "modernism" was also evident within the professional layers who exercised this power on behalf of the ruling class. Chabot's father had been *juge d'instruction* in Fontenay before him (17), but Chabot himself, tied to a declining class, seems impotent and outdated in comparison with the *procureur*, "a man barely thirty years old, hardly out of college" (62), who has little patience with the vanities and susceptibilities of the provincial *notables* (112) and who personifies the accelerating modernity of postwar French capitalism.

On the other side, the Fontenay ruling class is threatened by an increasingly militant and organized working class which forms street patrols in the wake of the murders and which is not afraid to show "a kind of hostility" (25) to the powers that be. The growing class consciousness and politicization of the Fontenay working class is embodied in Emile Chalus, a primary school teacher and left-wing militant, who engages in open class confrontation with Chabot when he attends the Palais de Justice for questioning:

> The hostility between the two men was palpable. Chalus was tense, too, and his manner of replying aggressive. He seemed to be challenging the magistrate to destroy his evidence....
>
> Maigret, who was watching him with interest, felt pretty certain that he took part in politics, belonged to a left-wing party, and was probably what is called militantly so. He was the kind of man to march in processions, to speak at meetings, the kind of man, also, to slip pamphlets in letterboxes and refuse to move on, in spite of injunctions from the police [54].

When Chabot suggests that Chalus is giving evidence because he believes it will compromise the Vernoux family, the latter makes it clear that what interests him are not individual personalities, but the struggle between social classes:

> "And I suppose you were delighted with the effect you were going to produce? You hate the Vernouxs?"
> "Them, and all like them" [57].

The narrator remarks that the tension between the classes has almost reached breaking point: "Perhaps at that moment, a word uttered by someone in the crowd, a shout, a gesture would have sufficed to make popular fury assert itself" (104). Further, when Chabot eventually decides to arrest Alain Vernoux (who is not, incidentally, the murderer), it is not from any real conviction of his guilt, but because of his fear of a riot by the Fontenay working class:

> I'm afraid that as tonight comes on, there may be an incident which could have grave consequences. It needs only the smallest thing, a youngster throwing a stone at the windows, a drunkard starting to shout insults outside the house. In the present state of public feeling... [112].

Maigret finds himself at the center of this almost open class warfare, to which is added a series of personal conflicts and questionings on his part. On the one hand, he has an almost instinctive dislike of Hubert Vernoux and his pretensions (82) and he is disillusioned by what his old friend Chabot has become (42). He sympathizes with Alain Vernoux's working-class mistress, whose rough treatment by the police is in marked contrast to the deference afforded the Vernoux family by the authorities (108) and he recognizes that Chalus is basically an honest man (60). At the same time, he sees Alain Vernoux as a prisoner of his class position, a man trapped by a situation he has not created (47). As elsewhere in the series, Maigret seems to view himself as rising above the conflicting class forces and behaving in a manner that he believes to be both humane and professional.

Yet the reader's overwhelming impression is that Maigret feels he is aging and that the author is describing a social milieu that is reaching the point of decrepitude. At the police conference he has just attended, Maigret feels old and outdated (7). Chabot, whom Maigret had once so admired, has become a provincial mediocrity (15, 117). The rural gentry, the bedrock of the society in which Maigret had grown up and to which he remains emotionally attached, but which is now represented by the likes of Hubert Vernoux, is in decline, both economically and morally. On the other hand, the *petites gens*, for whom Maigret has always declared his sympathy, offer no compensation or solution. He concedes that "the masses have an instinct" (130); but while the workers of Fontenay are capable of organizing and mobilizing to pursue their class enemies in the Vernoux family, Louise Sabati's neighbors are so blinded by their own class prejudice that they do not lift a finger to intervene to help her and feel that she has received her just deserts for sleeping with a member of the ruling class (109).

The society that Maigret encounters in *Maigret a peur* is one that fills him with foreboding. Although at the end of the novel when he returns home, his wife is able to offer comfort at a personal level—"Madame Maigret was tidying the room, as she always did before going to bed" (157)—the inescapable message of the novel seems to be that the commissaire has found himself in a society that is changing beyond recognition or return.

If *Maigret a peur* shows the disappointment of Maigret in his former university friend Chabot, an awareness of irreversible social change and a recognition by the author that the sociopolitical perspective outlined in his 1930s journalism has been lost, then this point is reinforced by *Un Échec de Maigret* (1956). In *L'Affaire Saint-Fiacre* (1932), Maigret is disappointed by his discovery that the countess de Saint-Fiacre, whom he had idolized as a boy, has been unable to live up to his childhood image of her. However, the novel ends on a positive note for Maigret with the implication that her son,

Maurice de Saint-Fiacre, may be able to restore the family fortunes and assume the kind of leadership role in society that Maigret and his creator seem to expect from the landed aristocracy. In *Un Échec de Maigret*, the commissaire discovers that the chateau has been sold; not only has it left the sphere of the aristocracy but it has been bought by Ferdinand Fumal, the son of the village butcher and a boyhood contemporary of Maigret (although definitely not a friend), who has become a highly successful capitalist, a wholesale meat seller. For Maigret, the loss of the chateau from the Saint-Fiacre family represents more than a simple property transaction. Rather, it is a symbol of the death of a social system to which he has always been sentimentally attached, just as for his creator the economic and social changes in 1950s France indicated the definitive defeat of Simenon's social worldview as expressed explicitly in his 1930s journalism and implicitly through his fiction.

The subsequent Presses de la Cité Maigret novels, of which there are a twenty-six, or a third of the total corpus, seem increasingly disconnected from contemporary French society. The class composition of the protagonists and the settings of the narratives are increasingly marginal to France's developing reality. On the one hand, this may be because the economic and social change of the 1950s not only continued but accelerated; on the other hand, it could be that Simenon felt that he had less and less in common with, and no sympathy at all for, the "new France" and therefore little desire to place its society at the center of his novels.

Maigret et les témoins récalcitrants (1959) is, in the phrase used by Wenger, "set under the sign of decrepitude" ("Maigret of the month: *Maigret et les témoins récalcitrants*"). The Lachaume house is old, of another age, but the mentality of the Lachaume family also dates from another time. Maigret, too, feels strongly his age in a way that he had not done in the Fayard novels such as *L'Ecluse numéro 1* (1933) and *Maigret* (1934), where he was on the brink of retirement in the former and actually retired in the latter. In *Maigret et les témoins récalcitrants* his childhood memories seem very far from his present life, he feels old in relation to his collaborators and to the new generation of magistrates represented by juge Angelot. By little touches, Simenon makes us feel Maigret's (and perhaps his own) nostalgia for the past and his disapproval of and reluctance in recognizing the present. The stove that Maigret finds at the Lachaume's house reminds him of his old office stove which has finally been removed; the new Parisian buses have no platform, so Maigret cannot smoke his pipe while traveling; Madame Maigret makes him wear a woolen scarf whereas in the past he had simply turned up his collar against the cold.

Maigret et les vieillards (1960) is set in an aristocratic milieu which, while it may serve to trigger Maigret's memories of the Saint-Fiacre estate, is increasingly irrelevant economically socially and morally to the contemporary France of industrial expansion, the Common Market, skyscraper construction and nuclear weapons. The time of composition of the novel was parallel to the autobiographical *Quand j'étais vieux*, although the latter was not published until 1970, and it is interesting to find many similar themes and reflections in the author's personal memoir and his fictional creation.

The issue is not that the author is unaware of social changes or that "modernism" in its day-to-day forms does not appear in the later narratives. It is more that contemporary French society is increasingly incidental to the novels, somewhat akin to a stage prop, part of a physical "staging" rather than integral to the development of narrative, character and themes. This can be seen strongly in the final Maigret novel, *Maigret et monsieur Charles* (1972) in which Maigret investigates the disappearance of a wealthy solicitor, Sabin-Levesque, who had been leading a double life as "monsieur Charles."

References to modernity are scattered throughout the book. The former stables at Sabin-Levesque's home on the boulevard Saint-Germain have been converted into garages (24); the Champs Elysées is full of automobiles (44) and there are traffic jams elsewhere in Paris (125); new HLM blocks are being constructed (126); and Maigret even falls asleep in front of the television (128). However, although these details help to situate the novel in contemporary Paris, the central characters seem to belong to an earlier age and the issues of social class which lie at the center of the plot essentially reflect the attitudes of a bygone period. Sabin-Levesque's professional activities involve him not with company law relating to the contemporary French economy but rather with the economic past. He has in large part inherited his clientele from his father (22) and, as his chief clerk explains to Maigret:

> He spent most of the day in his office and he saw nearly all the clients personally. He never gave the impression of being a busy man and yet he worked harder than I did.... Especially at anything which concerned the handling of private fortunes or buying and selling country houses and estates.... He had an appointment here more than a week ago with one of our clients, one of the largest, if not the largest landowner in France [35–37].

Sabin-Levesque's chauffeur reinforces the point in a later conversation with Maigret: "Sometimes we drove as far as fifty, or even a hundred kilometres out of Paris. Many of Monsieur's clients are very old and don't come into town any more. Some of them live in beautiful châteaux" (75).

Not only has Sabin-Levesque inherited his clientele from his father, he has also inherited a considerable family fortune. The salon is full of portraits of illustrious ancestors (111) and the apartment as a whole has "an atmosphere of wealth, the grand families of the last century" (31). The decor of the apart-

Road traffic in Paris, 1962. References to modernity are scattered throughout the final Maigret novel, *Maigret et monsieur Charles*: the Champs Elysées is full of automobiles and there are traffic jams elsewhere in Paris. (Courtesy Agence Roger-Viollet.)

Road traffic in Paris, 1929. However, the central characters seem to belong to an earlier age and the issues of social class which lie at the center of the plot essentially reflect the attitudes of a bygone period. (Courtesy Bibliothèque nationale de France.)

ment is sumptuous but old-fashioned: the salon has Louis-Philippe period furniture (25) and the decor of the solicitor's office is in Empire style (35). Although the library has thousands of books, these are "mostly old ones, with very few modern works" (34). The narrator twice refers to the home as a museum (31, 33) and Maigret has the impression that he has stepped back into the past:

> Maigret felt as though he had stumbled on a different world, a decayed world, turned in upon itself.
> They must have given balls and soirées here in the last century or the beginning of this one....
> The panelling which covered the walls had grown dark with age.
> The pictures hanging everywhere, portraits of gentlemen with sidewhiskers and very high starched collars, also spoke of a bygone era.
> It was as though at a given moment time had stopped [32].

The household servants and the solicitor's employees are not quite as old as the furniture, but they have all been in place for many years (31, 37) and the chief clerk even refers to his employer as "Monsieur Gérard," in the manner of a faithful old family servant, reminiscent of the manner of speech of Grand-maison's chief cashier in *Le Port des brumes/Maigret and the Death of a Harbor-Master* in 1932 (156–159): "We all love Monsieur Gérard ... I call him that because I've known him almost since his student days.... Everyone who works for him admires him.... They don't presume to judge his private life" (*Maigret et monsieur Charles/Maigret and Monsieur Charles*, 37). Although Maigret is at first somewhat disoriented by the apartment on boulevard Saint-Germain, the backward-looking social attitudes strike a chord with him. As he prepares to investigate Sabin-Levesque's double life in the nightclubs of the Champs-Elysées, "He ... changed his clothes. Not that it mattered what he wore, but he belonged to a generation which had always changed into tails to go to the opera and into a dinner jacket for going out to a nightclub" (43).

When Maigret eventually solves the case, he discovers that Sabin-Levesque has been killed by his wife, who had herself once been a nightclub hostess. Having married a wealthy haut bourgeois solicitor, she found herself isolated, ignored by her father-in-law because of her social origins (32), considered an outsider by the staff (150) and neglected by her new husband, who wished to continue his nocturnal escapades with new young women who he could pick up in nightclubs (121). The price of her social ascent is solitude and an inexorable slide into alcoholism, culminating in murder, as she is unwilling to divorce her husband and give up the life of luxury to which she had aspired (150). As in the Fayard novels of almost forty years previously, the attempt by an individual to move from one social class to another brings personal disaster in its wake.

Conclusion

Social class remains as powerful a force in the final Maigret novel, as it had been in the 1930s narratives. Once again, as in many of the Fayard novels, it seems that the gap between classes is too great to be bridged and any attempts to cross class lines will potentially set off a train of events leading to catastrophe. I have contended in previous chapters that the interwar Maigret texts present a portrait of a society divided by social class which is rooted in contemporary reality, albeit as viewed through a *passéiste* prism, which is a function of the author's own class position and perspective. In the later narratives, while Maigret's own views on class society remain broadly unchanged, as do those of the author, the classes portrayed and the nature of class relations within that society become increasingly divorced from the predominant features of contemporary French reality; as the series continues, the sense of contemporary realism progressively diminishes.

CHAPTER 6
Conclusions

Introduction

In my introduction, I outlined the aim of this book, namely to consider the role of social class and social change in the Maigret writings of Georges Simenon, especially those from the 1930s. My objectives were twofold: firstly, to analyze the importance of social class and social change to the stories in relation to the development of narrative, character, settings and themes; secondly, to assess the extent to which the fictional universe of the Maigret novels and short stories is an accurate representation of French society in the period. In Chapters 1 to 3, I presented a detailed study of the Maigret novels published by Fayard from 1931 to 1934; in Chapter 4, I considered the Maigret short stories and Simenon's journalism of the mid– to late 1930s; in Chapter 5, I examined the postwar Maigret corpus published by Presses de la Cité. In the present chapter, I will synthesize the conclusions that can be drawn from the foregoing analyses.

In the course of his early formative inquiries Maigret comes into intimate contact with characters from a wide range of social classes and milieus. All the significant social strata of interwar France are encountered: the aristocracy (*L'Affaire Saint-Fiacre*); the haute bourgeoisie (*L'Ombre chinoise, Le Port des brumes*, "La Vieille Dame de Bayeux"); the moyenne bourgeoisie (*Le Chien jaune, La Guingette à deux sous*); the petite bourgeoisie (*Monsieur Gallet décédé, Chez les Flamands*); what can be described as a plebeian popular layer, financially poor but not proletarian in the classical Marxist sense of wage-workers wholly separated from the means of production and the product of their labor power (*Le Chien jaune, Le Port des brumes, Le Charretier de la Providence, Au Rendez-vous des Terres-Neuvas*); the peasantry (more hinted at than actually penetrated in *L'Affaire Saint-Fiacre* and "Les

Larmes de bougie"); the proletariat, working in industry as either blue- or white-collar workers (*Chez les Flamands*); and what can best be characterized as déclassé elements, such as the criminal milieus encountered in *Pietr-le-Letton* and *Maigret* or those who have made a conscious decision to abandon their class origins, such as William Brown in *Liberty Bar*.

As I have shown above, the social and physical settings of the narratives act as more than "stage props" or local color. Rather, it is the conflict between classes, or within a class, and the relationship of each social layer to the society as a whole, and to changes within that society, which form the characters, drive the narrative and give an overall sense to each story. Maigret's interactions with the individuals he encounters and the treatment of the characters in the narratives also give us an insight into the attitudes of the commissaire and, I would argue, the novelist to the various social classes making up French society in the 1930s.

Maigret, Simenon and Social Class: A Petit Bourgeois Policeman, a Petit Bourgeois Author

The portrait Simenon paints of the haute bourgeoisie, whose wealth is inherited, is generally unflattering. Characters such as Grandmaison (*Le Port des brumes*), the mayor of Concarneau (*Le Chien jaune*), Belloir (*Le Pendu de Saint-Pholien*), Monsieur Delfosse (*La Danseuse du Gai Moulin*) and Deligeard ("La Vieille Dame de Bayeux") are revealed as self-assured, condescending and capable of duplicity or even criminality in the maintenance of their position. Secondary characters such as Couchet's in-laws (*L'Ombre chinoise*) and Ducrau's son-in-law (*L'Ecluse numéro I*) receive a similar treatment. The exception to this rule is Maigret's relationship to, and Simenon's presentation of, wealthy, self-made men. Couchet and Ducrau have an income derived from their business activities that places them in the highest social bracket, but they have started from humble origins. Maigret feels great sympathy for Couchet and Ducrau, but the author highlights the fact that their social ascent has not necessarily made them happy and that they are not accepted by the social class they have joined.

The moyenne bourgeoisie is often associated with the provincial *notables* (as in *Le Chien jaune* and *Le Fou de Bergerac*), generally members of the liberal professions or *rentiers*. Again the portrait is an unflattering one of a layer that is complacent, inward-looking and reliant on its social influence in a small-town setting. The nouvelle petite bourgeoisie fares scarcely better. The picture is often one of mediocrity (for example, Gallet in *Monsieur*

Gallet décédé, Martin in *L'Ombre chinoise*, Michonnet in *La Nuit du carrefour*) or driving ambition linked to a lack of moral scruples (for example, Mesdames Gallet and Martin). In contrast, the petite bourgeoisie traditionnelle is presented more favorably: Maigret is drawn to the values and lifestyle of the Peeters family in *Chez les Flamands* and he sympathizes with Anna Peeters despite his growing awareness that she has committed murder.

The aristocracy is represented by the emblematic Saint-Fiacre family (*L'Affaire Saint-Fiacre*): Sir Walter Lampson (*Le Charretier de la Providence*) and Andersen (*La Nuit du carrefour*) being defined more by their "foreignness" than by their social class. For Maigret, the Saint-Fiacres are more than a family—they represent the past (tradition and honor in the memories of the count), the present (hard times, economically and morally, in the character of the countess) and the future (rising above difficulties to promise renewal, in the person of Maurice) of the landed nobility.

The *petites gens*, plebeian but not proletarian, are viewed most sympathetically of all of the social classes by Maigret and, by implication, Simenon. Essentially they are passive characters in a social sense, with little control over their destiny. Emma and Léon (*Le Chien jaune*), Julie and Louis (*Le Port des brumes*) and Cécile ("La Vieille Dame de Bayeux") all achieve social advancement, but they do so through a combination of hard work, modesty and the benevolent intervention of Maigret and/or members of the ruling class. None of them is, properly speaking, ambitious and each represents, in some way, a state of innocence which is contrasted to the worldly corruption of the members of the haute and moyenne bourgeoisie with whom they come into conflict (the Concarneau *notables*, Grandmaison and Deligeard respectively).

The proletariat, in contrast, on the rare occasions when it appears, is presented unfavorably. The Piedboeuf family of *Chez les Flamands* is contrasted at every stage with the petit bourgeois Peeters family. The Piedboeufs are inclined to live for the short term, spending what money they have, engaging in promiscuity, living in squalor, while the Peeters are sober, hardworking, clean folk who attend Mass every Sunday. The world of the peasantry is perceived as backward-looking and often brutal ("Les Larmes de bougie") when it is removed from the "civilizing" influence of a stable aristocratic order.

Finally, there are the déclassés. By definition, this is a heterogeneous grouping, as it cannot be defined by a determined relation to the means of production. Maigret's essential criterion in his relations with the déclassé elements whom he encounters seems to be whether they pose a threat to the existing social order and its stability. Thus, characters like William Brown and Jaja (*Liberty Bar*), Jean (*Le Charretier de la Providence*), Nine, Adèle and Fernande (the mistresses and/or prostitutes in *L'Ombre chinoise*, *La*

Danseuse du Gai Moulin and *Maigret*) are all treated with indulgence, whereas the professional criminal milieu (*Pietr-le-Letton*, *Maigret*), the voluntary déclassés of the youthful *Compagnons de l'Apocalypse* (*Le Pendu de Saint-Pholien*) and the destabilizing influence of another Adèle (*Au Rendez-Vous des Terre-Neuvas*) are all frowned upon.

The attitudes to social class of Maigret and his creator can be understood in terms of their own class position in the sense outlined by Dubois (in Gothot-Mersche et al., 1980, 20):

> The class position of an individual is evidently a function of the class he or she belongs to but the two should not be confused. The class position of an individual consists in the manner in which this individual perceives, understands and lives his situation in society. Or even in the way in which he gives a sense to his personal life story as a function of class relationships.

Despite their incomes and social position, which place them within the moyenne bourgeoisie and haute bourgeoisie respectively, Maigret and implicitly Simenon consistently adopt a petit bourgeois class position in their relation to society. Although, as a commissaire of the Police Judiciaire, Maigret has effectively entered the moyenne bourgeoisie, and as a high-ranking police officer he has an important role in defending the existing state of class relations, his worldview is also marked by his origins as the son of the estate manager for the Saint-Fiacre family.

> Forever attached to the social layer from which he had come, Jules Maigret would always be more touched by the distress of the humble than by that of the rich. He was a man of the French heartland, a world of peasants and even nobles disturbed and even frightened by progress and modernism [Assouline, 1997, 93].

Simenon was to explain in later life when talking about his childhood:

> We were poor. But not really poor, not right at the bottom of the social ladder.... Right at the bottom were the factory workers ... next up came the craftsmen.... We were on the next rung up, the third. My father was a salaried employee.... Nowadays we would say "white-collar" [1981, 11].

The son of a hat-maker, Simenon's father was an accountant in an insurance company. The author's mother, the daughter of a timber merchant, was first a salesgirl in a large department store then, after her marriage, a housewife, letting out rooms to foreign students. Yet through hard work and ambition, the latter perhaps imbued in him by his mother's attitudes, Simenon rose from the artisan work of pulp fiction production, manufacturing a product, paid by the line (1981, 107), to the status of a successful businessman. Assouline comments that by 1931:

> People who had been in contact with Simenon during his nearly ten years in Paris noticed a change in his behavior. The man of letters was now a busi-

nessman too, formidable manager of his own affairs ... attending to the smallest details personally [1997, 103].

Yet, despite the great commercial success of the Maigret novels, Simenon's view of his work remained that of the *small* businessman. His involvement with the filming of three of the Fayard Maigret stories (*La Nuit du carrefour*, *Le Chien jaune* and *La Tête d'un homme*) led to frustration on his part:

> Individualistic novelist and solitary creator that he was, he was uncomfortable with the collective efforts and industrial procedures inevitably involved in film making. The ponderous chain of production annoyed him. Too many people had something to say about how the film came out. He was horrified by the sums of money and numbers of people involved and disoriented by a human and economic organisation whose functioning eluded him [Assouline, 1997, 108].

Although in the 1930s Simenon's finances and lifestyle were becoming those of a haut bourgeois, his own working methods and attitudes to production remained those of the hundreds of thousands of small French businessmen who felt themselves increasingly threatened by the advances of the big industrial monopolies and the modern working practices based on Taylorism and Fordism that were progressively arriving in France from the United States. And, like the millions of French petit bourgeois readers of the Maigret novels, Simenon feared the changes driven by historical forces beyond the control of the individual that were taking place in society. Many years later Simenon would assert, "You would look in vain through my 220 odd novels to find any traces of ideology" (1977, 54). However, this misunderstands the nature of ideology. Ideology is not reducible to a series of consciously considered and articulated thoughts about the world—rather, it is the way in which we see the world, the parameters of our thinking, which cannot be divorced from our life experience. And the ideological worldview of the Maigret novels bears a strong resemblance to Simenon's own experience.

Petit bourgeois ideology in the interwar period was founded in the growing marginality of this class, particularly in its traditional form, in relation to the two dominant classes, the bourgeoisie and the proletariat. Increasingly peripheral to the economy and society, disunited internally, fearful of its future existence, the petite bourgeoisie found itself torn between a defense of the extant capitalist society against the perceived threat of socialism and a desire to turn the clock back to a time when it felt that its position in society was more assured. For the petite bourgeoisie the key danger lay in change and instability. From one side, it felt threatened by the rising working class; on the other side it saw danger in the ongoing development of capitalism which constantly pushed it to the sidelines and reinforced the dominance of the most modern forms of monopoly capital.

Unable to exercise influence through its economic weight, which was in decline, the petite bourgeoisie sought to present itself as a mediator between the conflicting class forces: if it did not form part of either of the two main contending classes, it could portray itself as somehow rising above the fundamental class division and class struggle between capital and labor which characterized twentieth-century capitalist society. This is the sense in which Dubois describes "Maigret's Utopia" as "a social-democratic project" (1992, 188):

> He [Simenon] recognizes his own petit-bourgeois origins which he shares with his hero the commissaire. Through the latter, the petite bourgeoisie is assigned the semi-historical semi-utopian role of class conciliation or, better still, arbitration. The middle class is presented as the mediator of class conflicts: it promotes interaction and compromise but, knowing that in the final analysis there will be no significant changes, it favors above all class collaboration in place of exclusion and pretension [187–188].

Petit bourgeois ideology in the age of monopoly capitalism must seek to reconcile two distinct logical patterns. On the one hand, the petit bourgeois craves stability, therefore the existing order must be defended; on the other hand, there is a longing for a bygone period, in which the petite bourgeoisie imagines that its status was more central to society and hence more assured. This tension is closely reflected in Maigret's material situation as a high functionary of the existing bourgeois state apparatus and his ideological longing for a past order. As Bertrand (1994, 84) describes it:

> In this sense, Maigret's inquiries attempt to balance two conflicting logics: while society requires him to maintain the existing order, which is based on false premises ... the commissaire does his utmost to work towards a *restoration*, in itself utopian, of a paradise lost. And the conflicts within the narrative with the judicial, political or social hierarchies ... have their origin in this inevitable division between the logic of society, based on values of evolution, technique and movement, and Maigret's own logic, based on his nostalgia for unity, stability and the integration of all.

Unity, stability and integration are at the center of Maigret's ideological worldview. Unity is symbolized by the marriage of Jules and Louise Maigret and the calm, ordered atmosphere of the apartment on the boulevard Richard Lenoir. Although in the Fayard novels, Madame Maigret plays a minor part, Simenon will later endow her with a past in *Les Mémoires de Maigret* (1951, Chapter 4) which is fully consonant with her cameo roles in the 1930s texts. The daughter of an engineer in the Ponts-et-Chaussées branch of the civil service, she marries a police functionary who broadly shares her cultural background and class perspective, although his own origins are more modest. Despite numerous temptations, for example from Else in *La Nuit du carrefour* and Fernande in *Maigret*, the commissaire remains resolutely faithful to his marriage vows.

Stability is represented by Maigret's adherence to the notion of traditional values and his respect for France's past, in particular the landed aristocracy. The notion of "place" is central to the 1930s Maigret stories. Each person has an ordained position in society from which he or she can depart only at the risk of unleashing social disorder and personal disaster: the crossing of class lines, whether it be the ascent of a Couchet (*L'Ombre chinoise*) or Ducrau (*L'Ecluse numéro 1*), the descent of Jean, the *Charretier de la Providence*, or the inter-class dalliances of Captain Fallut with Adèle, in *Au Rendez-Vous des Terre-Neuvas*, carries risks. What is implicit in the Fayard stories will later be made explicit in Maigret's explanation that he became a policeman because:

> I felt dimly that too many people were not in their right places, that they were striving to play parts that were beyond their capacities, so that the game was lost for them before they started [*Les Mémoires de Maigret/Maigret's Memoirs*, 36–37].

Finally, the petit bourgeois ideology of Simenon's Maigret lauds integration insofar as while every person has his or her "place" in society, the powerful must not abuse their position (hence the disapproval of many haut bourgeois and even moyen bourgeois characters) and society must allow for individual social promotions on the basis of merit rather than disproportionate ambition. Hence, the ascent of Evariste Maigret to estate steward at Saint-Fiacre and Maigret's own rise to commissaire are justified on the basis of individual merit; the upward social mobility of Léon and Emma (*Le Chien jaune*), Julie and Louis Legrand (*Le Port des brumes*) and the lady's maid Cécile ("La Vieille Dame de Bayeux") promote integration without threatening stability; and the actions of Anna Peeters can be excused by Maigret on the grounds of her personal qualities.

At the same time, threats to social stability must be dealt with firmly, whether these come from members of the privileged classes abusing their power (*Le Chien jaune*, *Le Port des brumes*), overreaching ambition (*L'Ombre chinoise*, *L'Affaire Saint-Fiacre*), the criminal milieu (*Maigret*) or the vague menace posed by rootless cosmopolitans, foreigners and Jews (*Pietr-le-Letton*, *La Tête d'un homme*, *Le Fou de Bergerac*). Yet the petit bourgeois ideology of Maigret is in no way fascist. As Dubois (in Gothot-Mersche et al., 1980, 41) points out:

> In Simenon's heroes we do not find the resentment of his contemporary Céline. Neither do we find the fascist longing to re-establish order, to seize power, to violently purify society. There is none of this.

Rather, Maigret's ideology is a curious mixture of the desire for order and tradition of what would become Pétainism—*Travail, Famille, Patrie* (Work, Family, Fatherland) would in fact be a rather good motto for the commissaire—and the vacuous pronouncements of social democracy in favor of "fairness" while at the same time supporting the very capitalist system that creates and perpetuates inequality.

As subsequent historical developments would show, the petite bourgeoisie was a class in decline in the interwar period. The major political movements which sought to use petit bourgeois despair as a battering ram against the working class, such as Fascism and German National Socialism, would in their day-to-day economic policy promote the interests of national monopoly capitalism rather than small manufacturing and commerce; the perspective outlined by Simenon in his 1934 reports, *Inventaire de la France*, would lose rather than gain ground as the class whose interests it advanced became progressively enfeebled throughout the author's life. The British historian Richard Vinen in his introduction to the 2003 English-language translation of *Le Fou de Bergerac* recounts a story that seems to sum up the dead end of Maigret's ideological position:

> On 16 July 1942 walking along the rue de Turenne [the historian Annie Kriegel] saw a column of shabbily dressed people being led by a policeman. The policeman was carrying two suitcases, presumably belonging to people too frail to carry their own, and he was in tears. This sight probably saved Kriegel's life because it warned her that the deportation of Paris Jews had begun.... The crying policeman's combination of anguished sympathy for individual victims and unquestioning acceptance of authority will seem uncomfortably familiar to many admirers of Simenon's work [Vinen, 2003, b, xii].

Maigret, Simenon and Social Change: The Rejection of History

Maigret's creator is often reproached for his alleged failure to provide a historical backdrop to his fiction, and I have identified the question of History, in the sense of a process of social change existing independently of the sum total of the personal life "histories" of individuals, as one of my central areas of inquiry. The charge rests essentially on two foundations: firstly, the absence of references in the fiction to actual events taking place in the real world and secondly Simenon's own explicit comments about History.

It is certainly true that there is virtually no mention in the 1930s Maigret stories of the tumultuous events taking place in contemporary Europe: the rise of German National Socialism, the rise and fall of the Popular Front in

France and the Spanish civil war. Equally, there are few references back to the Great War or the Russian Revolution. However, it would be a mistake to assume that the absence of explicit historical references automatically implies the absence of History from a work of fiction. As Kettle (1977, 93) observes: "It is the silliest of criticism to blame Austen for not writing about the Battle of Waterloo or the French Revolution." Although these momentous historical events may not occupy a central place in Austen's novels, they nevertheless are crucial to the setting: if it were not for the Napoleonic Wars why otherwise would there be so many eligible young officers moving around the garrison towns of southern England? Moreover, Eagleton (1976, 126) argues convincingly that Austen's work "offers a peculiarly privileged focus for examining the conflicts and alliances between the aristocracy and the bourgeoisie in the early nineteenth century." How else can the relations between Darcy and Elizabeth be understood without taking into account the need for a historical compromise between their respective classes in the face of the threat posed by the French Revolution and rising popular discontent, which would culminate in the Saint Peter's Fields riots and massacre in 1817? A similar point could be made about the 1930s Maigret novels and short stories: both Austen and Simenon were, in their own way and like all authors, writing for contemporary readers who would be familiar with current events and would not therefore need them to be explicitly referenced as a means of providing a historical context.

I have contended that Simenon's narratives are often driven by questions of social class, and a close examination of the texts shows that the conflicts between and within classes, which frame and structure the stories, are often consequent upon the real historical changes taking place in interwar French society. It is difficult to fully grasp the situations, actions and motivations of the cases and characters Maigret investigates without recognizing their concrete historical setting in an era of rapid social change. The problems of the house of Saint-Fiacre are the result of France's drawn-out transformation from a rural, agriculture-based economy to an urban, industrial model which had begun in the nineteenth century and gathered pace in the years immediately before and after the 1914–1918 war. The rise of nouveau riche characters from humble origins, such as Couchet (*L'Ombre chinoise*) and Ducrau (*L'Ecluse numéro 1*), is partly explicable by the postwar boom and is partly the result of changes within French capitalism as a consequence of the transformations brought about by the introduction of new developments such as the horizontal and vertical integration of business (Ducrau) and production-line techniques (Couchet). At the same time, certain traditional sectors of the French haute bourgeoisie, such as Couchet's in-laws, faced decline as a result of their failure to embrace modernity. The provincial moyenne bourgeoisie and the petite bourgeoisie found themselves increasingly marginalized by the shifting balance between small towns and the major urban centers and the ever greater concentration of economic activity into larger units. They responded either by a desperate struggle to maintain their status (the *notables* of *Le Chien jaune*, Mesdames Gallet and Martin in *Monsieur Gallet décédé* and *L'Ombre chinoise* respectively) or the descent into mediocrity and apathy (Messieurs Gallet and Martin). New technologies such as the motor vehicle (*La Nuit du carrefour*) and the telephone (*Maigret*) were beginning to change the organization of economic activity, including that of professional criminals. Finally, the economic change of the 1920s was accompanied by major movements of population as France's postwar reconstruction and economic boom pulled in workers from other countries (*La Tête d'un homme*).

Clearly, social change is at the center of the 1930 Maigret texts, even if these are not explicitly linked to historical events with which the reader might be familiar. Yet Simenon himself, in a 1938 speech, went on record to deny what his fiction seemed to imply: "I raised my spirits by persuading myself that people do not live History with a capital *H*, but their own histories" (cited in Assouline, 1997, 169); and he was to restate this position on numerous occasions throughout his life:

> History is an everyday thing and the importance of events becomes clear only after the fact. One cannot live with History, or rather, one cannot live History. One lives one's own little life, or that of a group, of an instant of humanity, an instant in the life of the world [*Quand j'étais vieux*, 1970, 43].

In a sense, Simenon's words are a truism. The historical significance of events is only fully appreciated after the event: "The owl of Minerva spreads its wings only with the falling of the dusk," as Hegel puts it so memorably in his *Philosophy of Right* (1967, 13). Yet an understanding of the society in which we live and its development can only come through attempting to engage with History, in the sense of recognizing and participating in historical change, not by its denial. This is the essence of Marx's third thesis on Feuerbach: "The coincidence of the changing of circumstances and of human activity or self-change can be conceived and rationally understood only as *revolutionary practice*" (1977, 156, emphasis in original). The point is not to criticize Maigret and Simenon for the character of their political views, which were hardly likely to be revolutionary, but rather to demonstrate that Simenon's aversion to political activity (Assouline, 1997, 169–173) and his unwillingness to engage with the process of History in fact undermines his ability to understand the world.

Maigret's worldview, like Simenon's, looks backwards, not forwards, to an illusion of what Assouline describes as "an old Europe of indestructible, immanent values ... peopled with craftsmen, peasants and nobles ... a world resolutely hostile to progress and the machine age, to industrial society and technology" (1997, 167). The characters to whom the commissaire is most sympathetic in his inquiries often have a similar perspective. In *L'Ecluse numéro 1*, Ducrau, who at times appears to act as a kind of alter ego to Maigret, contemplates regaining happiness by abandoning his business, his houses, his money, his family—in short everything that ties him to his bourgeois life—and starting again as a simple bargeman, as he had begun his working life. Addressing his former colleague and subsequent employee Gassin, he proposes:

> Tomorrow you'll go off on the *Golden Fleece*. Then one fine day, when you least expect it, you'll hear someone hailing you from a tug. And it'll be me in a boiler suit. The chaps won't understand it at all. They'll think I've crashed. But that's not it. The truth is that I'm sick of dragging all this about after me [*L'Ecluse numéro 1/The Lock at Charenton*, 126].

Although Maigret's sympathy for the *petites gens* is genuine and although he attempts to confront some of the negative consequences of the class divisions of French capitalist society in the interwar period, he, like his creator, is shackled by his inability to recognize the inevitability of historical change or to understand that it is the process of social change ("History with a capital *H*") that creates the changing context in which "people live their own histories." The clock cannot be turned back at either a collective or an individual level.

In seeking to deny History, Simenon proclaims "his determination to write only stories—in the plural and not histories" (the original French plays on the two words *histoire*, a story, and *l'Histoire*, history) (Dumortier, 1985, 57) and in this he seeks to stake a claim for the universality of his fiction:

> So, people don't change. I think Neanderthal man would find himself in my work! People change on the surface, but very little deep down. I am particularly interested in people's fundamental passions, without looking for subtleties which vary according to country and custom [cited in Tauxe, 1983, 166].

Many of Simenon's admirers have seen this claim to universality, this *recherche de l'homme nu* as a strength of the author. De Fallois (1971, 72, 74) goes so far as to say that in this respect Simenon stands above such writers as Balzac and Zola:

> "What is a duchess?" Balzac seems to wonder. And Zola, what is a worker? But for Simenon the tramp and the managing director are almost interchangeable.... Most novelists try to explain man by his shell, but Simenon starts by removing the shell.

However, I have demonstrated in the foregoing chapters that the characters of the 1930s Maigret texts are in fact defined by their social class and that the action of the stories flows logically from the given historical conjuncture. Lukács (1972, 6, 10–13) sees the greatness of Balzac, Scott and Tolstoy in their ability to represent through their fiction the underlying social structure and forces of social change; the strength of Simenon's achievement is in the degree to which he is able to perform a similar feat for interwar France. Where Simenon differs from Balzac, as the latter is seen by Lukács, is in his response when the development of situations and characters he has created comes into conflict with his own convictions. Whereas Lukács argues that Balzac is able to "set aside his own prejudices and convictions and describe what he really sees, not what he would prefer to see" (11), Simenon is unable to do this consistently. The "discrepancy between intention and performance" (21) is with Simenon at times resolved by the emergence of the author's own worldview, which conflicts with the social reality he is describing. If, as Lukács contends, Balzac is able to lay bare the class structure of early nineteenth-century France *despite* his Legitimist political perspective, Simenon's petit bourgeois ideology acts on occasion as a brake on his ability to perform a similar function consistently throughout the Maigret saga.

The attempt to escape from History and seek refuge in universality sets up a contradictory logic in the Maigret series. Simenon articulates through Maigret a yearning for the stability and order of the Ancien Régime lightly seasoned with the conciliatory "fairness" of social democracy in which the petite bourgeoisie acts as a mediator and arbitrator between conflicting social classes. Such a society would rest on a "natural order," with the aristocracy at the summit, the artisans and peasantry accepting their place in the social hierarchy (with advancement strictly based on personal merit and hard work), and the petite bourgeoisie policing the whole, metaphorically in the case of Maigret's father, the estate steward, esteemed by the Comte de Saint-Fiacre and respected by the peasants, literally in the case of Maigret himself, seeking to extirpate the forces of disorder and decadence which threaten social stability.

However, closer examination demonstrates the untenability of this perspective. The denial of History and the notion of a "natural order" rest on a myth and a contradiction. The myth is of the Garden of Eden before the fall, a prelapsarian state of innocence, yet this requires a religious belief to which neither Maigret nor Simenon ascribe. The contradiction is in the identification of the "natural order" with a specific historically determined form of social organization. According to Dubois, "In refusing to accept, as he [Simenon] does, the dynamic of History and its transformations, he ends by conceiving of each *story* as a variation on an original theme, on a configuration of primary meanings" (1980, 13). But why should the world of Maigret's childhood on the Saint-Fiacre estate be any more "natural" than any other social system? Clearly, it does not represent an "original" order but is itself the product of historical development; therefore the identification of a particular social system with the "natural order" must suggest an implicit recognition of History combined with a belief that at some point an optimum of moral development has been reached while material social development has continued. Stripped of Maigret's and Simenon's proclaimed sympathy for *les petites gens* there remains a rationale for political reaction. In Fabre's words (1981, 77):

> It is beyond doubt that Simenon's biological humanism leads to the most conservative solution.... The Natural Order, always put forward by those in power, on account of its refusal of History, ideologically and practically, finds itself, despite its claims to high principle, limited to criticisms of concrete problems and the benevolent acceptance of "justice."

The denial of History often goes along with a denial of "Theory" or "Method." Maigret repeatedly claims that he has no particular method. This is plainly untrue: Maigret may have no explicitly formulated theories of social behavior—in this he typifies the empiricism of the petite bourgeoisie, which is underpinned by an unstated ideological worldview—but he does have a recognizable, consistent approach to his cases. Briefly, the Maigret method consists of soaking up the atmosphere of the environment within which the crime has been committed, progressively penetrating the social milieu in order to understand the psychology of the characters and applying pressure by his simple presence until the criminal reveals him- or herself. Alavoine (1999, 32) describes this method as "the phase of impregnation ... the phase of investigation and hypotheses ... the phase of resolution."

But the denial of historical change is itself a feature of History. As we have seen, the interwar period saw massive changes in French society; it was a time of transition from the classical capitalism of the prewar epoch to modern monopoly capitalism, which threatened small manufacturing and commerce with extinction. It was also a period of revolutionary change: the Russian Revolution and the emergence of communist parties throughout the world changed the political landscape. In France the labor union movement doubled its membership between 1918 and 1920 (Braudel and Labrousse, 1979–1980, 924), although it did not continue this growth. Even though the French Communist Party's membership fell from a high of 120,000 in 1921 to half of that figure by 1925 (Agulhon et al., 1993, 61) it nevertheless represented a highly visible opposition to the existing political model of the Third Republic. The resurgence of the organized workers movement in the 1936 strikes and factory occupations and the rise of the Popular Front would change the French political landscape permanently.

Squeezed between these two developments, the petite bourgeoisie endured a time of considerable instability. Economically threatened from "above" by the emerging monopoly capitalist businesses and fearing "descent" into the working class, the petite bourgeoisie was in a state of almost permanent disequilibrium. Hence the attraction of an author who spoke to their desire for a settled order and a character, Maigret, who identified with them and with whom they could identify. With his popular origins and his sympathy for the *petites gens*, yet having at the same time succeeded in rising to the rank of commissaire, Maigret was the perfect hero figure for millions of French readers, appearing to offer both a defensive shield for the petite bourgeoisie as a whole and a way forward for deserving individuals.

Herein lies one of the keys to understanding the success of the Fayard Maigret series. On the one hand, there is great realism in their description of a range of social class milieus in the contemporary society. On the other hand, there is an ideological orientation that meshes intimately with the situation and concerns of the contemporary readership of the texts.

Une Certaine Idée de la France: *Social Imagination and Social Reality*

This meshing of the fictional world of the Maigret texts and the ideological worldview of their readership can be more clearly understood if we consider the notion of the social imagination. Fiction whose intentions are realist is a source of information as to how a concrete historical conjuncture is lived in real time by its author and, if the literature meets with publishing success, by a wide readership. In this way, fiction is as much a valid historical source material as any other form of contemporary historical document, and later readers are permitted an insight into how a particular moment of economic, social and political reality is perceived by people at the time. If the aim of history as an intellectual discipline is to reconstruct a past reality, then a knowledge and understanding of how particular social groups responded to fictional representations of that reality is of great importance to the historian. At the same time, a knowledge and understanding of the economic, social and political context in which the fiction was created is essential for an informed analysis of literary production. These two approaches come together in the confrontation of the literary representation of a society with the reality of the contemporary socioeconomic landscape.

In his *Mémoires de la Guerre* (1954), Simenon's contemporary Charles de Gaulle famously described his *certaine idée de la France*:

6. Conclusions

> Throughout my whole life, I have held a certain idea of France, inspired as much by feeling as by reason. My sentimental side naturally imagines France, like the princess in a fairy tale or the Madonna in a fresco, as being intended for a special and distinguished destiny. ... If it should happen that her acts and gestures are marred by mediocrity, then it seems to me that this is an absurd anomaly, due to the mistakes of the French people and not the spirit of the motherland.... In short, in my opinion, France cannot be France without greatness.

I showed earlier that the Maigret texts of the 1930s also, in their own way, represent "a certain idea of France." Just as de Gaulle's notion is informed by his class position as the son of a wealthy and devout Lille haut bourgeois family, molded by his rise through the military hierarchy from the prestigious Saint-Cyr academy, Simenon's idea of France is the realization in literature of his petit bourgeois class position and its relation to the material situation facing the petite bourgeoisie in interwar France, a vision which is counterposed to the twin realities of monopoly capitalism and communism by which the petite bourgeoisie was threatened. For Maigret and, implicitly, Simenon, this ideal, and idealized, France must be patterned after a France of the past if it is to command the strength to unite the aristocracy, the petite bourgeoisie and the *petites gens* against the twin threats of the monopoly capitalists' and communists' visions of a France remade in the image of either the United States or the Soviet Union. As the 1960 preface to a Russian-language edition of Simenon's writings puts it:

> Simenon is the most troubling witness of the years from 1930 to 1940, the witness of the so-called middle class, one of whose characteristics was its penury. In reality, this class lived in *fear* of penury [cited in Lacassin and Sigaux, 1973].

The representation of interwar France in the petit bourgeois social imagination is as notable for what it omits as much as what it includes. In rejecting the practices of the classes which threaten his idea of France, Simenon marginalizes the representatives of these classes in his fiction. Hence the almost complete absence of those classes representing modernity: industrialists in the expanding industrial sectors, senior managers and civil servants, factory workers. When wage workers occupy center stage, they are almost invariably drawn from the maritime or river and canal transport sectors, that is, those workers whose conditions of employment and social lives corresponded least to the modern industrial worker. Small provincial towns are often selected as settings and the importance of heavy industry to Paris and Liège (in the Belgian-set Fayard novels, *Le Pendu de Saint-Pholien* and *La Danseuse du Gai Moulin*) is almost completely obscured. If France's economy and society in the period between the wars were characterized by a combination of progress and stagnation, Maigret's world offers only one side of the picture.

Only one side perhaps, but what a picture! The strength of Simenon's characterization and the force of his description of place and social milieu are such that his "certain idea of France" has succeeded in becoming part of the wider social imagination and has entered into the collective consciousness. According to Dubois (in Gothot-Mersche et al., 1980, 14):

> [Simenon's work] takes up and reinforces social stereotypes, confirming our ready-made ideas of a provincial town, a brothel, a minor civil servant, a barge on a rainy northern canal. In the end, we are no longer too sure if the clichés predate Simenon or if he is their creator.

The affective success of Simenon's writing is such that some readers and critics prefer the "stereotypical" Paris of Maigret, which, as I have suggested, becomes increasingly divorced from reality as the years go by, to the historically more accurate, and therefore "dated," in the precise sense of the term, portrait of Paris by Léo Malet in his Nestor Burma series.

> Therefore, Maigret and Simenon's Paris is a perfectly identifiable universe to the reader thanks to the "truthfulness" of the observation.... In this Simenon's Paris differs from Léo Malet's Paris in the *Nouveaux Mystères de Paris*: as Alfu argues, the Paris in which Nestor Burma operates is in the first place more limited geographically, but it is above all very dated: it is essentially the ambiance of the 1950s which we find immortalised in the *Nouveaux Mystères de Paris*. By little touches Malet evokes situations, ways and customs which are no longer current [Alavoine, 1999, 51].

In short, through the effectiveness of Simenon's writing, he succeeds in taking the world of Maigret beyond the limits of a purely descriptive realism into a deeper level of the social imagination, in which a literary output that is the product itself of a prevailing ideology becomes part of the succeeding ideology. In a certain sense, Dumortier is correct when he comments:

> We touch here on one of the limits of the corpus, which contributes to the author's originality and also the timelessness of his success. Lacking a firm historical anchoring point, Simenon's novels fade but do not age [1985, 57].

I have, on the contrary, shown that the 1930s Maigret texts have a very clear "anchoring point." The Fayard novels and the Gallimard short stories present a society that is very clearly identifiable in its moment and retrospectively as interwar France, an economy and a society that is in the process of transition, an economy and a society that despite its prevailing "classical" capitalist nature still contains elements of pre-capitalist production alongside elements of emerging "modern" monopoly capitalism. This is clearly realized in *La Nuit du carrefour*, with its juxtaposition of the various worlds. The setting is rural, with descriptions of peasants rising early to milk cows and harvest crops using horses and carts; but it is also a world of automobiles and trucks passing the crossroads transporting commodities. Road transport and motor vehicles were bringing formerly rural areas such as Arpajon and Arainville into the greater Paris conurbation, just as the railroads had transformed Argenteuil and similar areas in the 1870s from the rural idyll of Monet's paintings to industrial suburbs of Paris. In *L'Affaire Saint-Fiacre* the rural world of *La France profonde* is beginning to be opened to the modern world, but rests on the margins of economic and social development. In *L'Ecluse numéro 1*, a man who started his working life leading horses along the canal towpath has become head of a modern integrated capitalist freight transport business.

Simenon's project is rooted in the realist approach. The characters and settings are ones which readers can identify from their own lives; indeed, Simenon later insisted that they were people and places he himself had encountered, and there is no reason to doubt his account:

> I wanted to live ... not just for myself ... but because I understood that only one's own true experiences can be communicated to others by the intermediary of literature. I had to experience the world in every possible way, horizontally and vertically ... move in different social circles [lecture given in New York, 1945, in Simenon, 1988, 51–52].
>
> I am an echo, a sort of echo of life. I am happy to be compared to a sponge. I absorb life, you press on me, and novels come out [cited in Tauxe, 1983, 103].

Just as the raw materials for the Maigret texts are drawn from real life, so the technical approaches deployed by their creator are drawn from the canon of literary realism. Although references to events in the contemporary world are few in the 1930s novels and short stories, Simenon draws on a range of realist literary techniques. The Fayard and Gallimard narratives are strewn with references to real streets, restaurants, bars, markets and landmarks, described in such a way as to enable the reader to feel that he/she is reading an authentic account of a police investigation:

> In the realist text ... the recognizable detail makes the whole believable, the identifiable object makes the total picture authentic [Klinkenberg, 1980, in Gothot-Mersche et al., 130–131].
>
> You see that the story is believable, since the name of this *place* or that hotel is truthful [Blanc, 1991, 29].

Although the Maigret stories have a third-person narrator, Simenon employs a range of techniques, including heavy use of the impersonal pronoun *on* and a deliberately "non-literary" lexis and syntax, to draw the reader into an effect of reality.

> The distance between the author, the narrator, Maigret and the reader is tightly compressed: the narrator merges into Maigret and the reader follows the latter like a shadow ... the narrator is a reflection of the author and the distinction between the former and Maigret is blurred, finally the latter becomes one with the reader. Can we not see in the fusion of these four figures one of the reasons for the fascination that Simenon exercises over his readers, for his prodigious success and his ability to create atmosphere? After erasing his own presence as author and that of the narrator, having reduced Maigret to a "medium," all distance between the reader and the text is eliminated, one absorbs the other [Michel and Laurent, 1992, 29].

The opening of *La Tête d'un homme* is a classic example of this technique: the third person singular impersonal pronoun *on* is used repeatedly in the description of Heurtin's escape from prison, but to whom does it refer? Geoffrey Sainsbury's English translation (*A Battle of Nerves*) mostly uses the third person plural pronoun, "they," to translate *on*; but this is only one possible translation: the French *on* is an impersonal pronoun, which can just as easily mean "we," "you" or "one," or be used to give a passive sense to the verb. If the narrator is speaking, his repeated use of *on* conveys the impression that he must be present at Maigret's side and that we are also drawn into the collective *on* as witnesses to the escape rather than as distanced readers of a fictional account, as in the following extract where *on* is used no less than thirteen times in less than two pages.

> Le groupe était à moins de cinquante mètres du prisonnier invisible, dans un renfoncement, près d'une porte où il était écrit *Economat*.... Mais on entendait à intervalles réguliers le grésillement de sa [=Maigret] pipe. On devinait son [=Maigret] regard.... On ne pouvait distinguer le prisonnier, qui évitait les endroits éclairés. Mais quelque soin qu'il prît de ne pas faire du bruit, on l'entendait aller et venir, on le suivait en quelque sorte dans ses moindres démarches.... On n'avait pas entendu un soupir. On l'avait deviné. Et on devinait, on sentait la hâte fébrile de celui qui venait enfin de buter contre le paquet de vêtements et d'apercevoir la corde.... On distingua une tache plus claire le long du mur: le visage du 11, qui se hissait à la force des poignets. Ce fût long! Dix fois, vingt fois plus long qu'on l'avait prévu. Et quand il arriva au sommet, on put croire qu'il abandonnait la partie, car il ne bougeait plus. On le voyait maintenant, en ombre chinoise, aplati sur le couronnement [*La Tête d'un homme*, 125–126].

This realistic methodology continues in the postwar period with *Les Mémoires de Maigret* (1951), a unique piece of writing in which Maigret takes the place of Simenon to recount his career and his relations with his creator, not only "correcting" Simenon's narratives to give the "real" story but also offering his opinions of the author. *Les Mémoires de Maigret* are full of little touches intended to give a retrospective realistic feel to the series so far and to anticipate the coming stories which Simenon intended to write.

6. Conclusions

Maigret begins by insisting, "I have no memory for dates" (*Les Mémoires de Maigret/ Maigret's Memoirs*, 13), but he nevertheless deliberately dates his first meeting with Simenon to the period immediately preceding the composition of the first Fayard novels—"It was in 1927 or 1928"—thereby establishing the realistic tenor of the narratives as well as their historical setting. The biographical reality of the Fayard novels is deepened by a more extended account of Maigret's childhood and adolescence, his marriage to Madame Maigret and his early career (Chapters 3, 4, 5) and the purported authenticity of the police procedures in the novels is supported by Maigret's references to Simenon's visits to the Palais de Justice in the late 1920s (Chapters 1 and 2). The reality effect is further strengthened by the (fictional) Maigret's allusions to real criminal cases such as those of Mestorino, Bonnot, Landru and Sarret (Chapter 2) and to real senior police officers such as Guillaume and Guichard (Chapter 7). Finally, there is a developing intertextuality in the series. Characters and events are cross-referenced between narratives, giving the impression of authenticity and realism: for example the Fontenay *juge d'instruction* Julien Chabot, who is a central character in *Maigret a peur* (1953), is telephoned by Maigret when he needs information on the Vendéen politician Auguste Point in *Maigret chez le ministre* (1954).

Simenon's intentions are realist but, as I have noted earlier, the representation of French society in the 1930s texts is selective and incomplete. Nevertheless, this need not completely undermine the realistic status of the series. The principal function of a realist novelist is not to give a precise statistical reflection of the demography of the society he/she is describing, but to penetrate the social class structure of that society and to show how class relations and conflicts work their way out through the lives of his/her characters within a narrative. It would be normal that Simenon, with his urban petit bourgeois origins, had less familiarity with the lives of the urban working class and with rural life in general. It would be normal too that the author's petit bourgeois ideology would minimize the centrality of certain classes, such as "modern" monopoly capitalists and the industrial proletariat. Indeed, Pierre Macherey (cited in Eagleton, 1976, 34–35) argues that a work is tied to ideology not so much by what it says as by what it does not say. It is in the significant silences of a text, in its gaps and absences, that the presence of ideology can be most positively felt. Moreover, although the picture of French society is a partial one, the representation of the social universe throughout the series as a whole is sufficiently diverse to ensure that all significant social classes and fractions within classes are present to a certain extent at some point. Simenon's class position acts as a distorting mirror on his literary production, enlarging certain features, reducing others and showing the picture as a whole in a particular perspective: interwar French society is *refracted* rather than *reflected* in the Fayard and Gallimard Maigret stories, it is, in Eagleton's terms (1976, 51), r*eproduced* rather than *re*produced.

Moreover, Simenon's rejection of History results in a progressive distancing of the Maigret texts from contemporary social reality over the forty-one years of their publication. In the 1930s, the world of the Maigret stories is rooted in the author's acute sensibility to social class relations and the working out of the narratives flows from these same relations. However, in the absence of an understanding of the historical development of capitalism, the longevity and fecundity of production of Maigret novels is not matched by their development. By the time of the final Maigret novel, *Maigret et monsieur Charles* (1972), the reader may well feel that he/she is revisiting many of the same people and situations that were encountered at the very beginning of the saga in *Pietr-le-Letton* (1931). Although the settings of the later stories are updated to give a veneer of contemporary realism, the underpinning class structures remain those of the earlier texts. While it may be true, as suggested by Alavoine (1999, 29), that from the mid–1950s onwards the Maigret stories gain in psychological depth, they progressively move away from a sense of authenticity in their portrayal of social class relations. A frequent criticism of historical novels is that they often use a prevailing modern ideology to represent events and characters from a past time and that they consequently lack realism; in the case of the later Maigret novels, it is the reverse of this effect: events and characters from a superficially present time are realized through the ideology of a previous period, that is Simenon's and Maigret's interwar petit bourgeois worldview.

Social Class and Social Change: The Early Maigret Stories and the Development of Crime Fiction

Despite the reservations expressed above, the 1930s Maigret texts represent a significant step forward in crime fiction in terms of the portrayal and role of social class, especially in its lower ranges, and multilevel social change as a consistent subtext of the narratives. In the present context, an analysis of the relationship of the interwar Maigret writings to previous and subsequent crime fiction is inevitably rather sweeping. Nevertheless, a brief review of the question can help to signpost an evaluation of the extent to which Simenon's treatment is innovatory in the development of the genre. In pre–1914 crime fiction, from Samuel Warren's 1830s *Passages from the Diary of a Late Physician* (Worthington, 2005) and Poe's 1840s Dupin stories, the settings and characters are almost invariably drawn from the bourgeoisie and aristocracy. Even when the investigator is a policeman, as in William Russell's "Waters" stories in *Chambers' Magazine* of the 1850s, he is of genteel stock (Kayman, 2003, 42) and, while Gaboriau's Lecoq is a professional policeman of obscure class origins, the crimes he solves seem obsessively aristocratic in origin: as in English sensationalism, the conflict between bourgeoisie and aristocracy is played out in narrative terms.

This tendency continued in displaced form with the so-called classical detective stories of, among others, Agatha Christie, Dorothy Sayers and S.S. Van Dine, in Britain and America, and Pierre Véry, writing in French. The detective is still usually a nonprofessional, either an aristocrat, like Lord Peter Wimsey (Sayers); a wealthy bourgeois, such as Philo Vance (Van Dine); a *rentier* bourgeois like Hercule Poirot (Christie); or, in the case of Prosper Lepic (Véry), a well-to-do lawyer. The plots tend to be even further divorced from any real-world social setting than were the prewar stories, with the country house, or another *lieu clos* setting such as a train, a ship or an airplane, often providing the context in which the great detective can deploy his or her intellectual skills to resolve the puzzle of "who-dunnit?" Figures from outside the upper or middle classes tend to appear only in the form of servants or comic figures and there is no sense at all of the momentous changes taking place in the world. Mandel argues that this was in fact the very point of the "classical" detective stories:

> To reconcile the upset, bored and anxious member of the middle-class with the inevitability and permanence of bourgeois society. The subjective need to be filled by the classical detective story of the interwar years was that of nostalgia.... When the war ended and stability failed to return, the petty [*sic*] bourgeoisie, still essentially conservative, was consumed with nostalgia. The Republican administration in the United States, the Conservative Baldwin administration in Britain, Poincaré in France, Stresemann and Brüning in Germany, relied upon that sentiment politically. The classical detective story was its pendant in the field of "trivial" literature [1984, 29–30].

Simenon's work is remarkably innovative and independent. Though there is a 1920s English development of a petit bourgeois and mercantile focus, as in the work of Freeman Wills Crofts, it does not influence Simenon and is in any case of minor impact. And while I have argued that nostalgia is also a key feature of Maigret and Simenon's petit bourgeois ideology, there the similarity to the "classical" detective story ends. The crimes which Maigret investigates have social causes rather than being the actions of aberrant individuals: they are a necessary and inevitable part of the bourgeois society Simenon describes rather than a departure from normal behavior within a generally rational system. Maigret's ability to solve cases is based not on his superior intellect but on his ability to understand the different social milieus within which he moves. If order is restored at the end of a Maigret case, it is only in the most temporary of ways. The criminal is only "brought to justice" in five of the nineteen Fayard novels, the remaining inquiries ending in the madness or suicide of the guilty party or the matter being officially "unsolved." In two novels (*Monsieur Gallet décédé* and *L'Affaire Saint-Fiacre*) there is no crime in a legal sense. The reader is frequently left with the impression that any resolution is partial, as the social instability and class conflicts that lead to criminal actions remain.

In a sense, because they are inherently a social project, the interwar Maigret texts have more in common with the development of the style of crime fiction being pioneered by Dashiell Hammett in the United States. In Hammett's five novels and numerous short stories, social corruption, especially among the rich, is at the center of the narrative: crime is given a social context that is recognizably that of contemporary capitalist America, with the frantic struggle for wealth in the economic conditions of the postwar boom and the rise of organized crime in the wake of Prohibition. Yet for all of Hammett's sensitivity to social class and social change, his writings are somewhat limited in these respects in comparison to Simenon. Whereas Maigret investigates cases across a wide social spectrum, Hammett's investigators move in a narrower social circle. There are interesting insights into the conflict between "old wealth," represented by Senator Henry, and "new money," in the person of the political fixer Paul Madvig, in *The Glass Key* (1931); *Red Harvest* (1929) is underpinned by Hammett's own personal awareness, drawn from his experience as a Pinkerton agent, of the attempts by capital to smash organized labor; but overall the social vision is less comprehensive than that of Simenon. Although Simenon's portrayal of interwar France is a partial one and is distorted through the prism of the author's own petit bourgeois class position, it remains, nonetheless, more complete than Hammett's picture of American capitalist society in the same period.

Despite important differences, like Simenon, Léo Malet also locates his crime fiction in a class-divided social landscape. He attempts to survey a range of social settings of similar breadth to Simenon in his Nestor Burma series in the period following the Second World War. Burma makes his first appearance in *120, rue de la Gare* (1943) during the occupation of France, but it is with the *Nouveaux mystères de Paris* novels, published between 1954 and 1959, that he most fully explores the social class structure of 1950s Paris, with each of the fifteen novels set in a different *arrondissement*, each with its own social characteristics.

Crime fiction writers in other languages use the detective novel to present a similarly wide-ranging breakdown of class relations within their society. Among the most systematic are the Swedish authors Maj Sjöwall and Per Wahlöö in their ten-volume Martin Beck series (1965–1975), which presents an analysis of Swedish capitalist society under the hegemony of a social-democratic ideology. In 1967, Wahlöö defined their project as follows:

> The basic idea consists in a long novel of three thousand pages which cuts vertically through the structure of contemporary society. Criminality is to be studied as a function of society, its correlation with the material and moral reality of this society must be brought into the daylight [cited in Vanoncini, 2002, 111].

In *La donna della domenica* (1972) Carlo Fruttero and Franco Lucentini present a cross-section of Turin society, while Manuel Vasquez Montalban's Pepe Carvalho series (1972–2004) examines Barcelona from the period of transition from Francoism to the subsequent consolidation of bourgeois democracy. The Scottish author Ian Rankin uses his series of Rebus novels (1987–2007) to write what can be read as a social history of Scotland in the late twentieth century focused on questions of social class and social change. Among francophone writers, Jean-Claude Izzo's Fabio Montale trilogy performs a similar function for Marseille, and Didier Daeninckx builds on Simenon's awareness of social class to produce narratives in which crimes are the result of past (real) historical events. Class struggle, nationally and internationally, lies at the heart of novels such as *Meurtres pour mémoire* (1984), linking the deportation of French Jews in 1942, the massacre of Algerian demonstrators in Paris in 1961 and a murder committed in 1981, and *La Mort n'oublie personne* (1989), in which the memories of a retired industrial worker recounted to a young historian link wartime resistance and collaboration to the attacks on trade unionists and socialists in the postwar period. Not only does Daeninckx situate his stories by explicit reference to historical events with which his readers are familiar, but he insists on the importance of history to contemporary struggles for social change: "In forgetting the past, we condemn ourselves to relive it" (1984, Foreword).

The point is not to insist that all or any of these authors are necessarily directly influenced by Simenon's 1930s Maigret writings. Rather, it is to establish that the latter opened up a path in crime fiction that would be increasingly followed, particularly in France and mainland Europe, as the genre developed in the second half of the twentieth century. With all of their partiality and ideological limitations, the Fayard novels and Gallimard short stories involving Maigret stand at a crossroads in the development of crime fiction in their positioning of social class and social change as a central theme for many authors within the genre.

Bibliography

Primary sources

Simenon translations are listed with their French originals.

Simenon, Georges (as Georges Sim). (1928) *Les Cœurs perdus*. Paris: Tallendier.
_____ (as Christian Brulls). (1930) *Train de nuit*. Paris: Fayard.
_____ (1931). *Monsieur Gallet décédé*. Paris: Fayard. *Maigret Stonewalled*. (1963) (trans. Margaret Marshall). Harmondsworth: Penguin.
_____ (1931). *Le Pendu de Saint-Pholien*. Paris: Fayard. *Maigret and the Hundred Gibbets* (1963) (trans. Tony White). Harmondsworth: Penguin.
_____ (1931). *Pietr-le-Letton*. Paris: Fayard. *Maigret and the Enigmatic Lett* (1963) (trans. Daphne Woodward). Harmondsworth: Penguin.
_____ (1931). *Le Charretier de la Providence*. Paris: Fayard. *Maigret Meets a Milord* (1963) (trans. Robert Baldick). Harmondsworth: Penguin.
_____ (1931). *La Nuit du carrefour*. Paris: Fayard. *Maigret at the Crossroads* (1984) (trans. Robert Baldick). New York: Harvest/HBJ.
_____ (1931). *La Tête d'un homme*. Paris: Fayard. *A Battle of Nerves* (1950) (trans. Geoffrey Sainsbury). Harmondsworth: Penguin. Sainsbury's translation is "free" in the extreme, going as far as to change the name of one character from Crosby to Kirby!
_____ (1931). *Le Chien jaune*. Paris: Fayard. *The Yellow Dog* (2003) (trans. Linda Asher). London: Penguin.
_____ (1931). *Un Crime en Hollande*. Paris: Fayard. *Maigret in Holland* (1994) (trans. Geoffrey Sainsbury). Orlando, FL: Harvest.
_____ (1931). *Au Rendez-Vous des Terre-Neuvas*. Paris: Fayard. *The Sailors' Rendezvous* (1970) (trans. Margaret Ludwig). Harmondsworth: Penguin.
_____ (1931). *La Danseuse du Gai-Moulin*. Paris: Fayard. *Maigret at the Gai Moulin* (2003) (trans. Geoffrey Sainsbury). New York: Harcourt/Harvest.
_____ (as Christian Brulls). (1932). *La Figurante*. Paris: Fayard.
_____ (as Georges Sim). (1932). *La Maison de l'inquiétude*. Paris: Tallendier.
_____ (1932). *La Guingette à deux sous*. Paris: Fayard. *The Bar on the Seine* (2003) (trans. David Watson). London: Penguin.

_____ (1932). *L'Ombre chinoise*. Paris: Fayard. *Maigret Mystified* (1964) (trans. Jean Stewart). Harmondsworth: Penguin.

_____ (1932). *L'Affaire Saint-Fiacre*. Paris: Fayard. *Maigret Goes Home* (1967). (trans. Robert Baldick). Harmondsworth: Penguin.

_____ (1932). *Chez les Flamands*. Paris: Fayard. *Maigret and the Flemish Shop* (1990) (trans. Geoffrey Sainsbury). Orlando, FL: Harvest/HBJ.

_____ (1932). *Le Port des brumes*. Paris: Fayard. *Maigret and the Death of a Harbor-Master* (1989) (trans. Stuart Gilbert). Orlando, FL: Harvest/HBJ.

_____ (1932). *Le Fou de Bergerac*. Paris: Fayard. *The Madman of Bergerac* (2003) (trans. Geoffrey Sainsbury). Harmondsworth: Penguin.

_____ (1932). *Liberty Bar*. Paris: Fayard. *Maigret on the Riviera* (1989) (trans. Geoffrey Sainsbury). Orlando, FL: Harvest/HBJ.

_____ (1932). *Les 13 Coupables*. Paris: Fayard.

_____ (1932). *Les 13 Enigmes*. Paris: Fayard.

_____ (1932). *Les 13 Mystères*. Paris: Fayard.

_____ (1933). *L'Ecluse numéro 1*. Paris: Fayard. *The Lock at Charenton* (trans. Margaret Ludwig) in *Maigret Sits It Out* (1952). Harmondsworth: Penguin.

_____ (1934). *Maigret*. Paris: Fayard. *Maigret Returns* (trans. Margaret Ludwig) in *Maigret Sits It Out* (1952). Harmondsworth: Penguin.

_____ (1942). *Maigret Revient*. Paris: Gallimard/NRF.

_____ (1944). *Signé Picpus*. Paris: Gallimard/NRF.

_____ (1944). *Les Nouvelles Enquêtes de Maigret*. Paris: Gallimard/N.R.F. "Les Larmes de bougie"/"Death of a Woodlander"; "La Vieille Dame de Bayeux"/ "The Old Lady of Bayeux"; "La Fenêtre ouverte"/"The Open Window"; "Jeumont, 51 minutes d'arrêt"/"Jeumont, 51 Minutes' Stop" (trans. Jean Stewart), in *Maigret's Pipe* (1977). Harmondsworth: Penguin.

_____ (1945). *Je me souviens*. Paris: Presses de la Cité.

_____ (1947). *Maigret à New York*. Paris: Presses de la Cité. *Maigret in New York* (1979) (trans. Adrienne Foulke). London: Hamish Hamilton.

_____ (1947). *Maigret et l'inspecteur malchanceux*. Paris: Presses de la Cité. *Maigret and the Surly Inspector* (2003) (trans. Jean Stewart) in *Maigret's Christmas: Nine Stories*. New York: Harcourt/Harvest.

_____ (1948). *Pedigree*. Paris: Presses de la Cité.

_____ (1948). *Maigret et son mort*. Paris: Presses de la Cité. *Maigret's Special Murder* (1972) (trans. Jean Stewart) in *A Maigret Quartet*. London: Hamish Hamilton.

_____ (1948). *Les Vacances de Maigret*. Paris: Presses de la Cité. *No Vacation for Maigret* (1953) (trans. Geoffrey Sainsbury). New York: Doubleday.

_____ (1949). *La Première Enquête de Maigret*. Paris: Presses de la Cité. *Maigret's First Case* (1961) (trans. Robert Brain). Harmondsworth: Penguin.

_____ (1949). *Mon Ami Maigret*. Paris: Presses de la Cité. *My Friend Maigret* (2003) (trans. Nigel Ryan). Harmondsworth: Penguin.

_____ (1950). *Maigret et la vieille dame*. Paris: Presses de la Cité. *Maigret and the Old Lady* (1973) (trans. Robert Brain), in *The Second Maigret Omnibus*. London: Hamish Hamilton.

_____ (1951). *Les Mémoires de Maigret*. Paris: Presses de la Cité. *Maigret's Memoirs* (1978) (trans. Jean Stewart) in *Georges Simenon*. London: Heinemann/Octopus.

_____ (1951). *Maigret en meublé*. Paris: Presses de la Cité. *Maigret Takes a room* (1965) (trans. Robert Brain). Harmondsworth: Penguin.

_____ (1951). *Maigret et la grande perche*. Paris: Presses de la Cité. *Maigret and the Burglar's Wife* (2003) (trans. J. Maclaren-Ross). New York: Harcourt/Harvest.

_____ (1951). "Sept Petites Croix dans un carnet" in *Un Noël de Maigret*. Paris: Presses de la Cité.

_____ (1952). *Maigret, Lognon et les gangsters*. Paris: Presses de la Cité. *Maigret and the Gangsters* (1954) (trans. Louise Varèse). San Diego: HBJ.

_____ (1953). *Maigret a peur*. Paris: Presses de la Cité. *Maigret Afraid* (1965) (trans. Margaret Duff). Harmondsworth: Penguin.

_____ (1953). *Maigret se trompe*. Paris: Presses de la Cité. *Maigret's Mistake* (1988) (trans. Alan Hodge). New York: Harvest/HBJ.

_____ (1954). *Maigret à l'école*. Paris: Presses de la Cité. *Maigret Goes to School* (1992) (trans. Daphne Woodward). New York: Harvest/HBJ.

_____ (1954). *Maigret et la jeune morte*. Paris: Presses de la Cité. *Maigret and the Young Girl* (1973) (trans. Daphne Woodward) in *The Second Maigret Omnibus*. London: Hamish Hamilton.

_____ (1954). *Maigret chez le ministre*. Paris: Presses de la Cité. *Maigret and the Calame Report* (1996) (trans. Moura Budberg). New York: Harvest/HBJ.

_____ (1955). *Maigret et le corps sans tête*. Paris: Presses de la Cité. *Maigret and the Headless Corpse* (1985). (trans. Eileen Ellenbogen). New York: Harvest/HBJ.

_____ (1955). *Maigret tend un piège*. Paris: Presses de la Cité. *Maigret Sets a Trap* (2003) (trans. Daphne Woodward). New York: Harcourt/Harvest.

_____ (1956). *Un Échec de Maigret*. Paris: Presses de la Cité. *Maigret's Failure* (1962) (trans. Daphne Woodward). London: Hamish Hamilton.

_____ (1957). *Maigret s'amuse*. Paris: Presses de la Cité. *Maigret's Little Joke* (1973) (trans. Richard Brain) in *The Second Maigret Omnibus*. London: Hamish Hamilton.

_____ (1958). *Maigret voyage*. Paris: Presses de la Cité. *Maigret and the Millionaires* (trans. Jean Stewart) in *The Eleventh Simenon Omnibus* (1977). Harmondsworth: Penguin.

_____ (1958). *Les Scrupules de Maigret*. Paris: Presses de la Cité. *Maigret Has Scruples* (1988) (trans. Robert Eglesfield). Orlando, FL: Harvest/HBJ.

_____ (1959). *Maigret et les témoins récalcitrants*. Paris: Presses de la Cité. *Maigret and the Reluctant Witnesses* (1989) (trans. Daphne Woodward). New York: Harvest/HBJ.

_____ (1959). *Une Confidence de Maigret*. Paris: Presses de la Cité. *Maigret Has Doubts* (1971) (trans. Lyn Moir) in *The Third Simenon Omnibus*. Harmondsworth: Penguin.

_____ (1960). *Maigret aux assises*. Paris: Presses de la Cité. *Maigret in Court* (1965) (trans. Robert Brain). Harmondsworth: Penguin.

_____ (1960). *Maigret et les vieillards*. Paris: Presses de la Cité. *Maigret in Society* (1978) (trans. Robert Eglesfield) in *Georges Simenon*. London: Heinemann/Octopus.

_____ (1961). *Maigret et le voleur paresseux*. Paris: Presses de la Cité. *Maigret and the Lazy Burglar* (1994) (trans. Daphne Woodward) in *A Maigret Trio*. New York: Harvest/HBJ.

_____ (1962). *Maigret et le client du samedi*. Paris: Presses de la Cité. *Maigret and the Saturday Caller* (2003) (trans. Tony White). New York: Harcourt/Harvest.

_____ (1963). *La Colère de Maigret*. Paris: Presses de la Cité. *Maigret Loses His Temper* (2003) (trans. Robert Eglesfield). New York: Harcourt/Harvest.
_____ (1964). *Maigret et le fantôme*. Paris: Presses de la Cité. *Maigret and the Apparition* (2003) (trans. Eileen Ellenbogen). New York: Harcourt/Harvest.
_____ (1964). *Maigret se défend*. Paris: Presses de la Cité. *Maigret on the Defensive* (1987) (trans. Alastair Hamilton). New York: Avon Books.
_____ (1968). *Maigret à Vichy*. Paris: Presses de la Cité. *Maigret in Vichy* (1995) (trans. Eileen Ellenbogen). New York: Harvest/HBJ.
_____ (1968). *Maigret hésite*. Paris: Presses de la Cité. *Maigret Hesitates* (1993) (trans. Lyn Moir). New York: Harvest/HBJ.
_____ (1968). *L'Ami d'enfance de Maigret*. Paris: Presses de la Cité. *Maigret's Boyhood Friend* (2003) (trans. Eileen Ellenbogen). New York: Harcourt/Harvest.
_____ (1970). *Maigret et le marchand de vin*. Paris: Presses de la Cité. *Maigret and the Wine Merchant* (2003) (trans. Eileen Ellenbogen). New York: Harcourt/Harvest.
_____ (1970). *Quand j'étais vieux*. Paris: Presses de la Cité.
_____ (1971). *Maigret et l'homme tout seul*. Paris: Presses de la Cité. *Maigret and the Loner* (1975) (trans. Eileen Ellenbogen). London: Hamish Hamilton.
_____ (1972). *Maigret et monsieur Charles*. Paris: Presses de la Cité. *Maigret and Monsieur Charles* (1975) (trans. Marianne Sinclair). London: Hamlyn.
_____ (1975). *Un Homme comme un autre*. Paris: Presses de la Cité.
_____ (eds. Lacassin, F., and Sigaud, G.) (1976) *A la découverte de la France*. Paris: U.G.E. Editions 10/18.
_____ (1977). *Un Banc au soleil*. Paris: Presses de la Cité.
_____ (1978). *Vacances obligatoires*. Paris: Presses de la Cité.
_____ (1981). *Mémoires intimes*. Paris: Presses de la Cité.
_____ (1988). *L'Age du roman*. Brusells: Editions Complexe.
_____ (1998). *Police-Secours*. Paris: Mille et une nuits.

Secondary sources

Abbad, F. (1993). *La France des années 20*. Paris: Armand Colin.
Agulhon, M., A. Nouschi, and R. Schor (1993). *La France de 1914 à 1940*. Paris: Nathan.
Alavoine, B. (1999). *Les Enquêtes de Maigret de Georges Simenon. Lecture des textes*. Amiens: Encrage, Collection Références.
Allain, M., and P. Souvestre (1910–1914). *Fantômas, Tômes 1–3*. (2005). Paris: Robert Laffont.
Aplin, R. (1993). *A Dictionary of Contemporary France*. London: Hodder and Stoughton.
Ardagh, J. (1988). *France Today*. London: Penguin.
Asselain, J.-C. (1984). *Histoire économique de la France du XVIII siècle à nos jours. Tome 2: De 1919 à la fin des années 1970*. Paris: Editions du Seuil.
Assouline, P. (1997). *Simenon*. London: Chatto and Windus.
Baronian, J.-B., et al. (2004–2007). *Maigret: la Collection*. Paris: Hachette Collections.
Becker, J., and S. Berstein (1990). *Victoire et frustration, 1914–1929*. Paris: Editions du Seuil.
Bertrand, A. (1994). *Maigret*. Brussels: Editions Labor.

Blanc, J-N. (1991). *Polarville*. Lyons: Presses Universitaires de Lyon.
Bocquet, J-L. (1998). "Sentir les hommes," postface to the 1998 edition of Simenon, G., *Police-Secours*. Paris: Mille et une nuits.
Boileau, P., and T. Narcejac (1964). *Le Roman policier*. Paris: Payot.
Borne, D., and H. Dubief (1989). *La Crise des Années 30*. Paris: Editions du Seuil.
Boyer, R. (1973). *"Le Chien jaune" de Georges Simenon*. Paris: Collection Lire Aujourd'hui.
Braudel, F., and E. Labrousse (eds.) (1979–1980) *Histoire sociale et économique de la France, Tome IV, 1880–1950*. Paris: Quadrige/P.U.F.
_____ and _____ (eds.) (1982) *Histoire économique et sociale de la France, Tome IV, Troisième Volume, Années 1950 à nos jours*. Paris: P.U.F.
Bresler, F. (1983). *The Mystery of Georges Simenon*. London: Beaufort.
Bukharin, N. (1917). *Imperialism and World Economy*. New York: Monthly Review Press.
Carter, D. (2003). *Georges Simenon*. London: Macmillan.
Cobban, A. (1965). *A History of Modern France, Volume 3: 1871–1962*. Harmondsworth: Penguin.
Conan Doyle, A. (1887). *A Study in Scarlet*. (1981). London: Penguin.
_____. (1890). *The Sign of Four*. (1981). London: Penguin.
_____. (1892). "The Adventure of the Speckled Band," in *The Adventures of Sherlock Holmes*. (1994). London: Penguin Popular Classics.
Courtine, R. (1975). *Madame Maigret's Recipes*. New York: Harcourt Brace Jovanovich.
Cronin, V. (1994). *Paris: City of Light, 1919–1939*. London: HarperCollins.
Daeninckx, D. (1984). *Meurtres pour mémoire*. Paris: Gallimard.
_____. (1989). *La Mort n'oublie personne*. Paris: Editions Denoël.
Dard, O. (1999). *Les Années 30*. Paris: Livre de poche.
De Croock, G. "Maigret in France," at http://www.trussel.com/f_maig.htm.
De Fallois, B. (1961). *Simenon*. (1971). Lausanne: Editions Rencontre.
De Gaulle, C. (1954). *Mémoires de la Guerre, Tome 1*. Paris: Plon.
Dubois, J. (1970). "Pour une critique littéraire sociologique," in Escarpit et al. (1970).
_____. (1980). "Statut littéraire et position de classe," in Gothot-Mersche, C., et al. (1980).
_____. (1992). *Le Roman policier ou la modernité*. Paris: Nathan.
Dulout, S. (1997). *Le Roman policier*. Paris: Les Essentiels Milan.
Dumortier, J-L. (1985). *Georges Simenon. Un livre: une oeuvre*. Brussels: Editions Labor.
Eagleton, T. (1976). *Criticism and Ideology*. London: New Left Books.
Engels, F. (1888). "Letter to Margaret Harkness" in Solmon, M., ed. (1973).
_____. (1890). "Letter to J. Bloch" in *Marx, Engels, Lenin* (1972).
Escarpit, R., et al. (1970). *Le Littéraire et le social*. Paris: Flammarion.
Eskin, S. (1987). *Simenon: A Critical Biography*. Jefferson, NC: McFarland.
Evrard, F. (1996). *Lire le roman policier*. Paris: Dunod.
Fabre, J. (1981). *Enquête sur un enquêteur. Maigret. Un essai de socio-critique*. Montpellier: Editions du CERES.
Fruttero, C., and F. Lucentini (1972). *La donna della domenica*. Milan: Mondadori.
Gaboriau, E. (1867). *Le Crime d'Orcival*. (2005). Paris: Editions du Masque.
_____. (1868). *Monsieur Lecoq*. (2005). Paris: Editions du Masque.

Gallot, D. (1999). *Simenon ou la comédie humaine*. Paris: France-Empire.
Gorrara, C. (ed.) (2009). *French Crime Fiction: An Introduction*. Cardiff: University of Wales Press.
Gothot-Mersche, C., et al. (1980). *Lire Simenon*. Brussels: Fernand Nathan/Editions Labor.
Gouttefangeas, T. (1991). L'Imaginaire social des années 1930 à travers les "Maigret" écrits par Georges Simenon de 1929 à 1933. Mémoire de Maîtrise d'Histoire Contemporaine. Université de Lille III. Unpublished: available for consultation at the Fonds Simenon, Liège.
Gramsci, A. (1985). *Selections from Cultural Writings*. London: Lawrence and Wishart.
Hammett, D. (1929). *Red Harvest*. (2003). London: Orion.
_____ (1931). *The Glass Key*. (1972). New York: Vintage Books.
Hegel, G. (1820). *Philosophy of Right*. Oxford: Oxford University Press.
Hélias, P.-J. (1999). *Le Cheval d'orgueil*. Paris: Plon.
Hemingway, E. (1966). *A Moveable Feast*. Harmondsworth: Penguin.
Hobsbawm, E. (1995). *Age of Extremes: the Short Twentieth Century, 1914–1991*. London: Abacus.
INSEE. (1990). *Recensement de la population*. Paris: La Documentation Française.
Kayman, M. (2003). "The Short Story from Poe to Chesterton," in Priestman, M. (ed.), 2003.
Kettle, A. (1951). *An Introduction to the English Novel, Volume 1*. (1977). London: Hutchinson.
Klinkenberg, J.-M. (1980). "Réalités d'un discours sur le réel," in Gothot-Mersche et al. (1980), 117–138.
Knight, S. (1980). *Form and Ideology in Crime Fiction*. London: Macmillan.
Lacassin, F., and G. Sigaud (1973). *Simenon*. Paris: Plon.
_____ and _____, eds. (1976). *Georges Simenon, A la découverte de la France*. Paris: U.G.E. Editions 10/18.
Lemoine, M. (1991). *L'Autre Univers de Simenon. Guide complet des romans populaires publiés sous pseudonymes*. Liège: Editions du CLCPF.
Lenin, V.I. (1917). *Imperialism: the Highest Stage of Capitalism*. (1978). Moscow: Progress Publishers.
Leroux, G. (1907). *Le Mystère de la chambre jaune*. (1960). Paris: Livre de poche.
Lewis, A., and J. Picard (1996). *Normandy*. Bristol: Bristol Classical Press.
Lits, M. (1999). *Le Roman policier: introduction à la théorie et à l'histoire d'un genre littéraire*. Liège: Editions du CEFAL.
Lukács, G. (1948). *Studies in European Realism*. (1972). London: Merlin.
Malet, L. (1943). *120 rue de la Gare*. (2001). Paris: Livre de poche.
_____ (1954–1959). *Les Nouveaux Mystères de Paris*. (2006). Paris: Robert Laffont.
Manchette, J.-P. (1983). "Réponses," in *Littérature*, no. 49, February 1983.
Mandel, E. (1973). *An Introduction to Marxist Economic Theory*. New York: Pathfinder Press.
_____ (1984). *Delightful Murder: A Social History of the Crime Story*. London: Pluto.
Marnham, P. (1992). *The Man Who Wasn't Maigret*. London: Bloomsbury.
Marx, K. (1924). *Theses on Feuerbach*, in McLellan (ed.) (1980).
_____ (1845). *The German Ideology*, in McLellan (ed.) (1980).

_____ (1859). *Preface to "A Contribution to the Critique of Political Economy,"* in McLellan (ed.), 1980.
_____ and F. Engels (1848). *The Communist Manifesto*. (2004). London: Penguin.
_____, F. Engels and V.I. Lenin (1972). *Historical Materialism*. Moscow: Progress Publishers.
Mauriac, F. (1927). *Thérèse Desqueyroux*. (1987). Paris: Livre de Poche.
McLellan, D. (ed.) (1980). *Karl Marx: Selected Writings*. Oxford: Oxford University Press.
Menguy, C., and P. Deligny (1989). "Les Vrais Débuts du Commissaire Maigret" in *Traces*, Number 1. Liège: Université de Liège.
Michel, A., and F. Laurent (1992). *Chez les Flamands. L'Ecluse numéro 1: Georges Simenon*. Paris: Nathan Balises.
Michelin Tourist Guide: Paris (1981, fourth edition). London: Michelin.
Modenesi, M. (1996). "Rues, ruelles, impasses et boulevards: Maigret et l'espace parisien," paper delivered at the conference Les Ecritures de Maigret at the University of Florence, November 15–16, 1996. Available at http://www.trussel.com/F_maigret.htm.
Montero, M. (2001). *La France de 1914 à 1945*. Paris: Armand Colin.
Narcejac, T. (1950). *Le Cas Simenon*. Paris: Presses de la Cité.
Orwell, G. (1933). *Down and Out in Paris and London*. (1961). New York: Harvest/HBJ.
Palet, L. (ed.) (2006). *Les Brigades du Tigre*, Season 2, Episode 1. Paris: Editions Fabbri.
Perisset, M. (1986). *Panorama du polar français contemporain*. Paris: L'Instant.
Poe, E.A. (1841–1845). *Tales of Mystery and Imagination*. (1993). Ware, UK: Wordsworth Classics. This volume includes "The Murders in the Rue Morgue" (1841), "The Mystery of Marie Rogêt" (1842) and "The Purloined Letter" (1845).
Poulantzas, N. (1974). *Les Classes sociales dans le capitalisme d'aujourd'hui*. Paris: Seuil.
Priestman, M. (ed.) (2003). *The Cambridge Companion to Crime Fiction*. Cambridge: Cambridge University Press.
Shorley, C. (2009). "Simenon: a unique phenomenon" in Gorrara (ed.), 2009.
Solmon, M. (ed.) (1973). *Marxism and Art*. New York: Knopf.
Stevenson, R.L., and F.V.D.G. (1885). *The Dynamiter*. (2008). Cambridge: CSP Classic Texts.
Sue, E. (1842–1843). *Les Mystères de Paris*. (2005). Paris: Robert Laffont.
Symons, J. (1992, third edition). *Bloody Murder: From the Detective Story to the Crime Novel: A History*. London: Pan.
Tauxe, H.-C. (1983). *Georges Simenon. De l'humain au vide*. Paris: Editions Buchet-Chastel.
Tourteau, J.-J. (1970). *D'Arsène Lupin à San Antonio: le roman policier français de 1900 à 1970*. Tours: Mame.
Trotsky, L. (1979). *Leon Trotsky on France* (ed. D. Salner). New York: Monad.
Trussel, S. "Simenon's Inspector Maigret," at http://www.trussel.com/F_maigret.htm.
Vanoncini, A. (1990). *Simenon et l'affaire Maigret*. Paris: Editions Champion.
_____ (2002). *Le Roman policier*. Paris: P.U.F./Que sais-je?
Vinen, R. (2003a). Introduction. *The Yellow Dog*. London: Penguin Classics.

_____ (2003b). Introduction. *The Madman of Bergerac*. London: Penguin Classics.
Wenger, M. "Dans la garde-robe de Maigret: de l'élégance d'une charpente plébéienne" at http://www.trussel.com/F_maigret.htm.
_____. "Maigret of the Month: *La Première Enquête de Maigret*," at http://www.trussel.com/F_maigret.htm.
_____. "Maigret of the Month: *Maigret et les témoins récalcitrants*," at http://www.trussel.com/F_maigret.htm.
_____. "Maigret of the Month: *Maigret tend un piège*," at http://www.trussel.com/F_maigret.htm.
Worthington, H. (2005). *The Rise of the Detective in Early Nineteenth Century Popular Fiction*. Basingstoke: Palgrave Macmillan.
Zeldin, T. (2003). *Histoire des passions françaises. Tome 1: Ambition et amour*. Paris: Payot.

Index

abortion 152, 157
action crime fiction 5, 9, 21, 121
L'Affaire Saint-Fiacre 22, 63–70, 87, 91, 96, 99–101, 107, 109, 126, 128, 129, 132, 142, 153, 167, 173, 175, 179, 189, 194
L'Affaire Saint-Fiacre (film) 63
agriculture 24–25, 64, 116, 127, 138, 148–152, 181
Alavoine, Bernard 14, 111, 145, 185, 188, 192
alcohol 33, 35, 95, 152, 155
Allain, Marcel 121
Allier 64, 66, 126, 154, 160
Allingham, Margery 13
Alsace 137, 139
ambition 22, 28–31, 59, 69, 76, 90, 92, 98–99, 129, 159, 175–176, 179
L'Ami d'enfance de Maigret 154, 160
Ancien Régime 31, 67, 70, 184
animal imagery 38
Antibes 53, 63, 70, 81, 110, 123
anti–Flemish prejudice 72, 78–80, 102
Arainville 189
Argenteuil 189
aristocracy 18, 22, 24, 26, 31, 37, 63–70, 90, 92, 99, 142–143, 158, 160, 165, 168, 173, 175, 179, 181, 184, 187, 193
Arpajon 189
artisans 6, 75, 111, 139, 184
Assouline, Pierre 13, 14, 21, 22, 41, 50, 56, 66, 82, 92, 93, 94, 97, 98, 99, 104, 105, 106, 134, 176, 177, 182
atmosphere 45, 75, 80, 81, 101, 107, 109, 123, 169, 178, 185, 190

Au Rendez-Vous des Terre-Neuvas 69, 81, 176, 179
Austen, Jane 181
Auteuil 45–46
automobiles 34, 37, 38, 44, 67, 84, 86, 143, 152, 158
Avenue Carnot 162
Aymé, Marcel 32

Baker, Josephine 45
Baldwin, Stanley 193
Balzac, Honoré de 3, 10, 183, 184
Un Banc au soleil 109
Banlieue (suburbs) 24, 43, 45, 46, 57, 137, 142, 143, 150, 154, 189
The Bar on the Seine see *La Guingette à deux sous*
Barbès-Rochechouart 162
Barcelona 195
A Battle of Nerves see *La Tête d'un homme*
Baur, Harry 42
Belgium 44, 54, 71, 74, 79–80, 102
Bertrand, Alain 178
Black Mask (magazine) 12
blackmail 23, 30, 92, 96, 160
Blum, Léon 118
bohemianism 42
Boileau, Pierre 111
Bordeaux 83, 163
Boulevard Haussman 55, 56, 58, 94
Boulogne-sur-Mer 36
Boyer, Régis 32
Bresler, Fenton 146
Brittany 32, 35, 40

Brüning, Heinrich 193
Bukharin, Nikolai 12
Burgess, Meredith 42

Caen 81–87, 103, 129–133, 151
canal Saint-Martin 162
Carr, J.D. 13
Carter, David 145
Céline, Louis-Fernand 13, 179
Central Europe 12, 44
Le Charretier de la Providence 69, 72, 95, 96, 107, 108, 112, 123, 142, 153, 155, 173, 175, 179
Chautemps, Camille 119
Chesterton, G.K. 121, 132
Chez Florence (restaurant) 94
Chez les Flamands 22, 69, 70–81, 95, 101–102, 109, 111, 113, 142, 155, 173, 174, 175
Le Chien jaune 15, 22, 31–41, 81, 87, 93–94, 104, 107, 108, 110, 111, 112, 117, 119, 122, 134, 142, 153, 161, 173, 174, 175, 177, 179, 182
Le Chien jaune (film) 32, 177
Christie, Agatha 1, 7, 13, 106, 193
Citroën, André 27, 55, 137
class consciousness 109, 131, 166
class struggle 40, 78, 101, 178, 195
classic competitive capitalism 12, 18, 110, 112, 185, 188
classical crime fiction 125, 193
Cocteau, Jean 13
La Colère de Maigret 146, 157
Colette 13
colonies 29, 31, 72
Communist Party 118, 140
complacency 23, 28, 90, 119, 142, 174
Conan Doyle, Arthur 121, 125
Concarneau 32–41, 93, 104, 110, 122, 142, 153, 174, 175
condescension 98, 104, 108, 129, 132, 159, 174
Une Confidence de Maigret 47, 154
conservatism 3, 35, 105, 112, 143, 158, 160, 185, 193
consumerism 67, 117, 158
contraband 40, 72
Côte d'Azur 26, 86
La Coupole (bar) 43–52, 94
Courier Royal (journal) 97
Un Crime en Hollande 107, 122
crime fiction and commodity production 10–11

crime fiction and short stories 120–122, 124, 132, 135

Daeninckx, Didier 195
Daladier, Edouard 106
La Danseuse du Gai-Moulin 98, 107, 108, 111, 174, 176, 187
Dard, Frédéric 11
"Death of a Woodlander" *see* "Les Larmes de bougie"
Deauville 26
déclassés 46, 48, 50, 61, 108, 157, 174, 175
De Gaulle, Charles 15, 186
Delannoy, Jean 1, 63
Deligny, Pierre 22
demographic changes 24, 34, 44, 61, 64, 66, 73, 127, 137, 149–150, 154, 182
Depression (1930s) 11, 12, 23, 33, 50, 54, 71, 72, 82, 84, 113, 115, 116, 117, 118, 119, 124, 130, 135, 139, 140, 141
Détective (magazine) 121
devaluation 24, 33, 83, 118
Dijon 150
Dubois, Jacques 7, 11, 14, 22, 63, 74, 77, 100, 101, 102, 104, 108, 176, 178, 179, 184, 188
Dulout, Stéphanie 9, 11
Dumas *père*, Alexandre 13
Dumortier, Jean-Louis 183, 188
Duvivier, Julien 42

Eagleton, Terry 2, 9, 10, 18, 181, 191
Eastern Europe 12, 44
Un Échec de Maigret 154, 157, 160, 167, 168
L'Ecluse numéro 1 62, 72, 107, 108, 142, 146, 153, 168, 174, 179, 181, 183, 189
economic dualism 34, 43, 72
Ehrenbourg, Ilya 50
electricity supply 26, 66, 78, 85, 128
L'Empreinte (magazine) 13
Engels, Friedrich 9, 16, 17, 41
Eskin, Stanley 14, 21, 22, 32, 41, 42, 44, 45, 53, 63, 66, 81, 97, 105, 115, 122, 145
Etretat 154
Evrard, Franck 10, 11

Fabre, Jean 7, 14, 15, 16, 47, 75, 76, 99, 111, 134, 135
Fallois, Bernard de 183
Fascism (Italy) 12, 115, 180

Index

Fayard, Arthème 13, 21, 22
February 6, 1934 106, 118
Fécamp 69, 81, 122
"La Fenêtre ouverte" 120, 122, 124–126, 132, 133, 142
feudalism 17, 18, 37, 70, 101
fishing 36–37, 69, 81, 137, 138
Fitzgerald, F. Scott 45
fonctionnaires 39, 59–60, 63, 111, 178, 188
Fontenay-le-Comte 154, 163, 165–167, 191
Fordism 72, 177
Le Fou de Bergerac 96, 107, 110, 142, 153, 174, 179, 180
Fouquet's (restaurant) 134
Fourth Republic (France) 159
Franco, Gen. Francisco 12, 115
Fruttero, Carlo 195

Gabin, Jean 1, 63
Gaboriau, Emile 106, 121, 193
Gazette de Liège (journal) 97, 105, 135
Germany 5, 12, 43, 52, 105, 115, 116, 133, 134, 140, 193
Gide, André 13
Giraudoux, Jean 51
Givet 71–80
Goldman, Emma 51
Gouttefangeas, Thierry 14, 15, 143
Gramsci, Antonio 14, 16
Great Britain 5, 6, 12, 23, 36, 40, 83, 110, 115, 116, 119, 121, 129, 140, 148, 193
Great War (1914–1918) 1, 10, 18, 43, 54, 55, 60, 61, 63, 64, 65, 66, 83, 84, 112, 121, 124, 126, 128, 141, 142, 154, 159, 181, 193
Grenoble 150
La Guinguette à deux sous 95, 97, 107, 108, 111, 123, 153, 173

Hammett, Dashiell 2, 194
Hanotaux, Gabriel 73
haute bourgeoisie 37, 47–49, 57–59, 86, 90, 103, 108, 129–132, 142–143, 160, 162, 172–176, 179, 181, 187
Hegel, Georg Wilhelm Friedrich 182
Hélias, Pierre-Jakez 40
Hemingway, Ernest 45
Hitler, Adolf 105, 115
Holmes, Sherlock 2, 9, 121
homme nu 6, 93
housing 24, 31, 33, 46, 56, 150, 162

ideology 39, 117, 134–135, 177–180, 184, 188, 191–193, 195
immigration and foreigners in France 43–52, 78–79, 95, 108, 143, 149–151, 155, 179
industry 24, 25, 29, 43–44, 55, 72, 74, 82–84, 115–116, 137, 139, 141–143, 148, 151, 152, 155, 165, 174, 177, 181, 183, 187
inequality 34, 107, 108, 180
inflation 24, 30, 33, 37, 58–60, 65
inheritance 23, 28, 49, 54, 82, 129, 166
Inventaire de la France 136–144, 180
Issy-les-Moulineaux 45–46, 142
Italy 5, 12, 44, 115
Izzo, Jean-Claude 195

Je me souviens 98, 102
"Jeumont, 51 minutes d'arrêt" 122, 123, 124, 133
"Jeumont, 51 Minutes' Stop" *see* "Jeumont, 51 minutes d'arrêt"
Jögiches, Leo 52
Le Jour (journal) 120, 136

Kayman, Martin 121, 193
Knight, Stephen 1–3, 15
Kriegel, Annie 180

labor unions 118–119, 134, 140, 185, 194
La Chapelle 162
Lakeville, Connecticut 163
Lalou, René 53
"Les Larmes de bougie" 120, 122, 124, 126–128, 132, 133, 174, 175
Laughton, Charles 42
Leblanc, Maurice 121
legal profession 6, 48, 132, 146, 166
Le Havre 51, 84, 118, 133, 137
Le Mans 151
Lenin, V. I. 12, 16, 17, 18
Leroux, Gaston 121
Liberty Bar 95, 123, 174, 175
Liège 13, 79, 102, 122, 134, 135, 187
literary realism 18, 188–192
Lits, Marc 10, 11
Little Caesar (film) 13
The Lock at Charenton see *L'Ecluse numéro 1*
Lorient 36
Lorraine 137, 139

Lucentini, Franco 195
Lukács, Georg 3, 184
Luxemburg, Rosa 52
Lyon 34, 84, 118, 133, 137, 150

Macherey, Pierre 191
The Madman of Bergerac see *Le Fou de Bergerac*
Maigret 98, 108, 114, 147, 153, 155, 157, 168, 176, 179, 182
Maigret à l'école 160
Maigret à New York 147, 154, 159
Maigret a peur 146, 154, 158, 160, 162–167, 191
Maigret à Vichy 154
Maigret Afraid see *Maigret a peur*
Maigret and Monsieur Charles see *Maigret et monsieur Charles*
Maigret and the Apparition see *Maigret et le fantôme*
Maigret and the Burglar's Wife see *Maigret et la grande perche*
Maigret and the Calame Report see *Maigret chez le ministre*
Maigret and the Death of a Harbor-Master see *Le Port des brumes*
Maigret and the Enigmatic Lett see *Pietr-le-Letton*
Maigret and the Flemish Shop see *Chez les Flamands*
Maigret and the Gangsters see *Maigret, Lognon et les gangsters*
Maigret and the Headless Corpse see *Maigret et le corps sans tête*
Maigret and the Hundred Gibbets see *Le Pendu de Saint-Pholien*
Maigret and the Lazy Burglar see *Maigret et le voleur paresseux*
Maigret and the Loner see *Maigret et l'homme tout seul*
Maigret and the Millionaires see *Maigret voyage*
Maigret and the Old Lady see *Maigret et la vieille dame*
Maigret and the Reluctant Witnesses see *Maigret et les témoins récalcitrants*
Maigret and the Saturday Caller see *Maigret et le client du samedi*
Maigret and the Surly Inspector see *Maigret et l'inspecteur malchanceux*
Maigret and the Wine Merchant see *Maigret et le marchand de vin*

Maigret and the Young Girl see *Maigret et la jeune morte*
Maigret at the Crossroads see *La Nuit du carrefour*
Maigret at the Gai Moulin see *La Danseuse du Gai-Moulin*
Maigret aux assises 147, 157, 158
Maigret chez le ministre 147, 159, 191
Maigret, commissaire Jules: age 64, 68, 147, 168; anti–Semitism 51, 96, 97, 101, 142; attitudes to nationality 159, 180; attitudes to social class 39, 48, 70, 89, 93, 100–101, 103–104, 124, 132–133, 154, 158, 166, 174–180; automobiles 143, 158; childhood and adolescence 63, 64, 66, 68, 69, 91, 99, 126, 128, 153, 159, 160, 161, 167, 168, 185, 191; clothes 111, 172; colleagues 112; conclusion of inquiries 71, 81, 89, 93, 193–194; conservatism 3, 52, 112, 143, 158, 160, 175, 179–180; creation of 21–22; domestic life 158, 167, 169, 178; early appearances 21; father (Evariste Maigret) 63, 69, 99, 160, 179, 184; food and drink 111; humanism 3, 93–94, 104, 111–112, 160–161, 167; identification with Simenon 91, 104; identification with the narrator 68, 74, 92, 96–97, 142–143, 189–190; location of enquiries 24, 35–36, 42, 54, 64, 73–75, 83–85, 110, 122, 127, 154–155, 189; Madame Maigret 158, 167, 168, 178, 191; method 5, 94, 111, 122–124, 185; nostalgia 68, 100–101, 128, 159, 168, 178, 193; physical characteristics 39, 47, 68, 159; plots 81, 106, 107, 109, 115, 146, 169, 171; professional criminals 140, 142, 155, 159, 176, 182; reasons for popularity 110, 186; series launched 21–22, 42, 94; social origins 39, 63, 65, 104, 111, 160, 176, 178, 186; speech 39, 68; time span of inquiries 122; translations 1, 13, 22; unofficial inquiries 71, 111, 114; use of *vous* and *tu* 39, 49–50, 89, 112
Maigret en meublé 154, 161–162
Maigret et la grande perche 154, 157, 159, 160, 162
Maigret et la vieille dame 157
Maigret et le client du samedi 157, 158
Maigret et le corps sans tête 157
Maigret et le marchand de vin 157
Maigret et le voleur paresseux 154

Maigret et les témoins récalcitrants 168
Maigret et les vieillards 154, 157, 159, 161, 168–169
Maigret et l'homme tout seul 147, 154
Maigret et l'inspecteur malchanceux 140, 153
Maigret et monsieur Charles 13, 158, 169–172, 192
Maigret et son mort 47, 155, 157–158
Maigret Goes Home see *L'Affaire Saint-Fiacre*
Maigret Goes to School see *Maigret à l'école*
Maigret Has Doubts see *Une Confidence de Maigret*
Maigret Has Scruples see *Les Scrupules de Maigret*
Maigret Hesitates see *Maigret hésite*
Maigret hésite 159
Maigret in Court see *Maigret aux assises*
Maigret in Holland see *Un Crime en Hollande*
Maigret in New York see *Maigret à New York*
Maigret in Society see *Maigret et les vieillards*
Maigret in Vichy see *Maigret à Vichy*
Maigret, Lognon et les gangsters 159
Maigret Loses His Temper see *La Colère de Maigret*
Maigret Meets a Milord see *Le Charretier de la Providence*
Maigret Mystified see *L'Ombre chinoise*
Maigret on the Defensive see *Maigret se défend*
Maigret on the Riviera see *Liberty Bar*
Maigret Returns see *Maigret Revient*
Maigret Revient 114, 153
Maigret se défend 157
Maigret se trompe 157, 160, 162
Maigret Sets a Trap see *Maigret tend un piège*
Maigret Stonewalled see *Monsieur Gallet décédé*
Maigret Takes a Room see *Maigret en meublé*
Maigret tend un piège 146
Maigret voyage 155, 160
Maigret's Boyhood Friend see *L'Ami d'enfance de Maigret*
Maigret's Failure see *Un échec de Maigret*
Maigret's First Case see *La Première enquête de Maigret*
Maigret's Little Joke see *Maigret s'amuse*
Maigret's Memoirs see *Les Mémoires de Maigret*
Maigret's Mistake see *Maigret se trompe*
Maigtret's Special Murder see *Maigret et son mort*
Malet, Léo 188, 194
The Man on the Eiffel Tower (film) 42
Manchette, Jean-Patrick 10
Mandel, Ernest 10, 193
Mandel, Georges 106
Marais 96, 97
maritime commerce 81, 83
Marlowe, Philip 2, 9
Marnham, Patrick 14, 91, 101, 102, 112, 122, 135
marriage 29, 35, 59, 61, 76, 84, 92, 178
Marseille 34, 137, 150, 151, 195
Marx, Karl 16, 17, 41, 52, 182
Marxism 16–18
Le Masque (magazine) 13
Mauriac, François 13, 50, 51
Maxim's (restaurant) 94, 134
mediocrity 30–31, 37, 60, 98, 108, 160, 167, 174, 182, 187
Les Mémoires de Maigret 44, 136, 140, 154, 178, 179, 190–191
Menguy, Claude 22
Meung-sur-Loire 158
La Michaudière 32, 110
Miller, Henry 45
modernity 27, 34, 41, 45, 139, 158
Mon Ami Maigret 154, 155, 157
Monet, Claude 189
monopoly capitalism 12, 18, 110, 151, 178, 180, 185, 187, 188
Monsieur Gallet décédé 22–31, 33, 91–92, 96, 106–107, 111, 112, 122, 142, 147, 153, 173, 174–175, 182, 194
Montalbán, Manuel Vásquez 195
Montmartre 56, 141, 155
Montparnasse 42, 45, 94
Montpellier 150
Moulins 63, 64, 66, 67, 109
moyenne bourgeoisie 26, 29, 173–176, 181–182
My Friend Maigret see *Mon Ami Maigret*

Namur 71, 76, 79
Nancy 71, 72, 79
Nantes 28, 83
Narcejac, Thomas 7, 14, 111
National Socialism (Germany) 12, 105, 115, 133, 180
natural order 101, 184–185
Neuilly 94, 134, 162
new money 33, 57–59, 90, 181, 194
Nice 150
Nilson, Sven 153
No Vacation for Maigret see *Les Vacances de Maigret*
Normandy 81, 83–85
notables 37–38, 143
nouvelle petite bourgeoisie 18, 57, 59, 76, 101, 174–175
Les Nouvelles Enquêtes de Maigret 114–115, 120–135, 140, 142, 153
La Nuit du carrefour 107, 108, 142, 175, 177, 178, 182, 189
La Nuit du carrefour (film) 177
Les Nuits de Chicago (film) 13

"The Old Lady of Bayeux" *see* "La Vieille Dame de Bayeux"
old money 33, 59, 90, 194
L'Ombre chinoise 22, 53–63, 70, 98–99, 108, 132, 142, 153, 173, 174, 175, 179, 181, 182
"The Open Window" *see* "La Fenêtre ouverte"
Orléans 151
Orwell, George 44, 50
Ouistreham 69, 81–83, 85–87, 89, 103–104, 110, 123, 129

Paray-le-Frésil 66, 99, 110
Paris 6–7, 22, 24, 32, 34, 35, 37, 38, 41, 43–50, 53, 55–57, 63, 66, 67, 71, 73, 78, 79, 81, 84, 86, 92, 95, 96, 118, 119, 122, 126, 131, 132, 133, 134, 141, 143, 150, 151, 152, 154, 156, 158, 161–164, 169–171, 176, 180, 187, 188, 189, 194, 195
Paris-Soir (journal) 114, 135, 136
Paris-Soir Dimanche (magazine) 114, 135
Parmenides 9
passéisme 143, 172
peasantry 18, 37, 65–68, 100, 132, 137–138, 173, 175, 184
Pedigree 98

Le Pendu de Saint-Pholien 22, 96, 108, 111, 122, 153, 174, 176, 187
Pétain, Philippe 180
petite bourgeoisie 12, 18, 26, 28–30, 46, 57, 71, 73–75, 88, 90, 101–102, 104, 109–110, 112, 118, 134, 151, 177–187; traditionnelle 59, 75, 175
petites gens 6, 31, 49, 62, 88, 93, 100–101, 111, 134, 142–143, 157, 161, 167, 175, 183, 185–187
Pietr-le-Letton 22, 47, 52, 95–96, 107, 112, 122, 142, 146, 155, 174, 176, 179, 182
Pigalle 55–56, 61, 159
Place des Vosges 53–56, 61, 110
plebeians 90, 173, 175
Poe, Edgar Allan 120, 121, 125, 192
Poincaré, Raymond 33, 83, 105, 193
Poirot, Hercule 2, 9, 193
police 6, 26, 39, 50, 78, 89, 109, 111, 123, 124, 136, 140, 176, 191; procedural crime fiction 9, 106
Police-Film (magazine) 114, 120, 135
Police-Roman (magazine) 114, 120, 129, 135
Police-Secours 136, 140–142
Popular Front 12, 118, 119, 124, 134, 140, 180, 185
Porquerolles 94, 134
Le Port des brumes 22, 48, 69, 81–89, 102–106, 108, 109, 110, 111, 112, 113, 117, 119, 123, 129, 132, 134, 142, 153, 172, 173, 174, 175, 179
post–Great War economic expansion 11, 33, 60, 65, 110, 112, 125, 126, 130, 132, 133, 136, 139, 181, 182, 194
post–Second World War economic expansion 147, 149, 151, 154, 157, 158, 162, 164
Poulantzas, Nicos 16, 18, 57, 59, 75, 76
Pound, Ezra 45
La Première Enquête de Maigret 147, 154, 159, 161
production line 27, 43, 57
prohibition (USA) 33, 45, 194
proletariat 38, 45–46, 48, 71, 77, 90, 101–102, 134, 142–143, 174–175, 177, 191
property development 25, 33
prostitution 61–62
provinces 31, 33, 35–37, 48, 73–75, 84–85, 93, 107, 129–133, 137, 143, 150,

158, 159, 161, 162, 165–167, 174, 181–182, 187–188
psychological crime fiction 5, 9
pulp fiction 1, 13, 21, 176
Puteaux 162
puzzle crime fiction 9, 106, 193

Quand j'étais vieux 169, 182
Queen, Ellery 13

race 41, 51, 75, 79–80, 90, 95–96, 102
racism 50, 142
Radek, Karl 52
Radical Party 34, 105, 118
Rankin, Ian 195
ratiocinative crime fiction 120–122
religion 35, 67, 184
Rennes 32, 39, 151
retail commerce and distribution 24, 73, 75, 116, 151, 185
river and canal transport 72, 73, 85, 123, 142, 187, 189
roman semi-littéraire 21
Rothschild, Baron Edmond 106
Rouen 84
royalism 10, 23, 29
Russell, William 193
Russia 11, 50, 52, 96, 112, 181, 185
Russian revolution 11, 112, 181, 185

Les Sables d'Olonne 154, 161
Saigon 28
The Sailors' Rendezvous see Au Rendez-Vous des Terre-Neuvas
Sainsbury, Geoffrey 190
Saint-André-sur-Mer 154
Saint-Cloud 42, 43, 45, 46
Saint-Fargeau 23–25, 31, 33, 122
Sancerre 23, 24, 26, 122
Sayers, Dorothy 13, 193
Scarface (film) 13
Scotland 195
Scott, Walter 3, 184
Les Scrupules de Maigret 48, 158
Second World War (1939–1945) 1, 2, 10, 12, 15, 19, 114, 194
"Sept Petites Croix dans un carnet" 140
servants 26, 88, 172
Shorley, Christopher 15
Signé Picpus 114, 140, 146
Simenon, Désiré (father of Georges) 98, 101, 102, 176
Simenon, Georges: anti–Semitism 97, 101, 105; attitudes to history 15–16, 180–186, 192; attitudes to nationality 75, 78, 90, 95–96, 101; attitudes to social class 14, 93–94, 98, 99, 100–101, 103–104, 108–109, 132–133, 141, 143, 161, 162, 172, 174–180, 184, 191, 192; causes of crime 5, 108, 128, 140–141, 193; childhood and adolescence 13, 97, 101, 102, 134, 176; commercial success 1, 2, 5, 13, 19, 22, 92, 94, 105, 134, 135, 176–177; conservatism 3, 105, 185; creation of Maigret 9, 13, 22, 63, 109; critical acclaim 1, 5, 7, 9, 13–14, 19, 32, 53, 188; detection stories before Maigret 21, 121–122; humanism 6, 93–94, 100, 103–104, 106, 185; identification with Maigret 91, 104; journalism 13, 97, 105, 135–144, 168; lifestyle 94–95, 144, 177; literary style and narrative techniques 1, 2, 93, 109, 122, 188, 190–191; moves to Paris 13; moves to Switzerland 156; moves to United States 2, 156; Nazi Germany 1, 105, 134; past, importance of in the Maigret narratives 70, 108, 153–154, 157, 169, 171, 175, 178, 179, 187, 192; periodization of the Maigret series 114, 146–147; politics 101, 104–106, 138, 159, 182, 185; pre- and postwar Maigret stories compared 145–147, 153–155, 161–162, 172, 192; publicity and marketing 22, 42, 94, 153; pulp novels 1, 13, 21, 110, 176; *romans durs* 1, 7, 135, 145; social attitudes 98–102, 142–143, 176–177; titles in the Maigret series 3, 42, 53, 146, 153, 157; travels 7, 23, 110, 134, 135
Simenon, Henriette (mother of Georges) 41, 98, 99, 101, 102, 134, 176
Simenon, Régine ("Tigy," first wife of Georges) 56, 94
simple commodity production 18
Sjöwall, Maj 194
snobbery 26, 58, 130
social democracy 178, 180, 184
social disorder 51–52, 179, 184
social imagination 7, 11, 17, 186–188
social mobility 24, 53, 65, 77, 108, 110, 125, 132, 179
social origins and status of detectives 192, 193
social place 70, 160, 179, 184
socialism 177

Socialist Party 118
Souvestre, Pierre 121
Soviet Union 187
Spain 12, 115, 133, 181
Spanish Civil War 115, 133, 181
speculation 29, 30, 33, 36, 65, 92, 116, 130, 137–139, 140
Stavisky, Alexandre 106, 117, 136
Stavisky affair 106, 117, 136
Stein, Gertrude 45
Stevenson, Robert Louis 121
Stresemann, Gustav 193
strikes and factory occupations 118, 119, 140, 185
suicide 23, 42, 47, 54, 60, 63, 71, 89, 92, 106, 107, 124, 141, 146, 194
Sweden 195
Switzerland 141, 154
Symons, Julian 121

Tarride, Abel 32
Tarride, Jean 32
telephone services 66, 74, 127, 152, 182
La Tête d'un homme 22, 41–52, 55, 94–97, 107, 108, 112, 122, 132, 142, 155, 177, 179, 182, 190
La Tête d'un homme (film) 42, 177
Third Republic (France) 13, 29, 31, 38, 70, 73, 77, 81, 104, 105, 106, 117, 119, 120, 132, 151, 161, 185
Tigy *see* Simenon, Régine
Tolstoy, Leo 184
Toulouse 34, 84, 118, 133, 137, 150
Tours 151
Tourteau, Jean-Jacques 10
Tracy, Jacques, Marquis de 23, 66, 92, 99, 101, 117
Les 13 Coupables 122
Les 13 Enigmes 122

Les 13 Mystères 122
Trotsky, Leon 52, 105, 118, 119
Turin 195

Underworld (film) 13
unemployment 36, 50, 61, 72, 116, 137
United States 12, 32–33, 39, 43, 44, 45, 82, 110, 115, 116, 140, 146, 148, 154, 159, 177, 187, 193, 194

Les Vacances de Maigret 154, 161
vacations 26, 37, 86, 118, 134
Van Dine, S.S. 106, 193
Vanoncini, André 9, 14, 15, 70, 100, 121, 195
Vendée 159, 163, 191
Véry, Pierre 193
Vichy 154
"La Vieille Dame de Bayeux" 120, 123, 124, 129–132, 133, 134, 142, 173, 174, 175, 179
Vinen, Richard 15, 146, 153, 180
Vitry-aux-Loges (forest of Orléans) 126–128
Voilà (magazine) 105
vulgarity 24, 39, 57–58, 126 160

Wahlöö, Per 194
Wall Street crash 12, 23, 33, 71, 113, 115
Warren, Samuel 192
water supply 26, 66, 85, 151
Wenger, Murielle 111, 146, 161, 168
West Germany 148
Wills Crofts, Freeman 193
women (social position of) 29, 38, 40–41, 61–62, 66, 77, 116, 128, 152

The Yellow Dog see *Le Chien jaune*
Young, Arthur 84

www.ingramcontent.com/pod-product-compliance
Lightning Source LLC
Chambersburg PA
CBHW032055300426
44116CB00007B/749